Llewellyn's Celtic Wisdom Series

Isle of Avalon

OPEN A DOORWAY TO THE ETERNAL

For centuries, the Isle of Avalon has cast a spell over inhabitants and travelers. The ancient Celts and their predecessors believed Avalon to be an earthly paradise containing the gateway to the Otherworld, where the souls of the deceased waited for rebirth. They developed an entire cosmology around Avalon's reputation as a meeting place between physical and spiritual reality. Avalon is the world mountain in the early shamanic tradition. Avalon is a magical presence in Arthurian legend, and is also the place where Joseph of Arimathea planted the flowering staff of Christianity in Britain. Today, Avalon attracts countless spiritual seekers drawn by its mysteries and unusual properties. What is it that makes it a place of such mystical power and holiness?

The Isle of Avalon explores the Avalonian mysteries from a perspective based solidly in the features of its unique landscape. Sitting within a global context of powerful ley lines, Avalon is a locus for subtle and elemental forces which here meet in a dynamic polarity. With its red and white springs, prominent hills, surrounding plain, sacred trees, and cavernous underground system, the natural features of the landscape create a powerful "spirit of place."

This is the first book to consider the incredible aspects of the Avalonian landscape that have been uncovered in this century—such as the Glastonbury Zodiac, the St. Michael Ley Line, the Glastonbury Tor Maze and the sacred geometry of Glastonbury Abbey—as part of the larger geomythical properties of Avalon. Discover how and why Avalon is the point of connection and of journeying between the physical world and the Otherworld—and understand how nature and spirit combine at this sacred place to open a doorway to the eternal.

ABOUT THE AUTHOR

Nicholas Robin Mann was born in Britain in 1952. His degree from Univeristy College, London, is in ancient history and anthropology. First drawn to the Isle of Avalon in the 1970s, he made his home there in 1983. His original fieldwork included geomancy, dowsing, sacred geometry, folklore and mythology. He has written several guidebooks to Avalon and conducted many visitors around the ancient sites there and throughout the British Isles. He currently lives in New Mexico.

TO WRITE TO THE AUTHOR

If you wish to contact the author or would like more infomration about this book, please write to the author in care of Llewellyn Worldwide and we will forward your requst. Both the author and publisher appreciate hearing from you and learning of your enjoyment of this book and how it has helped you. Llewellyn Worldwide cannot guarantee that every letter written to the author can be answered, but all will be forwarded. Please write to:

Nicholas R. Mann
℅ Llewellyn Worldwide
P.O. Box 64383-K459, St. Paul, MN 55164-0383, U.S.A.

FREE CATALOG FROM LLEWELLYN

For more than 90 years Llewellyn has brought its readers knowledge in the fields of metaphysics and human potential. Learn about the newest books in spiritual guidance, natural healing, astrology, occult philosophy, and more. Enjoy book reviews, new age articles, a calendar of events, plus current advertised products and services. To get your free copy of *Llewellyn's New Worlds of Mind and Spirit*, send your name and address to:

Llewellyn's New Worlds of Mind and Spirit
P.O. Box 64383-K459, St. Paul, MN 55164-0383, U.S.A.

Llewellyn's Celtic Wisdom Series

Isle of Avalon

Sacred Mysteries of Arthur and Glastonbury Tor

Nicholas R. Mann

1996
Llewellyn Publications
St. Paul, MN 55164-0383, U.S.A.

FIRST EDITION
First Printing, 1996

Cover design by Tom Grewe
Illustrations by Nicholas R. Mann
Photographs by Nicholas R. Mann and Kevin Redpath
Design, layout, and editing by Pamela Henkel

Library of Congress Cataloging in Publication Data
Mann, Nicholas R.
Isle of Avalon : sacred mysteries of Arthur & Glastonbury Tor / Nicholas R. Mann. — 1st ed.
      p.   cm. — (Llewellyn's Celtic wisdom series)
      Includes bibliographical references and index.
      ISBN 1-56718-459-6 (pbk.)
      1. Celts—England—Glastonbury—Religion. 2. Glastonbury Abbey. 3. Arthur, King. 4. Britons—Kings and rulers—Folklore. 5. Glastonbury (England)—Religion. I. Title. II. Series.
BL980.G7M36   1996
942.3'83—dc20   95-51433
                                             CIP

Llewellyn Publications
A Division of Llewellyn Worldwide, Ltd.
St. Paul, Minnesota 55164-0383, U.S.A.

ABOUT LLEWELLYN'S CELTIC WISDOM SERIES

Can it be said that we are *all* Celts? Certainly Western civilization owes as much, if not more, to our Celtic heritage as to Greek and Roman influences.

While the origins of the Celtic peoples are shrouded in mystery, their distinctive culture emerged as a powerful force in Central Europe during the second millennium BC. During the first millennium BC, Celtic civilization spread across Europe, challenging Rome in the fourth century BC and occupying areas from Spain to Russia, Turkey to Ireland.

The Celtic tribes were politically independent, and—in contrast to the Roman Empire—never truly united under a single ruler. That same independence brought Europeans to the New World, then pulled them westward across the continent through a continuous need to create a "new order for the ages" and a nation of people free of social, religious, political and economic oppression. Today, the same Celtic spirit asserts itself as peoples everywhere struggle for a new political reality.

Celtic art, music, magic, and myth are unique, and are enjoying a renaissance today. Of particular interest is the Grail legend, which Carl Jung called the most recent of the great myths to surface from the collective unconscious, constituting the primary myth of Western civilization. The Grail legend offers us the means to find our way to the Otherworld and come back again richer, wiser, healed and whole, having gained the knowledge and power to live consciously and fully.

Basic to the Celtic tradition is the acceptance of personal responsibility and realisation that all of us constantly shape and affect the land on which we live. Intrinsic to this notion is the Celtic interrelationship with the Otherworld and its inhabitants. The Celtic world view is a magical one, in which everything has a physical, mental, and spiritual aspect and its own proper purpose, and where our every act affects *both* worlds.

It is true that we are all Celts—for even the most humble of us must face the challenges of Arthur and Guinevere, of Merlin and Morgan le Fay in our own lives. Like the Knights of the Round Table, we all seek the Holy Grail in some shape or form. Like all great myths, the Grail legend is the model for the life we must live to bring this world and the Otherworld together, and thus to restore the wholeness we were all meant to possess.

The books of the Celtic Wisdom Series comprise a magical curriculum embracing ideas and techniques that awaken the soul to the myths and legends, the psychological and spiritual truths, and the inner power each of us can tap to meet the challenges of our times.

OTHER BOOKS BY NICHOLAS R. MANN

His Story (Llewellyn, 1995)

The Cauldron and the Grail (Glastonbury: Annenterprise, 1985)

Glastonbury Tor (Glastonbury: Triskele, 1986, revised 1993)

The Keltic Power Symbols (Glastonbury: Triskele, 1987)

Sedona: Sacred Earth (Prescott: Zivah Publishers, 1989, revised, expanded edition 1991)

The Red and White Springs: The Mysteries of Britain at Glastonbury (Glastonbury: Triskele, 1992)

The Giants of Gaia (co-author Marcia Sutton Ph.D., Albuquerque: Brotherhood of Life, 1995)

To Maya

TABLE OF CONTENTS

Introduction 1

Part 1

1. The Island 7
   Geography. The Tor. Geology. The Tor Springs. Ponter's Ball. The Avalonian Traditions. Joseph of Arimathea. The Red and the White.

2. Prehistory: The First Comers 29
   Somerset: 4,000-2,000 BC. The Prehistoric Monuments. A Ceremonial Monument? Somerset 2,000-0 BC.

3. Early History: The Old Church and King Arthur 39
   Caradoc of Llancarfan. William of Malmesbury. The Excavations on the Tor. The First Settlement. Somerset in the Dark Ages. Cadbury Castle. The Second Settlement. Glastonbury Abbey.

4. Later History: The Abbey and the Tor. 57
   The Last Abbot. Frederick Bligh Bond. The Monastery on the Tor. St. Michael's Tower. The Fairfield. The Terraces on the Tor. Agriculture on the Tor. The Present Day. The Mystery of the Terraces.

Part 2

5. The Geomantic Mysteries: Labyrinths, Lines, and Zodiacs. . 81
   Ley Lines. Glastonbury Global Alignments. "Arthur's Hunting Path." Chalice Hill Geometry. The Tor Stones. The Tor Labyrinth. The Tor Labyrinth and its Astronomical Alignment. The Glastonbury Zodiac. The Floorplan of the Temple.

6. Myth and Legend: Cave, Cauldron, Mountain, and Tree . . 123
   *Caradoc and King Arthur. Morgan le Fay. The Goddess at
   Beckery. Bride's Well. The Landscape Goddess. The Hollow
   Hill. The World Axis. The World Mountain and Tree.*

7. The Underworld: Red Spring and White Spring 155
   *The Chalice Well. The Vesica Piscis. The Tor Springs. The
   White Spring. The Underworld. The White Spring to the
   Present Day.*

8. The Matter of Britain: Dragons, Blood, and Heavenly Dew 175
   *The Red and the White Dragons. The Blood Mysteries of
   Avalon. The Twice Born. The Red and the White Rose. The
   Alchemy of Avalon*

Appendix: Dualism and Deity 199
Bibliography 203
Index 207

ACKNOWLEDGEMENTS

Diana. Howie, who pointed out the landscape diamonds. Stanley. Alexis Manzi Fe. Roger, Jag, and Nigel who measured the true dimensions of the Mary Chapel. Sig Lonegren, whose skill and computer, verified them and the astronomical alignments. Terry Walsh, who insisted on accuracy and provided the global alignments. Ann Morgan, who insisted on the equivocal. Kevin Redpath, who provided photographs. Palden, who first told me about the King of Faery. Kristen, who helped so much with the illustrations. Patrick Whitefield. Willow. John Michell. John Brunsdon. Ella and Andy Portman. The Glastonbury Antiquarian Society. All the many researchers, writers, archaeologists, engineers, and frequent flyers on the Avalonian Dreamtime who provided the basis for this book and endured my constant badgering, thank you all very much indeed.

▲ *The Tor.*

INTRODUCTION

After a long period of early European culture, during which time ages of ice and flood came and went, people began to settle around the inland sea of the Summer Land. The abundance of game, the easily travelled waterways, and the rich soil supplied all their needs. From the surrounding countryside, the Isle of Avalon stood out in the centre of the marshes. The island's unusual hills and groves of trees, watered by two strange and prolific springs, made it an attractive and compelling destination. One spring bubbled out from a white grotto that led into a mysterious realm below the highest hill; the other spring flowed blood red. At times the isle could not be seen because of the strange mists that encircled it. Over the ages an otherworldliness grew up around the island. It was not to be idly visited.

At length the isle on the sea of glass became a place of initiation. Men and women, old and young, journeyed there in anxiety and anticipation. Who was willing to climb its sacred mountain? Who was willing to dive into its waters? The springs flowed with the same juices of their bodies. Blood would be let so they could share in the mystery of the greater cycles of existence. Songs were sung to the cries of boys beginning to understand their powers. Stories were told as girls cried at the onset of their mysteries. Spirits entered into the lives conceived during the trance-inducing dances on the isle. The dying asked that their spirits return through the rites and ceremonies performed there.

As people discovered their power in shaping the landscape with works in earth and stone, they were inspired to consecrate the isle in a unique way. They cleared the high hill of vegetation and began to give it a shape. The form they selected for the hill was one that allowed a great assembly to gather on seven terraces upon its slopes. The huge concentric rings of the terraces were similar to the great ceremonial enclosures of the day, but they also possessed a vertical dimension. There was a way up and a way down. The vertical axis allowed movement between above and below, between light and darkness, between the inner and the outer, between heaven and hell—or whatever the cosmic polarity was conceived to be. At certain times of the year—determined by astronomical lines of sight—the people gathered to honour the opening between heaven, earth, and the underworld. Ceremony increased the flow of energy between them. The surrounding landscape began to mirror this order of the cosmos.

Times changed, ideas altered, different people built different monuments across the land. But the Isle of Avalon, with its shining waters, its sacred groves, its hallowed springs, its yawning cave, and now with its marvelously sculpted world mountain, remained. The Celtic tribes, coming to the island as people had always done by causeway or by boat, felt the need to demarcate the holy place with a ritual boundary that separated it from the outside. They built the rampart known as Ponter's Ball. The Celts renewed the ancient and venerated traditions of the isle by building nothing more within the precincts they so enclosed.

As a sanctuary and as the gateway between the heavens and the underworld, only those initiated into the ancient mysteries could stay on the Isle of Glass. An eremetic tradition sprang up—perhaps it had always existed. A certain number—seven, nine, twelve, thirteen?—of Druidic priests, priestesses or shamans dwelt upon the island. They kept the mysteries of the other worlds, of the subterranean and celestial realms. They kept the mysteries of the Great Goddess and the Twin Gods. They kept the mysteries of the astronomical cycles and the Zodiac, of the Blood Spring and the White Spring, of the World Tree, the Spiral Castle, the Sword, the Spear, and the magical Cauldron of Rebirth. Perhaps, at some point, they provided a school for initiates. The rule was to build nothing but simple huts from saplings and cover them with reeds gathered from the marshes.

When the Christians came to Britain, they went to the Isle of Avalon and discussed the mysteries with its inhabitants. Over time, ideas melded and contributed to the creation of the Celtic Church with its unique doctrines. Perhaps by the sixth century, Christianity was the defining doctrine of the isle. The souls of the dead—including the great King Arthur—went to the Christian paradise, heaven, or hell through its portal. Just to be buried in the holy soil of Avalon secured one's salvation. But when Celtic Christianity had to capitulate to Rome, the order which replaced the hermits of Avalon rewrote the history of the isle.

The Avalonian Tradition, the Romans said, had really been Christian all along. The nature-worshipping shamans or Druids were the early monks. The ancient tradition of withy and reed huts was originated by St. Joseph of Arimathea, if not by Christ himself. The mysteries of the two springs—especially the terrible secrets of the Blood Spring—were inaugurated by the blood and sweat of Christ. The death and rebirth of the initiates was the "Virgin Birth" of Christ and his crucifixion and resurrection. The spiral or revolving castle on the Tor was a mount that traced the footsteps of Christ at Calvary. The celestial patterns in the surrounding landscape were the twelve hides of land granted to the Abbey. The magical Cauldron of Rebirth was in fact the Holy Grail. The Great Goddess was the Virgin Mary. The World Tree was the Cross. The sacred geometric ratios to be found in the natural order of the Isle of Avalon were employed in the design of the "Motherchurch" of Christendom.

The sovereign mystery was taken from the springs, the hills, the trees, the earth—these were merely trappings of the greater, transcendent truth—and placed within the churches. In this monotheistic, bright new world of faith there was no place for the chthonic deities of hill and cave. There was no place for the alchemical mysteries of the breast and womb. There was no place for the sexual whirl of genes, semen, and blood. There was no place for the wild dance, ecstatic trance, death, and rebirth of the high initiates. So the entrance to the Underworld upon the Tor was sealed by the exorcism of St. Collen and the constant vigilance of St. Michael.

This interpretation is not to repudiate the Glastonbury Legends, but to deepen the understanding of them. It is to ground the traditions in the dream of the spirit of a place that always was, and—if we follow the prophecies of the Isle of Glass—will be in the future.

The Mysteries of Avalon have a profound place in the wisdom-teachings of the Native European Tradition. The Mysteries of Avalon lie beyond the boundaries of any prevailing orthodoxy in the time and space beyond time and space. The Avalonian Dreamtime is the synthesis of polarity. It is the comprehension of the dual nature of mind. It presents the threshold between the round of the inner and the outer worlds. To pass through its portal requires . . . what? A ride with the God of the Wild Hunt? A surrender to the Cauldron of the Goddess? Ecstasy? Death? Rebirth? Or if the challenge is not to pass through into any singular world, but into one that embraces the totality of birth, life, and death—earth, heaven, and hell—then Avalon is a state of perception where all dimensions meet in the heart of those who seek wholeness.

PART
ONE

1

THE
ISLAND

The town of Glastonbury lies about fifteen miles from the sea on the eastern edge of the Somerset Levels in southwest Britain. This is low, flat, farming country bounded by rolling hills to the south, the Severn Estuary to the west, and the steep escarpment of the Mendip Hills to the north. The Levels are divided down the centre by the long finger of the Polden Ridge. The Levels were, until recently, a huge marsh subject to frequent tidal inundations. People ventured into its misty interior to hunt for fish and fowl. Before the marsh, when sea levels rose after the last Ice Age, it was a shallow inland sea.

For thousands of years Glastonbury was an island on the edge of an indeterminate meeting of earth, sky, and sea. It was known as the Isle of Avalon, "apple orchard," or Ynis Witrin, the "Isle of Glass." It is possible that the name of Glastonbury, Glass-town-borough, originates from the experience of those sailing the calm waters of the inland sea. In the late twelfth century, Caradoc of Llancarfan wrote "Glastonia … that is, the glassy city, which took its name from glass."[1] The isle was connected to the mainland only by a narrow strip of land to the east. A high, strangely shaped hill dramatically rose above

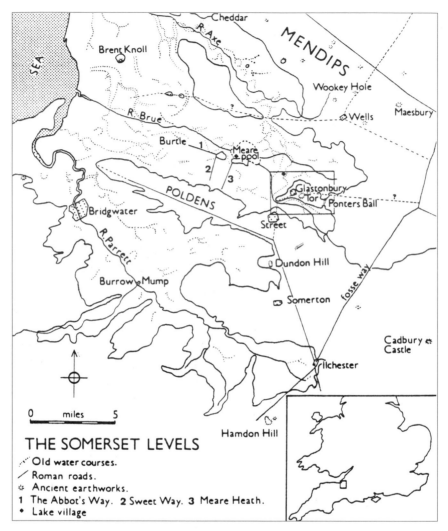

THE SOMERSET LEVELS

Old water courses.
Roman roads.
Ancient earthworks.
1 The Abbot's Way. 2 Sweet Way. 3 Meare Heath.
Lake village

▲ *This map of the Somerset Levels shows some of the old waterways and the original coastline—approximately the 20-foot contour. Many more trackways ran across the marshes than are shown here. The trackways, along with hill forts and other earthworks, reveal the extent of settlement and use of the Levels from as early as 4,000 BC. The Romans constructed several roads into the area and drained huge tracts of land.*

the centre of the island. On occasion, the hill was all that could be seen of the island as it protruded above the peculiar mists of the marsh.

Oak, ash, elm, hawthorn, and hazel covered the island. The woods opened here and there into groves of yew and wild apple. Along the edges of the marsh the reeds, willows, and alders thrived. In the centre of the isle, amid a dense grove of yew, there rose two perennial springs. Each spring had a different source of origin. One filled its course with red minerals and the other deposited an unusual accretion of white.

The Christians came and made the island a home. They fashioned a reputation for themselves based upon the early date of their arrival and upon the ancient sanctity of the place. Over the centuries they built one of the greatest abbeys and places of pilgrimage in Europe. Before the Christians, the information becomes scarcer, more deeply hidden in the mists. But we know the ancient people of Britain honoured the isle. It may be that those who created the "lost" cultures of early Europe—the sculptors and cave artists of the Magdalenian, for example—were the first to revere the lonely isle. It is likely that it was the Neolithic people who saw fit to sculpt the giant terraces that spiralled around the prominent hill. It was probably the British Celts who built the giant earthwork, Ponter's Ball, which separated the island from the outside world. Whatever their purpose and beliefs, when the visitors came to Avalon they all paused at the foot of the strangely shaped hill and drank at the two unusual springs.

Over time, the isle in the mists, the odd hill, the bounteous trees, and the two springs entered the stories, the myths. The features of the island existed to be contemplated and, for the visitors, the message of the inner and the outer worlds could be read from them. The landscape itself gave a hand in shaping the nature of knowledge. At length, matters of life and death, of this world and the next, of kings and queens, of sovereign goddesses and dying and rising gods, were located on this, the "Fortunate Isle," the "Blessed Isle of the Dead," this Avalon of the Britons.

GEOGRAPHY

The island is roughly circular and consists of four hills: the Tor—a regional name for a rocky outcropping on a hilltop—Chalice Hill, and St. Edmund's Hill. Chalice Hill is gently rounded and therefore quite distinctive. The fourth hill, Wearyall Hill, forms a limb out to the southwest. The land descends steeply to the west and more gently to the east. The Tor stands out above the other hills in the centre of the island and dramatically dominates the entire plain.

The glacial sheets of the last ice age did not reach Somerset but stopped a few miles to the north. It is possible a wall of ice a mile high towered over a dry and barren scene. The Tor would have stood in a landscape much lower in its valley floors than now. When the ice melted some 10,000 to 12,000 years ago, the sea level rose and flooded the valleys. For around 5,000 years, the Somerset Levels were under sea water and Glastonbury was a rocky island cut off from the mainland at high tide. It should be mentioned here that the tidal differences in the Bristol Channel and Severn Estuary are very great, being in the order of forty feet.

As fresh water ran off the surrounding hills and the flooded valleys slowly silted up, conditions were established for the formation of vast reed beds. As a result, the sea further retreated, and there began the process of the continual growing and dying of the reeds. This laid down a substantial depth of peat. On the platforms made by the peat, scrub and rough woodland gained a foothold. By about 4,000 BC, enough dead organic material, failing to decompose in the oxygenless water, had piled up to create a raised bog. This was a rich but rather wet and unpleasant environment.

Nevertheless, the evidence shows that people were attracted by the plentiful food supply and used the inland sea and surrounding hills intensively from about the ninth millennium BC. As the marsh built up, they laid wooden trackways down on the surface. These trackways are found preserved in the layers of peat. They reveal a similarity in their method of construction that lasted for over 5,000 years. By the Iron Age, the first millennium BC, Lake Villages appear. These are settlements raised on platforms above the level of the water. Artefacts found at Godney Lake Village just to the north of Glastonbury reveal that its inhabitants employed a wide variety of sophisticated techniques in activities ranging from glass bead making to boat building.

Aerial photography shows that the rivers Axe and Brue originally formed a myriad of waterways and often changed their course. It is likely that large ships found their way through these waterways—perhaps as far as Glastonbury—during the period 1,000 BC to AD 300. Tradition says ships from the Mediterranean came to ports at Axbridge and Cheddar from as early as 800 BC for Mendip silver and lead. It is also said that some of these ships belonged to the merchant Joseph of Arimathea and on occasion he visited the region accompanied by his young nephew, Jesus.

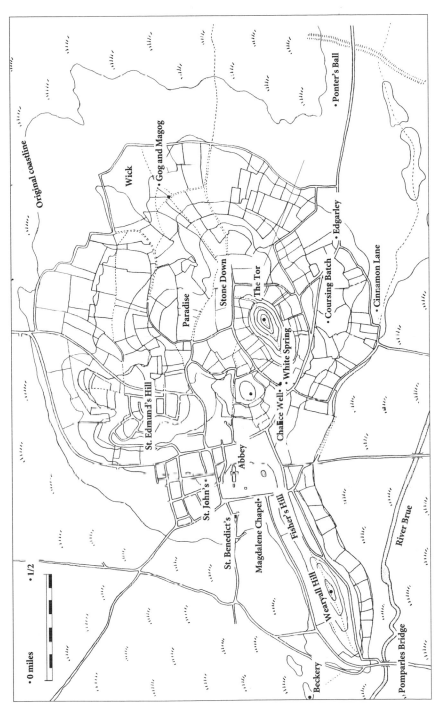

Original coastline

Wick

• Gog and Magog

• Ponter's Ball

Paradise

Stone Down

• The Tor

St. Edmund's Hill

• Edgarley

• Coursing Batch

• Cinnamon Lane

Chalice Well •

• White Spring

St. John's •

Abbey

St. Benedict's •

Magdalene Chapel •

Fisher's Hill

River Brue

• Beckery

Wearyall Hill

Pomparles Bridge

• 1/2

• 0 miles

▲ *The Isle of Avalon.*

The Levels were particularly prone to flooding from the sea, especially in the period AD 250 to400. This led to the beginning of drainage and flood prevention and the ending of the raised bog conditions. The Romans (AD 43 to 410) reclaimed large areas of land, especially in the Axe valley and to the west of Glastonbury at least as far as Burtle. Many villas, surrounded by their estates, lie in these areas. This was followed by centuries of work organized by the monks of Glastonbury Abbey. This included the construction of huge drainage ditches and sea walls, for which St. Dunstan (tenth century) is particularly credited. Canals capable of transporting barges brought people and goods right up to the Abbey. The inland sea was a busy place.

Until quite recently there was an undrained inland area known as the Meare Pool. This provided a rich source of food for the Abbey. It is said to be the place of origin of King Arthur's sword, Excalibur.

Today, large areas of the Levels are only a few feet above sea level. The land is sinking as the peat dries out, and skilful use of lock gates and continuous pumping is required to protect the land from salinity and flooding. Around Glastonbury the marsh has gone, the plain is drained and fertile, and the town with its 6,500 souls spreads over the western part of the old island. One Glastonbury tradition says that to resume and fulfill its original spiritual purpose it must once more become an island. To that end the town sees many and strange revivals of the ancient tradition.

THE TOR

Sitting high above the inverted saucer of earth that forms the island, Glastonbury Tor is a steep natural hill rising 518 feet above sea level. From some angles it resembles a conical pyramid. From other angles a thousand foot long whale-backed ridge sloping away to the southwest creates a longer, more streamlined impression. A variety of trees girdles the base. Apart from these trees, the Tor is covered in grass. There is a small area on the southeast flank where erosion—mostly caused by badgers and rabbits—have exposed underlying soil and rock and a few trees gather.

On the summit once stood the cluster of buildings that formed the Monastery of St. Michael on the Tor. Possibly founded as early as 600 but no later than AD 800, the monastery existed until the Dissolution of 1539. Now all that remains is the fourteenth-century church tower. Judging from the archaeological record, the summit of the Tor was occupied before this

▲ *The Tor from Chalice Hill.*

time by those who had intentions more militaristic than monastic. The history and legends around this "fortress" tell of associations with King Arthur. From some period, perhaps in the depths of prehistory, there is the evidence of enormous labour upon the Tor's slopes.

Huge artificially cut terraces lie in concentric rings over every flank of the Tor. Their purpose is a mystery. They are variously interpreted as a spiral path, a three-dimensional labyrinth, a Calvary mount, the steps of a pyramid, a fairy castle, labia, a variety of animistic forms, and as agricultural lynchets. Estimates of the era of construction range from Atlantean, through Neolithic and Celtic times, to the last few centuries. In recent years it is as popular to be extreme in interpretation of the terraces as it was in the scientific age to be skeptical.

We can be certain that during the Medieval period the terraces around the Tor were farmed by the monks and the concept of the Tor as a sacred or Calvary mount was enhanced by them. But it cannot be said that the monks originally built the terraces. In fact, the terraces are quite likely to have originated in a world so different from our own that their significance is hard to understand or even imagine. Although this subject will be investigated throughout this book, at this point all that can be said with any certainty, is that the Tor's uniquely dramatic shape was determined over the millennia by a diverse combination of geological, agricultural, and spiritual activities.

Two footpaths run to the summit of the Tor. One, the "Pilgrim's Path," ascends from the junction of Well House Lane and Chilkwell St.reet, through the old Fair Field and along the back of the Tor. The other departs south from the lane on the top of Stone Down and, although steeper, is a shorter climb. These ancient ways were recently made up with concrete and wooden steps. Farm animals have made closely spaced horizontal paths on almost every section of the Tor. Sheep have a predilection for leaving their droppings on the concrete of the new paths, necessitating adroit maneuvering in rain or at night.

Birds and insects congregate around the tower in summer. A cool breeze can be expected by all who climb to the top. Dawn and sunset are especially spectacular times to visit the Tor, when low-lying mists may be observed rising from the rivers and wet lands. After heavy winter rains, the Levels often flood and from the summit of the Tor it is possible to gain an impression of Glastonbury as an island, surrounded once again by the waters of marsh and sea.

GEOLOGY

The land around Glastonbury is composed of a mixture of Jurassic Blue Limestone, softer marlstone, and clays. Midford Sandstone lies on the high ground and forms the Tor. Once, this sandstone, rich in fossils, completely covered the area. It has long since eroded by the combination of water and the uplift of the land. Few places display this better than the Tor, where ammonites laid down under the sea more than a 100,000,000 years ago could recently be seen on the summit. It is suggested that the Tor survived as a proud pinnacle in a level plain as iron from even higher deposits was carried into the sandstone by the action of the spring that subsequently became Chalice Well.[2] This had the effect of hardening the sandstone so it could successfully resist erosion. At the same time the land was being pushed upward, in the case of the Tor to a height of over 500 feet. The uplift of the land may have been contributed to by the weight of northern ice sheets, which never reached further south than the Mendips.

An unusual feature of the sandstone is the presence within it of much harder round, oval, or egg-shaped boulders. A good example can be seen on the eroded section of the Tor's southeast face. Locally known as "Tor burrs," they are anything from a fraction of an inch to a few feet in diameter. The exact cause of their formation is unknown. They are composed of red rather than yellow sand, which suggests the presence of iron. It may be that iron-rich water percolating through the sand began to accrete around a small nodule that eventually grew into an eggstone.

One of the largest of these Tor burrs came to light in the excavations of the Abbey grounds. Found near the crossing of the nave and south transept, it gave rise to speculation that it was set up on the site for religious purposes long before the arrival of Christianity. It was an omphalos that may have subsequently been used for the base of a cross, having a socket cut into it. The pagan stone now lies unregarded behind the Abbot's Kitchen.

The marlstone and limestone strata below the sandstone are fairly soft and probably contain flowstones and calcite crystals. Other hills in the area reveal spectacular examples of calcite crystal formations, including geodes with a variety of crystalline mineral content.

▲ *Eggstone on the eastern flank of the Tor.*

THE TOR SPRINGS

A spring rises under the Tor, cutting tunnels and caverns into the soft limestone. This has contributed to the limestone strata becoming unstable, causing slipping and fissuring of the overlying sandstone. The summit of the Tor is literally falling apart. This has led to the instability of any buildings on the Tor and was probably the cause of the destruction of the first recorded church built there. The source of the subterranean water could be rain falling on the Tor and surrounding high ground, but the volume of the spring and other springs, including the minerally different Chalice Well, suggests water of an older and more remote origin.

The outlet for this source of water is known as the White Spring, which rises at the bottom of Well House Lane. The water is calciferous (calcium carbonate) and perennial, although its rate of flow does vary considerably. Tradition has it that the spring water emerged from the mouth of a cave made beautiful by the accumulation of white tufa or flowstone deposits. It was also said that the water-worn tunnel was large enough to allow access into the Tor itself. This is not the case now. The spring was capped and diverted into a reservoir at the end of the last century, destroying a popular local beauty spot.

Fifty yards away rises the water of Chalice Well. This spring, also perennial, does not share the same source as the White Spring. It does not fluctuate as much, flowing at an average rate of 1,000 gallons an hour. It has a chalybeate or iron content. Upon every surface the water touches, it leaves a coat of rust-red deposit. The water of the "Blood Spring" flows through a grove of yew trees, which appear to have always made their home there. As we shall see in Chapter Seven, the little valley between Chalice Hill and the Tor must once have been uniquely beautiful—and mysterious—with its trees and bubbling springs rising side by side.

PONTER'S BALL

Ponter's Ball is an eastward facing ditch and bank just under three-quarters of a mile in length. It was built to cut across the causeway that connects the island to the mainland. It is hard to see from the road. To get an inkling of the original scale of the earthwork it is worth obtaining permission and walking the fields to the north. Originally, the ditch was full of water and the ends of the bank.lost in difficult marshland.

The time of construction of Ponter's Ball is uncertain. The name comes from the monastic period of Glastonbury. It originates in the Latin *pontis vallum,* which means "the bridge over the ditch or moat." But the earthwork is atypical of anything done by the medieval monks or the Romans. It is far more in keeping with the great earthworks built in the Bronze and Iron Ages—or possibly in the Anglo-Saxon period—for defensive and boundary marking purposes. Excavation at the site revealed a few Iron Age pottery shards. This suggests the most likely date of construction was between 800 and 100 BC. The excavators could not be conclusive as the shards could have been deposited on the site earlier and there were indications that the ditch was worked at a later date, even during the time of the Abbey. The monks may have enlarged a preexisting ditch in order to control traffic, and thus revenues, to and from the great monastery on the Isle of Avalon.

If Ponter's Ball is Iron Age, it seems the Celtic people of that time were going to uncharacteristic trouble to defend very little of any strategic or economic value. The island is small and was not located on any major communication route. Hardly anything from the Iron Age has been found on the island, although there was plenty of activity nearby, with the Lake Villages to the north and Dundon Hill Fort to the south. It may be that the Celts valued the island for a different reason and felt it worthy of demarcation. If Ponter's Ball is earlier, for example from the Neolithic period, when we know the people were constructing huge monuments of earth for ceremonial purposes, then we are faced with a similar conclusion. This is a conclusion that upholds the isle as a sacred place of extreme importance for not just the people of the area but for the whole of southern Britain.

With the lack of any evidence of settlement upon the island during the pre-Christian periods when it was most likely to have been built, it is hard to determine the purpose of Ponter's Ball. It is only possible to conclude that it was constructed across the causeway as a temenos—a ritual boundary separating the outside world from the sanctified land within. If this is true, then the Isle of Avalon was held to be a sacred place from at least the time Ponter's Ball was made. This recognition was continued by the Christians who distinguished Avalon with the claim to be the site of the first church in Europe, and who would have considered it worthwhile to enhance an already existing ditch.

THE AVALONIAN TRADITIONS

To gain insights into the nature of the ancient traditions concerning the Isle of Avalon, the view taken in this book is that these traditions must be seen in the context of the surrounding landscape. It is the combination of all the landscape's natural elements that makes Avalon so powerful.

It is important that Avalon was once an island in the western part of the land—the place of the setting sun. It is important that the countryside is so flat—without the Levels, the Tor would not stand out. It is important that the two most prominent hills on the island, Chalice Hill and the Tor, should so contrast—one rounded, gentle, and soft and the other peaked, rugged, and hard. And it is important that two springs, each so different, should flow out of a cavernous underground system right where the two hills meet in the centre of the island.

Taken as a whole, the natural features of the landscape create a powerful "spirit of place." They create a setting in which practitioners of geomancy or "earth divination" say the subtle and elemental forces of the landscape meet in a dynamic polarity that can create tension or harmony. Long term residents say Glastonbury is a place of conflict, a place of the shadow and the higher self—a place of heaven or hell. A place to dive to normally inaccessible depths. It is possible to hear comments around town such as: "Where the light is brightest, the shadows are darkest." Or: "Newcomers arrive with their own ideas about the place, but after a while they get their Glastonbury initiation."

In the pre-Christian British tradition, Avalon was both an "Isle of the Dead" and an "Isle of the Blessed." It was an earthly paradise where the souls of the deceased went for rebirth. It contained the gateway to the Underworld. The broader Celtic tradition describes this gateway being within a fairy mound or a magical castle. This was always located to the west and surrounded by water. Several islands with Underworld entrances upon them were said to lay in the western seas.

The otherworldly island is said to have a tree within its boundaries. On the Isle of Avalon this was an apple, the food of otherworldly beings. Avalon may mean the "apple orchard" or the "Isle of Apples." Apple in Welsh is *aballon*. A fairy king called Avallach or Evalake presided there. Little is known about him. The Welsh tradition says he was the father of a Mother Goddess figure known as Modron. We also know from the ancient sources that the Celts developed a doctrine of immortality or metempsychosis in which the soul passed freely from the world of the living to the world of the dead and back again.

In the Glastonbury tradition, the entrance to the Underworld Realm of Annwn is located on the Tor. The guardian of the doorway is Gwynn ap Nudd, "White Son of Night." He is the Lord of the Underworld, leader of the Wild Hunt, and a "King of Faery." The entrance to the Underworld upon the Tor is not merely an abstract idea. It is physically present in the cave and the strange white mineral deposits of the White Spring.

According to the twelfth century authors Giraldus Cambrensis and Geoffrey of Monmouth, the island was the abode of Morgan le Fey. They wrote that she was the chief of nine priestesses and the daughter of the shadowy Avallach. Morgan, or Modron, like Gwynn was a guardian of the mysteries of Avalon. She may be regarded as an aspect of the Great Goddess, concerned with the Underworld, death, and rebirth. She is closely related to a keeper of the Celtic Cauldron of Rebirth, the Earth Mother or the hag Cerridwen. It was Morgan—and two queens—who received the dying King Arthur on the Isle of Avalon to prepare him for the next stage of his journey.

The departing soul, it was said, was collected by the Wild Hunt with Gwynn ap Nudd at its head, and taken into Annwn. The Cwm Annwn or the "Hounds of Hell" and the horses of the Wild Hunt were Otherworldly beings who are usually described as red and white. In *The Mabinogion* when Pwyll made his journey into Annwn and traded places with the Underworld King Arawn, not only were the creatures he encountered coloured red and white, but so were the clothes and furnishings of the people he met there.

When the soul entered the Underworld, it did not remain there for long. A magical cauldron appeared, immersion in which ensured rebirth. In the Celtic Tradition, there are several prominent cauldrons. The cauldron of the Daghda, the Irish father god, provided unfailing nourishment. The great cauldron of Bran restored the life of warriors, but not their speech. Drafts from other cauldrons were the source of wisdom. Despite their often being kept in the hands of men, the cauldron is really a symbol of the transformative and nourishing power of the Great Goddess. It would be highly significant if Cerridwen, the creator and keeper of a cauldron of poetry, wisdom, and rebirth, should have her abode on Avalon, the final resting place of the Grail in Christian mythology.

After meeting the dark face of the Goddess in her form as Cerridwen or Morgan, the soul was reborn. In later Christian literature, Glastonbury is described as being "hungry for the death of pagans." This is a specific reference to it being a place where lay the doorway to the other worlds.[3]

▲ *The Isle of Avalon from Wearyall Hill. The Holy Thorn is in the left foreground. The Abbey ruins lie left of centre. Chalice Hill and the Tor lie in the background.*

▲ *St. Joseph of Arimathea. Stained glass in St. John's Church, Glastonbury.*

In some cases, the soul dived into the waters, the cauldron, for the healing that came from retrieving and integrating lost or repressed aspects of the self. In other cases, the soul, in a shamanic-like trance, sought entrance to the Underworld for the knowledge and transformation that came from communion with spirits. Among the children of the ancient goddess Don or Danu, it was Gwydion who sought the secrets of the Underworld. Gwydion was taken by its ruler Pwyll to a mysterious island called Caer Sidi and imprisoned there. As a result he received the gift of poetic inspiration. This was the same gift that Cerridwen had prepared in her cauldron for her son. It was won by the bard Taliesin after he was transformed into several animals, then consumed by Cerridwen and reborn. Gwydion and Taliesin are thus twice-born. The stories of Arthur at Avalon may preserve an account of how he, as a shaman-leader of his people, attempted such Underworld journeys. Arthur sought the restoration of his ailing kingdom through gaining the talismans of sovereignty, which included the Cauldron of Annwn. It is possible to argue that subsequent

Glastonbury traditions built upon this ancient British foundation, perhaps most elaborately in the legend of the coming of Joseph of Arimathea.

JOSEPH OF ARIMATHEA

The story goes that Joseph of Arimathea came from Palestine, via southern France and Cornwall, carrying with him two cruets and, in some versions, the Holy Grail.[4] Whatever else the Grail may have been, it was popularly held to be the cup used by Christ at the Last Supper. The gold and silver cruets, usually depicted as red and white, contained the holy blood and water that issued from Christ's wounds at the crucifixion. When Joseph and his party reached the Isle of Avalon late in December, they were exhausted, giving name to the location "Wearyall Hill." There Joseph struck his staff into the ground and a miracle occurred. The staff instantly took root and blossomed. As an allegory of the taking root of Christianity in Avalon the miracle is exact. For Joseph was said to have remained in Avalon, to have built the "First Church in Christendom" from nothing more than withies and reeds, and buried the Grail and the two cruets near Chalice Hill. From that day forth, the tradition says, the spring that rose at the foot of Chalice Hill flowed red with the healing blood of Christ.

The legend is peculiarly satisfying, if quite unable to be proven true. Its details are mythically congruent and evolve rather than disappear when examined closely. The species of thorn Joseph brought is a Levantine variety. An offspring of the original which blossoms each Christmas stands on the hill today. The eastern end of Wearyall Hill is called Fisher's Hill and in local lore it has become the Castle of the Fisher King, the wounded keeper of the Holy Grail. As Bron in the Grail Legends, the Fisher King is the heir of the Celtic cauldron bearer Bran. He spends his time fishing on the waters which surround the Grail Castle. When the Glastonbury Zodiac was uncovered and Wearyall Hill proved to be one of the two fishes of the sign of Pisces, not only was the Grail connection amplified, but the story of the planting of the staff could be read as the ushering in of the Age of Pisces. This age of the fish, the zodiacal era in which Christianity was born, took root and flourished.

The Joseph legend is central to Glastonbury's claim for being the earliest Christian foundation outside of Palestine. The "Old Church" said to be built by Joseph from withies was on the site of what is now the St. Mary Chapel in the Abbey grounds. This extraordinary claim—at once primal and profound—was widely respected and resulted in the Abbey's enormous reputation as a place of pilgrimage. The development of its great power and wealth continued until the dissolution of the monasteries by Henry VIII.

Whatever the historic truth of the Joseph legend, it is remarkable for the structural consistency it shares with the older traditions. The Grail is strongly suggested by the cauldron of its Celtic forebears. The wounded king fishing on the waters of the lake is strongly reminiscent of the concerns of the Celtic shamans. Could the first church—dedicated to Mary—be one modelled upon an earlier Druidic sanctuary—sacred to the Earth Mother? And is it possible the two cruets are allegorically related to the Red and the White Springs?

It is pleasant to speculate that when early Christians arrived at the pagan sanctuary of Avalon, they found a flourishing and ancient initiatic tradition based upon a doctrine of immortality, an entranceway to the Underworld, and a cauldron of divine dispensation, sovereignty, healing, and rebirth. This tradition was preserved by shaman-like hermits who maintained the simplest of lifestyles. This was geomantically located beside two unusual hills and two springs. One spring, the white, emerged from out of a cave entrance below the Tor, and the other, the blood or the red, emerged from out of a grove of sacred trees. As the Christians established themselves on Avalon, and especially as esoteric ideas developed in the thirteenth century, they required a strong alternative myth to dispel this tradition and assimilate it into their religion. The legend of Joseph is just such a myth of incorporation and it reveals the very things it was meant to conceal.

The legend of Joseph with its underlying theme of Christ's death and resurrection contains the Celtic doctrine of metempsychosis or reincarnation. The powers of death and rebirth represented by the springs flowing from the entranceway to and exit from the Underworld become the water and blood of Christ's wounds. The regenerative power of the springs—originally belonging to a divine presence conceived as Earth Mother—is subsumed by the story of Christ's crucifixion and resurrection. The Holy Grail of Joseph assimilates the transformational, inspirational, and nourishing functions of the Celtic cauldrons. Holy Grail in Latin, "San Greal," easily becomes "Sang Real," Royal Blood, making evident the association between the Blood Spring and the Grail. The little huts of the initiates or shamans become the foundation of Joseph's church. The Joseph legend even reveals the sacred powers attributed to trees by the Celts in the story of the blossoming of the Holy Thorn. The details change, but the power of the place remains the same.

Although the legends of Joseph were developed by the Glastonbury Brothers in order to increase the reputation of the Abbey, they retain a mythical link to the far older pagan tradition embedded in the trees, springs, and landscape of the Isle of Avalon. From the Christian tradition it is therefore possible to read the ancient story of the island.

THE RED AND THE WHITE

The themes outlined above are repeated throughout the Avalonian Tradition and reveal a structural consistency which turns upon a polarity of red and white, a mystical vessel, a cave, baptism or transformation through water, truth to the laws of nature, and death and rebirth. These themes occur throughout the mystical traditions of the Western world, especially in the practice of alchemy. The two cruets, for example—and their associated symbolism of blood and sweat, red and white, gold and silver—find exact parallels in the alchemical processes of transmutation. The presence of these themes in the Avalonian Tradition is likely to lie in the extremely ancient honouring of the presence of the two springs. The reason for such power being imputed to the springs originates in a primary cognitive dualism—often present in myths of creation—in which red and white are forces charged with ancient, primordial, and sacred power.

An example of this process at work on the Isle of Avalon is provided by John Dee, scholar and astrologer to Queen Elizabeth I. He reported finding the red and white "alchemical powders" of St. Dunstan—Glastonbury's greatest abbot—in the Abbey grounds. It is hard to know exactly what Dee meant by this, just as it was hard to know what was meant by his comments about "the starres which agree with their reproductions on the ground," until the Glastonbury Zodiac emerged. But we do know that the monks diverted the waters of the red and white springs along Chilkwell Street down into the Abbey grounds, and that this work was probably ordered by St. Dunstan. To this day water from the Chalice Well fills the Abbey Fishpond and emerges, briefly, in Magdalene Street. As for St. Dunstan being an alchemist there is a tract by him in the British Museum called the "Philosopher's Stone." It is likely John Dee saw this.

Other examples of the primary colour dyad of red and white are provided by the creatures which appear in the Avalonian Tradition. One of the crests of the Abbey was the white pelican piercing its breast, allowing drops of red blood to feed its young. Another bird mentioned by John Dee and present in the Glastonbury Zodiac is the mythical phoenix, white in a nest of red flame. A red dragon appears in several accounts of the Tor and happens to be the emblem of Somerset. The name Cerridwen means "great white sow" and a great white sow features in a Glastonbury foundation legend. Then there are the creatures of Annwn mentioned above, the spectral red-eyed, red-eared, red-tongued, white-bodied hounds of hell, and the red and white horses of the Celtic Otherworld. The horses generally carry a beautiful woman who cannot be overtaken—such as the Underworld Queen Rhiannon. They always effortlessly remain ahead of any rider sent to engage her.

Although this is explored in the final chapters, something that may help to understand the primary qualities attributed to the colours red and white is provided by their relationship to procreation and the natural mysteries of blood, semen, and milk. White milk, distilled directly from blood, is nutritional food whose quality is unmistakable. Given that the Tor is breast-like in shape, the waters issuing from it with their white and red mineral content may be seen in this way. Semen is also white and, like milk, it is life-creating. In this case, it comes from a man. The water of the White Spring may be symbolically associated with the life-enhancing power of a woman giving milk or a man giving his seed.

In the case of the Red Spring and blood, it is not so straightforward. On the one hand, blood is a sign of death. Released uncontrollably from the body, it leads to death. In menstruation any accompanying pain may not so much suggest the fertility of the body but its opposite. During the clearly fecund state of pregnancy, the menstrual flow ceases. On the other hand, blood is a sign of life. In flowing through every part of the body or flowing in menstruation, it shows the regenerative life force is present. When a woman gives birth a mixture of blood and water is released. The waters of the Red Spring may have been seen by the early European peoples as a representation of the flow of the life force of the fecund feminine spirit throughout the land.

These associations suggest that in the past the meeting place of the two springs was as much about death as it was about birth and development of new life. The mysteries of Avalon centre upon these dual themes, and although represented by red and white symbols—and eventually the two cruets—they probably had their origins in the far older initiatic mysteries of red blood and white semen. Red and white, feminine and masculine, life and death, also find symbolic corollaries in the sun and the moon.

We can never be certain how the ancient peoples of Britain viewed the springs. The ambiguous character of red blood can signify both death and life. Meaning switches from one to the other. The same is true for the White Spring. The name Gwynn ap Nudd contains both "white" and "black." The white waters rise from under his dwelling in the Tor. The cave there is both the entranceway to the world of the dead and the emergence place of new life.

It is likely that here on Avalon, we must look at the character of transformation itself. We must allow for an invisible third force that resolves the ambiguity around the dual symbolism of red and white and makes the mysterious cycle of life, death and rebirth a complete whole. This eternal and creative process underlies the meaning of the Celtic Cauldron and the Holy Grail. The following chapters will follow the clues provided by the landscape and the Glastonbury traditions in an attempt to understand what Avalon meant to the people of the past, or failing that, what Avalon may mean to us today.

ENDNOTES

1. "Life of Gildas" in *Baring-Gould, S. & Fisher, J., Lives of the British Saints,* 1911.

2. Philip Rahtz, *Glastonbury,* London, 1993, p. 18.

3. John of Glastonbury, *Chronicle,* trans. Carley, B., Boydell 1985.

4. *Joseph of Arimathea,* Robert de Borron, circa 1200.

2

PREHISTORY:
THE FIRST COMERS

The archaeological evidence from the Isle of Avalon is very scanty for the period before the Roman invasion and the arrival of Christianity. Apart from a little detritus from the Roman period, thirty-seven seasons of excavations on the Abbey site found nothing before the sixth century. There have been no digs on the terraces or lower slopes of the Tor. Professor Philip Rahtz and colleagues partially excavated the summit during the summers of 1964-66.

A few of the flints found on the Tor are similar to some from the cave at Wookey Hole below the Mendip Hills. They date to an interglacial period of about 20,000 BC. Flints and implements from 75,000 BC onward are common on the Mendips. In the dry caves, preservation is excellent. About 12,000 years ago, after the retreat of the last ice sheets, more people moved into the area. They left evidence of their presence on the small "islands"of higher ground between Glastonbury and the Mendips.

The Neolithic period—7,000-2,000 BC— saw the beginning of permanent settlement and intensive use of the rich resources of the wetlands. Hill forts and sites with a spiritual purpose such as long barrows, henges—circles of earth—and stone circles begin to ring the area. Archaeologists turned up some Neolithic flints on the Tor and a greenstone axe. This strongly shaped and weathered stone didn't look like it was ever used. It may have been a votive offering. Other finely worked axes have been found in the marshes, notably along the trackways.

The Bronze Age—2,000 to 800 BC—and the Iron Age—800 BC to AD 40—are also not represented on the island, although plenty of material was found at the Lake Villages nearby. Not enough evidence has been found to make any conjectures about the early history of the Tor or the island as a whole. It is a mystery where the inhabitants of the Lake Villages buried their dead. To gain a full picture of the prehistoric period, the Isle of Avalon needs to be set in its greater geographical and cultural contexts.

SOMERSET: 4,000-2,000 BC

The evidence from the peaty depths of the Somerset Levels shows the introduction of a mixed farming and hunting economy from at least as early as 4,000 BC. This replaced an earlier hunter-gathering and nomadic way of life. The settlers used stone tools to cut timbers for raised trackways over the marshlands. These trackways were remarkable structures. Made of split planks laid on piles of brush and wickerwork, they were held in place by stakes and long pegs driven into the marsh. The "Abbot's Way" between the isles of Westhay and Burtle was over a mile and a half long. It required for its construction over 10,000 trees, mostly alder—which does not rot—oak, ash, and hazel. The trackway was built around the middle of the third millennium—2,500 BC. The "Sweet Track" is even earlier, around 3,800 BC.

Studies of the Meare Heath Track show that the planks, cross-beams, and stakes that went into its construction were part of a single, concerted effort carried out with stone tools over one summer. The trackway is over a mile in length and dates to about 1,500 BC. It is similar to the earlier examples. The evidence suggests that the trackways were not built by small, independent bands of semi-agricultural hunters. They were the product of a large organized society capable of mobilizing considerable amounts of labour.[1]

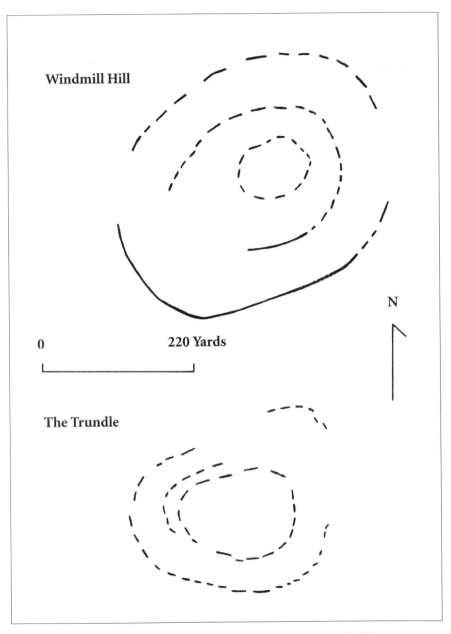

Windmill Hill

The Trundle

N

0   220 Yards

▲ *Two examples of Neolithic Causewayed Camps: Windmill Hill near Avebury above, the Trundle in Sussex below. Each "camp" is delineated by a broken series of ditches and banks arranged in rings, circa 4,000 BC.*

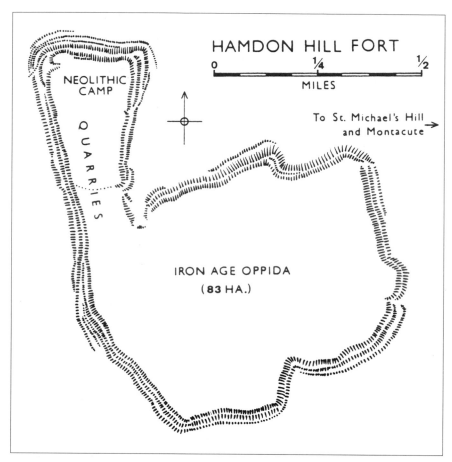

HAMDON HILL FORT

0   ¼   ½

MILES

NEOLITHIC CAMP

QUARRIES

To St. Michael's Hill and Montacute →

IRON AGE OPPIDA
(83 HA.)

▲ *Hamdon Hill. In contrast to the Neolithic Causewayed campus, the earthenworks here are methodical and continuous. They were constructed for defensive purposes, not ritual.*

THE PREHISTORIC MONUMENTS

The first great permanent settlements in southern Britain, or if not settlements, then oddly broken enclosures known as "causewayed camps," were built in the same period as the first trackways. These are regionally distributed across southern Britain. Whether ceremonial, economic, or political in their purpose—or, most likely, a mixture of all three—they marked the centres of population. Several camps lay near the Levels and the inland sea was an important part, if not the major component, of their resource base. The Levels allowed ease of transportation. They provided rich, easily worked soil as well as a limitless supply of fish and game. To avoid the agues of the damp environment, people may have delayed entering the marshes for prolonged periods until summer. This provides a possible origin for the name the "Summer Country," the "Summer Sea," or "Somerset."

The settlements on Dundon Hill, Brent Knoll, Cannington, Dolebury, Maes Knoll, and Maesbury reveal occupation from at least the late Bronze Age circa 1000 BC. It is likely some of these hill forts had much earlier periods of occupation. The excavations at Cadbury Castle indicated Neolithic occupation from about 3,000 BC. The henge at Gorsey Bigbury on the Mendips comes from the same period. Hamdon Hill to the south of the Levels not only has a claim to being one of the largest continually occupied hill tops in the country, but reveals Neolithic usage from the late fifth millennium BC. The Mendip Hills to the north show the beginning of highly intensive settlement from around this time. Life around the Summer Sea was rich, protected, and without interruption.

All these early works, like the trackways, required massive organization of labour. It took years to construct, basket by basket, the concentric rings of earthworks at Cadbury. The same effort was required for the construction of the henges and other monuments on the Mendips. The long barrow at Stoney Littleton circa 3,200 BC, the three circular henges at Priddy circa 3,000 BC, or the stone circles at Stanton Drew, built around 2,500 BC, required thousands, probably millions, of hours of labour. From these Neolithic contexts, can any comparisons be drawn with the construction of Ponter's Ball or the terraces on Glastonbury Tor?

A CEREMONIAL MONUMENT?

Assuming for the time being the terraces on the Tor were not built solely for defensive or agricultural purposes, the people of the late Neolithic period were more than capable of organizing the huge amount of labour necessary for their construction. The Neolithic axe found on the Tor was in its day a highly prized object and may have been a votive offering left at a place of special significance. A similar axe head, made of polished jadeite imported from Brittany, was found beside the Sweet Track. It was probably deposited as a consecrational offering of the raised trackway in about 3,800 BC. There was also a beautifully made long-bow of yew and, by contrast, an extremely crude wooden figurine of a woman.

From about this time, throughout the fourth millennium BC, the Neolithic people began the undertaking of building massive ceremonial monuments. The mysterious causewayed enclosures appear to be for large gatherings devoted to highly ritualized purposes. They also built the chambered mounds or long barrows. The well known West Kennet long barrow in Wiltshire may date to as early as the middle of the fourth millennium. The classic examples of decorated and astronomically oriented chambered mounds in Ireland, Newgrange, Knowth, and Dowth were built circa 3,200 BC. The exact purpose of the chambered barrows is unknown. They were more than likely to have been the scene of ritual practices for the dead. Such practices nearly always involved a cult of lineage or of mythologized ancestors.

Somerset, with its access to the sea, enjoyed connections with northwestern Europe, especially Brittany. Megalithic monuments were constructed here from about the middle of the fifth millennium—much earlier than in Britain. Chambered mounds or dolmens (capped stones), standing stones, or menhirs—eventually organized at places like Carnac into complex circles or rows—were common features of the landscape. The regional distribution of the Megalithic sites shows that each farming community had its own dolmen or chambered mound, and that each distinct topographical area had its highly revered, greater "tribal" monument.

After about 2,600 BC, stone circles begin to be built by the people of southern Britain. These were usually preceded or accompanied by a circular inner ditch and outer bank. This is known as a henge. One of the most famous henge monuments is Avebury—which boasts the largest stone circle in the world. The vast henge at Durrington Walls lay near Stonehenge, and Mount Pleasant and Maumbury Rings lay to the east of Glastonbury in Dorset near the river Frome. These, like the causewayed enclosures of the fourth millennium, could accommodate thousands of people, but are not quite so haphazardly built. On the Mendips, the local henge monuments at Gorsey Bigbury and Priddy are smaller, but Priddy did have three circles close together in a row. Such regional diversity is typical of the Neolithic age, where hardly a single ceremonial monument resembles another. The average-sized henge enclosure at Neolithic Stonehenge, for example, has an avenue running to it, a larger avenue—the cursus— nearby, a wooden structure at its centre, and a few megaliths with some fairly complex orientations to sun and moon. Another henge of similar size and orientation lay nearby. The carved standing stones and their spectacular lintels came much later.

Unlike Brittany, Ireland, or central southern Britain (Wessex), the area around the Summer Sea does not have any recognizable major monuments. The Priddy circles, which in total approach the size of the great henges, each amount to only a small enclosure and are part of a grouping that appears to look north rather than south. This left a vacuum in what is now central Somerset. This is very strange given the numerous settlements, the labour-intensive trackways, and the large population base. Although it is always possible another henge was totally obliterated or the people preferred to follow a different local tradition, it is a mystery where the "tribal" monument of the Summer Sea people lay. It is also a mystery as to why there is not more evidence of occupation on the Isle of Avalon. Perhaps the archaeologists have just not looked in the right place.

Although it would be a mistake at this point to jump to any conclusions, the intense efforts that went into the terraces on the Tor were probably made during the Neolithic period after about 3,000 BC. The diversity of monumental undertakings at this time shows that the Neolithic people were not adverse to the unusual and moving earth around was standard practice. Indeed, beginning in about 2,700 BC, the populace moved millions of baskets of soil to make the seven tiers of Silbury Hill, the largest prehistoric mound in Europe. Glastonbury Tor can be seen in this context as fulfilling the role of the greater ceremonial monument for the peoples of the area around the Summer Sea. This would give the Tor a significance comparable to the great henges. The concentric terraces on the Tor are similar to the circular monuments, except of course, they also possess a vertical dimension. The evidence for this at present can only be by inference. It is also possible the terraces were carved before the third millennium, when the first great causewayed enclosures had several rings to them.

Why couldn't the terraces have been built later?

SOMERSET 2,000–0 BC

By 2,000 BC—the early Bronze Age—social changes and the influx of different cultural styles into southern Britain meant that the huge collective ceremonial centres were no longer being built or even maintained. The Avebury complex had gone through several phases of construction during the third millennium—including the building of Silbury Hill—but by its end the locals were building farm walls across the great avenues. They abandoned Durrington Walls and destroyed Mount Pleasant. Stonehenge is an exception to this. The last phases of building there—the sarsens and their lintels, completed about 1,500 BC—can be understood in terms of a social elite expressing its power in traditional forms whose earlier purpose they emulated but no longer really understood. The structure that previ-

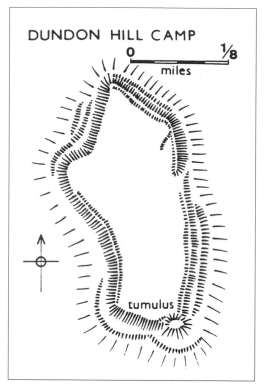

DUNDON HILL CAMP

0 ⅛

miles

tumulus

▲ *Dundon Hill, five miles south of Glaston-bury, is a fairly typical Iron Age hill fort. It occupies the whole hill top, about eighteen acres, the same as Cadbury, but has only one major bank and ditch.*

ously stood on the site with its complex lunar alignments, was replaced by a grandiose carved stone monument with a simpler, single solar axis.

Increase in social stratification, especially in the second millennium BC, led to the construction of more individually oriented monuments. The round barrows, unlike the long barrows, were clearly built to feature the burials of powerful leaders. Social change also led to the strengthening of the existing hill forts, as well as to the building of new forts and other utilitarian agricultural and defensive systems. Colossal ramparts, dozens of miles long, spread across the landscape. Ponter's Ball at Glastonbury could be a defensive outwork of some Bronze Age tribal chieftain of the Summer Sea.

Around 800 BC—the beginning of the Iron Age—British society was transforming into the European Celtic culture described in historical sources. In fact, some of the best material evidence of these people comes from the Lake Villages at Glastonbury and Meare. Settled from about 450 BC, the lake dwellers built trackways using techniques that began over 3,000 years before. They fashioned metal for tools, weapons, and personal finery. They were part of a sophisticated society capable of building sea-going vessels, smelting glass, and weaving extremely fine robes and tapestries. Given their proximity to the Isle of Avalon and the profusion of their cultural artifacts, it is strange that hardly anything belonging to these people is found there. A few shards at Ponter's Ball, Beckery, Chalice Well, and on the natural raised platform known as the Mound just to the north of Wearyall Hill, shows they did at least frequent the island.[2]

During this time, society possessed a priestly class—the learned and respected Druids. Spiritual practices focused on the initiation of the individual and on the local spirits of place. The Druids turned away from the colossal ceremonial works of earlier days and concentrated on education, the development of the bardic arts, the sanctification of the hearth, the holy wells and the sacred groves. Like the early Neolithic nomads, their concern was to preserve the qualities of the natural landscape. What the British Celts did not do was expend enormous amounts of energy on religious works. The intention of the Druids was to maintain the sanctuary of Avalon in its pristine state.

As the British tribes went through these social changes, and as new technology offered better weapons of war, they often came into conflict. It seems likely that the Wessex people who built the last stage of Stonehenge—and later the great hill fort at Maiden Castle in Dorset—were seeking to maintain their control of trade with the continent. Through the monopoly of prestigious items such as axes and swords, emphasis upon social ranking escalated. The description of the fiercely competitive, proud, and vainglorious warrior class, found in the written sources of Iron Age Celtic society, seems accurate. These people built defensive earthworks around large hilltops which could accommodate many inhabitants and their herds of cattle. They also built linear ramparts across the countryside, dividing their territory from that of the neighbouring tribe. Glaston-

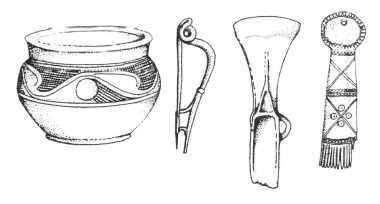

▲ *Objects from the Glastonbury Lake Villages, circa second century BC.*

bury Tor cannot possibly qualify as a hillfort, and only remotely can Ponter's Ball qualify as a tribal boundary. There was nothing on the Isle of Avalon—no herds of cattle, no mines, no towns, no harbours, not even any strategic significance—for a tribe to protect.

Lacking direct archaeological evidence from the Isle of Avalon, it is only possible to conclude that the most substantial prehistorical hypothesis for the Tor is that the terraces imply an undertaking comparable with the great ceremonial monuments of the British Isles built between 3,300 and 2,000 BC. The terraces may be earlier, but not later. If this is true, the Tor served primarily as a local ceremonial centre for the many people of the Neolithic age who lived on the surrounding mainland, and secondarily as a greater centre of unique spiritual significance for the peoples of at least southern and western Britain. There was nothing else quite like it to be found. This spiritual significance probably continued into the Bronze and Iron Ages. Although the Celtic peoples worshipped at the natural sacred sites and were unlikely to have made the terraces, the Tor no doubt had a meaning for them, the roots of which reached deep into the ancient past. The second part of this book will explore what that meaning may have been.

ENDNOTES

1. Bryony and John Coles, *Sweet Track to Glastonbury: The Somerset Levels in Prehistory,* London, 1986.

2. Arthur Bullied, *The Lake Villages of Somerset* (5th edition), Glastonbury, 1958.

3

EARLY HISTORY:
THE OLD CHURCH
AND KING ARTHUR

The first references to the Isle of Avalon appear in twelfth-century sources. Geoffrey of Monmouth's *History of the Kings of Britain*, written about 1140, describes Avalon as the place to which the mortally wounded King Arthur was carried. Giraldus Cambrensis, writing slightly later, does the same. Both claim to have much older information, as do the monks of Glastonbury Abbey. Specific references to the history of the Tor also come from the twelfth and thirteenth centuries and are very much the product of myth-making by the monks.

CARADOC OF LLANCARFAN

In the mid-twelfth century, Caradoc, a monk of Llancarfan, wrote a *Vita Gildae*, translated as *Life of Gildas*. Gildas was a sixth-century monk who included in his rhetoric an account of the early history of Britain. Gildas focused on a description of the struggle between the Britons and the Saxons in which King Arthur prominently featured. Although Gildas does not mention Arthur, Caradoc does, and connects him with

Avalon. This, as we shall see, is a peculiar kind of fabrication that does find some confirmation in the archaeological record.

Caradoc wrote that in the early sixth century Arthur besieged Melwas, king of the Summer Country, in his Tor-top Glastonbury stronghold. Melwas had abducted Guinevere and was holding her prisoner there. This is only one of many abductions of Queen Guinevere that appear in the Arthurian legends. Arthur raised an army in Devon and Cornwall and marched to Avalon. Due to the marshy nature of the surrounding land, he could not secure her release. The situation seemed locked in stalemate until Gildas and the Abbot intervened. They held a service in the "Old Church"—St. Mary's in the Abbey—and Guinevere was restored to Arthur.

The story appeared improbable as excavations in the Abbey grounds could find no conclusive evidence of a church being there during this time. Caradoc seemed involved in the traditional pastime of creating an ancient and august history for the Abbey. All Caradoc really had to go on was the fact that Gildas was alive at the time and may have visited Glastonbury. To this Caradoc added information of uncertain and mythical origin. Then the excavations took place on the Tor. The evidence suggested that some kind of late fifth- or early sixth-century military outpost had been there. Despite Caradoc's efforts to make Church history appear older than it really was, some details of the abduction story are borne out by the facts. With just a few men, Melwas—or someone like him—could have held out on the Tor. By placing more men on Ponter's Ball he could have caused any opponent great difficulty in bringing forces across the marshes to the island.

It will be necessary to dwell upon further historical and archaeological evidence to evaluate the truth of this story. For how did Avalon acquire strategic military importance after the Roman withdrawal when it never had any before? Or perhaps the question is, who or what exactly did Melwas or Avalon have that Arthur wanted?

WILLIAM OF MALMESBURY

William of Malmesbury, a renowned and reliable historian, wrote a history of Glastonbury Abbey in about AD 1130, *De Antiquitate Glastonie Ecclesie*. It contains the first account of the story of Joseph of Arimathea. It also includes a Charter of St. Patrick, but unfortunately—like the rest of William's work—it can be shown to have many later interpolations.

The Charter, supposedly written by St. Patrick, asserted that two missionaries, Phagan and Deruvian, visited the "Old Church" of Glastonbury in AD 166. They attributed its foundation to the twelve disciples of St. Philip who came to Yniswitrin in AD 63. At that time three pagan kings granted "twelve hides" of land to the Christians. From here it is but a short step to the story of the coming of Joseph of Arimathea and the Holy Grail. Phagan and Deruvian renewed the monastic community with twelve of their companions and restored the Old Church. A King Lucius reconfirmed the rights to the land. This is exactly the kind of history the monks of the Abbey were seeking to substantiate their claims to an early foundation.[1]

The charter also includes a description of Patrick's own visit to Glastonbury in which he claimed to have found the successors to the original twelve monks. He reorganized them and became their first Abbot. "Much later," Patrick was said to have written, "taking Brother Wellias with me, I climbed with great difficulty through a dense wood to the peak of a hill which rises on the island. When we reached it we saw an old oratory, almost destroyed yet suitable for devotion .... We found writing to the effect that saints Phagan and Deruvian had built the oratory in honour of St. Michael." [2]

St. Patrick and another Irish saint, Brigit, were important figures in the history of the establishment of Christianity in the British Isles. Both were said to have visited Glastonbury in the fifth century after completing their work in Ireland. St. Brigit traditionally was the founder of the chapel at Beckery. It is just possible Patrick was the first Abbot of Glastonbury. While Patrick was on the Tor, he further decided "there would always be two brothers in that place. And I, Patrick ... grant one hundred days of indulgence to all who shall hew with axe or mattock the wood that covers this hill."

Apart from spurious facts such as pagan kings making grants of land when Britain was under Roman rule and the indulgence—an ability of Medieval priests to grant time off from purgatory—the Charter does contain the interesting information that the Tor was densely wooded in the early Christian era, whenever that may have been. And that there was a hermitage—an incipient monastery—there from an early time. The Glastonbury traditions would have it there from the first or second centuries AD. The archaeological and historical evidence suggest otherwise. In the first place, the monastic movement did not get under way until at least the late fourth and fifth centuries—the time of Patrick. In the second place, Caradoc's sixth-century military stronghold on the Tor is somewhat at variance with any monastic claim.

William also included in his history an alternative account of how Glastonbury was founded and how it received its name. There were twelve brothers from the north, one of whom, Glasteing, settled at Wells. He had a huge white sow, said by some to have eight feet, who became pregnant. One day she took off across the marshes with Glasteing in pursuit. Eventually he caught up with her. She was suckling newly born piglets beneath an apple tree on the Isle of Avalon. Glasteing brought his family to the island of the apple trees, which then bore his name, Glasteing-burgh. The route the sow took subsequently became known as the Sow's Way.[3] The story sounds apocryphal, but it also sounds as though it retains truth regarding the ancient sanctity of the Isle.

THE EXCAVATIONS ON THE TOR

Paleolithic flints, the Neolithic greenstone axe, and a leaf-shaped arrowhead—found in 1918—are among the few pieces of prehistoric evidence from the Tor. The axe was quite weathered and looked as though it was thrown to its resting place just below the trig point by later construction work. It is probable that a similar fate happened to all the prehistoric material.

Finds from the Roman period (AD 43 to 410) consist of a few tile fragments, some shards of coarse local pottery, and much finer imported Mediterranean ware. Little can be made from the evidence. Someone may have carried it up the Tor in a later period. Nothing was found resembling the hill top temples at nearby Lamyatt, Priest's Hill at Pedwell, Pagan's Hill, or Brean Down (all circa AD 300). This is surprising given the attractive qualities and, no doubt, the long standing pagan traditions of the Tor. But

▶

*Key to the main features found on the Tor: **Prehistoric:** (1) Neolithic axe head. **Dark Age:** (2) cairn, (3) north-south graves, (4) hearth, (5) south platform and bronze head. **Early Monastic:** (7) post holes of north-south building, (8) building platforms, (9) cells, (10) cross head, (11) "hollow way," (12) cross base. **The Medieval Monastery:** (13) foundations of the first church—1100s, (14) buttresses of the second church—1300s, (15) wall, (16) corner of a large building with ovens, (17) wall trench, (18) steps.*

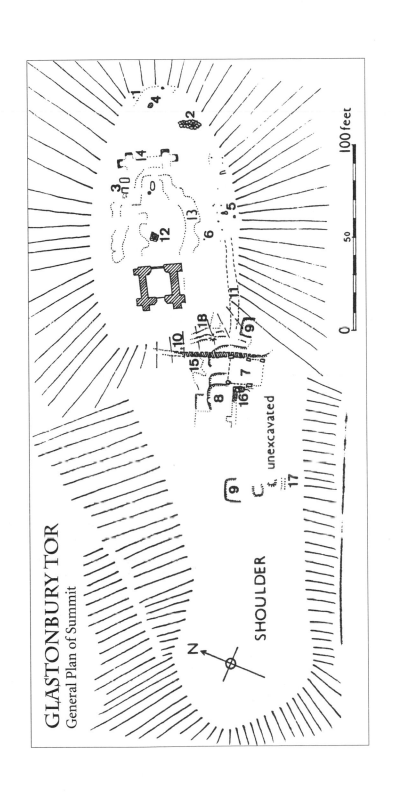

GLASTONBURY TOR
General Plan of Summit

SHOULDER

N

unexcavated

100 feet

0   50   100feet

the thin scattering of Roman evidence on the island suggests that the whole island was the temple, and continued observation of the ancient Avalonian Tradition drew the line at the construction of any artificial features. Evidence for the first period of occupation of the Tor dates to the fifth and sixth centuries.

THE FIRST SETTLEMENT

The excavations of 1964-66 extended over the summit and part of the western shoulder of the Tor. The finds were nearly all around the crest. Builders had levelled the summit for the churches and dug out the shoulder in rock quarrying and construction operations in the Saxon and Medieval periods.

What Professor Rahtz called the "Dark Age" or the "Arthurian" settlement consisted of a series of platforms cut into the bedrock to make it level. This first phase of occupation lay on the more sheltered southern and eastern sides of the summit. A small collection of buildings, half buried in the ground, huddled together out of the prevailing winds. They contained several hearths, in two of which archaeologists found crucible fragments and bronze residue. It is likely the hearths were used for metal working. A helmeted bronze head in the "long" Celtic style was discovered nearby, and Rahtz thought it was made on the Tor.

A southern platform consisted of a long, broad, fairly level shelf some four or five feet below the present church area. Most of this was removed by erosion. Such features as remained—timber slots and post-holes—suggested to the excavators that the largest building of this period had once stood there. Could this have been an early chapel?

The rubbish from this settlement included two hundred pounds of food remains, mostly bones of cattle, sheep, and pigs. They were slaughtered elsewhere and only the joints carried up the Tor. Professor Rahtz thought that from what is known of Celtic monks the heavy emphasis on meat-eating was at variance with their ascetic practice. Two graves oriented north-south in conformity with pagan practice also reduced the likelihood of this being a Christian site.

Other finds from this period included the base of a cairn, ten by five feet in area, and fragments of imported Mediterranean amphorae. These containers are only found at post-Roman sites of some significance in southwest Britain. They originally carried wine or oil. On the west coast, excavations at the site of Tintagel revealed a progression from military

Bronze head found in the earliest "Dark Age"
level of occupation on the Tor. It fitted over
a larger object such as a handle. The eyes
were probably enamelled. The narrow
face with a slit mouth is characteristic
sixth century "long" Celtic work.

stronghold to monastery. It is from the evidence of Tintagel that the date of this similar settlement on the Tor is fixed through the sixth to the mid-seventh century AD.

The excavator's interpretation of the evidence favoured either a small outpost—a look-out for a permanent but small number of soldiers—or a fortress-stronghold of a local chieftain. The site was adequately protected from attack and there was plenty of water at the foot of the Tor. So while the archaeological evidence does not support the second-century oratory found by St. Patrick, or the fifth-century hermitage he claimed to have established there, it does support Caradoc's account of Melwas, the sixth-century chief of the Summer County, who held off Arthur from his Glastonbury Tor stronghold.[4]

SOMERSET IN THE DARK AGES

The dates usually attributed to King Arthur lie somewhere between AD 450 and 540. To assess the possibility of someone like Arthur besieging the Tor at this time, we need to look at the greater context of Britain.

After the Roman withdrawal from Britain circa AD 400, there was a renaissance of Celtic culture. This is often misleadingly called the "Dark Ages" because of bias toward literate and urban cultural forms. The Celts possessed a rich oral tradition, not a written one, and a decentralized social order that was no less "civilised" than the highly centralized Roman.

Evidence from sites across the country shows that the Roman rule left the traditional Celtic way of life pretty much alone. Of course, almost four hundred years had an impact, but Celts and Romans shared pantheistic beliefs—and eventually Christian ones—and the Roman system allowed and fostered cultural diversity and regionalism. As long as the Celts paid their taxes, they were free to think and behave as they had always done. The Druids, whom the Romans persecuted, fled to Scotland or Ireland. So when the Romans withdrew, due to external pressure felt in the centre of their empire, the Britons were able to pick up where they had left off and combine the best of the Roman experience with their own.

The burning questions of the time were identical with those faced by the Romans: How to keep the "barbarians," in this case the Saxons and the Picts, from invading, and who had the authority to unite the diverse regions of the land against them.

One possibility lay in the Church. The Romans had sponsored it after the third century, but it was forced to retreat with them. By the sixth century it was developing its uniquely Celtic flavoured religious practices in Wales, Ireland, and other remote strongholds. It held the promise of restoring Roman urban, legal, and administrative traditions that had once brought unity, law, and order. But Christian activity in Britain as a whole was weak—Gildas complained a great deal about that—and there is nothing definitely ecclesiastical in Somerset until about AD 700.

In the secular arena, there was a struggle for authority. The historical traditions around Vortigern, a British chieftain, Uther Pendragon, and Ambrosius Aurelianus indicate internal chaos among the powerful. Theirs was a long history of warfare against the people who came in ships across the eastern sea. They fought many battles; some successful, some not. As part of this struggle the British reoccupied some of the old Celtic hill forts. These included Eddisbury in Cheshire and Dinas Powys in Wales. In most cases only a small fraction of the original acreage was used, but this was not so for Cadbury Castle.

CADBURY CASTLE

Excavations at Cadbury, eleven miles southeast of Glastonbury, in 1966 and 1967 revealed substantial structures in the centre of the site. Considerable amounts of other fifth- to sixth- century occupation material lay all around. During this period, the British had rebuilt the walls and constructed gate towers. The quality of finds indicated a rich and powerful settlement.

Given the Arthurian traditions around Cadbury Castle—the locals always held it to be the site of Camelot—the archaeological evidence sug-

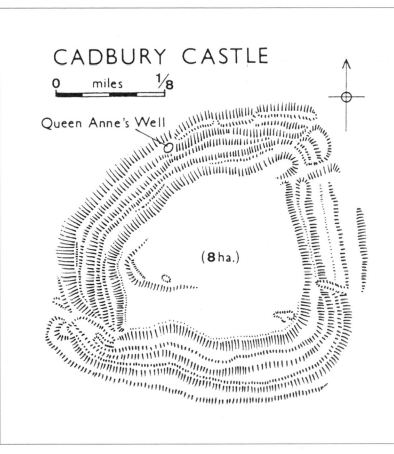

CADBURY CASTLE

0   miles   ⅛

Queen Anne's Well

(8 ha.)

▲ Plan of Cadbury showing the complex defenses. Four sets of ditches and three
entrances are discernible. The two main entrances had gate houses and breast-
works to outflank attackers. The hill was first occupied in the Neolithic period
and then became the capital of the Celtic tribe known as the Durotiges in the
Bronze and Iron Ages. The British abandoned Cadbury during the Roman
period and then strongly rebuilt it during the "Dark Ages." Here, the
Britons, led by a "King Arthur," maintained a vital centre from which
to resist the Saxons. The Saxon victory at Deorham in AD 577 drove a
wedge between the Britons of Wales and those of the Southwest.
Cadbury and outlying posts like Glastonbury Tor, were on or
near the front line of this confrontation. After AD 600, Saxons
appeared in the area and the British abandoned Cadbury.
It was occupied again in the early eleventh century
and became an important administrative centre.

gests that when a powerful leader finally arose to unite the Britons against the Saxons he made his base at Cadbury. At some point, probably about AD 518, this ruler had a great victory over the Saxons at a place called Mount Badon. This was almost certainly in central southern Britain, and possibly not far from Cadbury near Bath. Contemporary authors are reluctant to name this leader, but the Welsh sources have no difficultly with this—it was King Arthur.

Geoffrey Ashe has argued that a king, known as Riothamus, was around with the right credentials at the time, and he was a heroic figure around which the Arthurian legends could coalesce. Riothamus is historically shadowy as, first, his name could be a title, such as "High King," and secondly, after his initial successes he vanished quickly from the scene. Geoffrey Ashe suggests he fits the description of a British king who took an army onto the continent to fight the invaders there, but mysteriously disappeared. After a short but heady rule, Riothamus could be reported neither dead nor alive—the perfect candidate for a "once and future king."[5]

In the British context, "Dark Age" Somerset, with its tracts of easily defended marshy ground, was far enough away from the invading Saxons to form a power base. It was likely to have had a string of military outposts across it that were controlled from Cadbury. If any local chieftain felt secure enough to go against his Cadbury king, then — like Melwas — he may well have found soldiers at his door.

The details of Caradoc of Llancarfan's story are thus borne out quite well by the historical and archaeological evidence. But as Chapter 6 will show, the tale of Melwas and Arthur does have some other rather unhistorical mythological resonances.

THE SECOND SETTLEMENT

The second period of occupation on the Tor, dated to between AD 800 and 1100, is characterized by Saxon and Christian finds. Although it is possible that this phase began earlier and independently of the Abbey, it was not long before it came under the Abbey's control. In the early 600s, Saxon names begin to occur on the list of Abbots. Worgret circa 601 seems to be the last Celtic Abbot, but this may be a fabrication. Excavations on the Abbey site reveal nothing specifically Christian there at this time.

It is not until AD 700, the traditional date of King Ine's gift of land, that foundations for a substantial church can be shown to exist in the Abbey grounds. While it is conceivable that the first settlement on the Tor transformed into a monastic colony from as early as AD 600. It is hard to be certain.

On the shoulder of the Tor, excavation revealed a set of platforms cut into the rock to provide the basic shape for small, square buildings. Some of these "cells" contained hearths. One larger structure with several post-holes for supporting large timbers was rendered with stucco and probably used as a public space. Its north-south orientation made it unlikely to be a chapel. The archaeologists gave a ninth century date to this level.

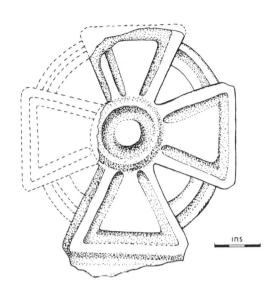

▲ *The wheel-headed cross from the Tor. The pattern is repeated on both sides and is similar to examples from the tenth or eleventh centuries. The cross on its shaft may have stood alone on the summit with a few low buildings to the south and west. (After Philip Rahtz.)*

One of the more spectacular finds was the top of a wheel-headed cross. Carved from a block of Doulting stone, it had originally surmounted a short column. This cross probably stood on a square base oriented to the compass found in the centre of the summit. It was located before any churches were built there. Comparison with other crosses suggested a date of around AD 1000.

By the tenth century, a small monastic community or hermitage existed on the summit of the Tor. The refuse from this period, in contrast to the one before, was mostly made up of the bones of fish and fowl. This would be in conformity with Benedictine practice. The small buildings on the shoulder were probably monk's cells. There was a path the excavator called the "hollow way" cut into the rock leading up to the summit where the wheel-headed cross stood. Perhaps a small chapel stood beside it.

So the thirteenth-century texts of the Abbey point to a monastic tradition on the Tor at least three hundred years old. It may even be older, as the sixth- to eighth-century settlement levels cannot conclusively be shown to be secular. The evidence of meat eating does not entirely rule out a monastic site. There are plenty of bones in the early levels of the Celtic monasteries at Tintagel and Iona. If the Christians were here from the beginning, or at least the end of the first period of occupation, then the Tor would be among the earliest sites of this kind in England. This is exactly the kind of antiquity the monks of the Abbey always claimed.

GLASTONBURY ABBEY

As described above, the archaeological evidence from the Abbey grounds begins telling an ecclesiastical story from about the seventh century AD. The written record would have it begin far earlier. It is possible that both views are correct. As the claim of the monks for a foundation "by God himself" is an allegory of the sanctity Avalon had enjoyed for millennia. Furthermore, the claim that Joseph of Arimathea built a church from "withies twisted around in a circle," may allude to an Avalonian tradition—ancient even in the days of the Druids—of building nothing more on the holy isle than huts made from bent saplings and reeds. Such a tradition would, of course, be entirely unexcavatable.

It is this tradition that points toward an ancient mystery, echoes of which are still alive today, whereby the spiritual way of life is maintained upon the earth through simple communion with the natural world. By living directly with the elements and introducing nothing to overly manipulate them, a nomadic, tribal or shamanistic culture remains in harmony with the primal forces of creation. In this state they possess extraordinary psychic and spiritual powers. Such a tradition upon the Isle of Avalon may even point to nakedness on the part of the inhabitants—a condition the Romans reported elsewhere in Britain. It is certainly indicated by the lack of archaeological detritus, especially metal objects, as well as the complete absence of temples or other artificial shrines upon the island.

It is entirely possible that when the Christians did come: either St. Joseph and his twelve followers in AD 63, or St. Phagan and St. Deruvian in 166, or St. Patrick and St. Brigit in the fifth century, or St. David in the sixth, or Paulinus in 625 to enclose the Old Church tended by these saints, or finally because of the gift of land from the Saxon King Ine just after 700, that the Avalonian spiritual tradition had never lapsed. Each newcomer added their contribution to it, while maintaining the original patterns and mysteries of the ancient tradition.

In his work *New Light on the Ancient Mystery of Glastonbury,* John Michell presents a splendid case for the continuation at Glastonbury of a mystical tradition of remote antiquity, and indeed one that originated from a heavenly source. He argues that this tradition can be recognized by certain features, not least of which is a twelve-fold division of spatial and social forms. He points out that the City of Revelation of St. John has this structure, that Israel had twelve tribes, that Christ had twelve disciples. Twelve was the traditional number of the missionaries who accompanied St. Joseph to Avalon and twelve was the number of monks maintained there through the reorganization by St. Patrick. Then there are the twelve brothers of Glasteing, the twelve knights of the Round Table and the twelve hides that make up the traditional amount of land originally given to the Abbey. Finally, the stellar zodiac—said to take terrestrial form around Avalon—is composed of twelve astrological signs.[6]

John Michell claims that the geometry of the Old Church—which contained the original wattle hut—perpetuates this twelve-fold scheme. This geometry can be recreated by combining the written sources with the archaeological evidence. The primary evidence is the dimensions of the Mary Chapel which stands on the site today. After the great fire of 1184 that destroyed the Old Church and all its priceless relics, the monks took extreme care to conserve the original pattern. When William of Malmesbury saw the original church in 1130, he wrote the following cautious statement:

> One can observe there upon the paving, in the form of triangles and squares, stones carefully interlaced and sealed with lead. If I believe that some sacred mystery is concealed under them, I do no harm to religion.[7]

This "sacred mystery," Michell argues, was maintained in the new church. It is found in all architectural traditions able to invoke the sacred source. It is not exclusive to any religion. Thus it is found in the design of Stonehenge as well as in Indian and Japanese temples. According to the Knights Templar and their fellow Masons, the prototype for the mystical pattern lay in the ancient temples of Egypt and, above all, in the Temple of Solomon in Jerusalem. It is really the quest of John Michell and others like him—including the Masonic fraternity—to recover the exact order of this

▲ *The ruins of Glastonbury Abbey. A view from the east along the main axis. The Tower of St. Benedict's is visible over the Mary Chapel.*

pattern, to recreate it and so make the earthly order a mirror of the heavenly. Before we continue with a description of the mysteries surrounding Glastonbury Abbey, it will be convenient at this point to state where the views of this author depart from those inclined toward the ideas of the Masons and of the excellent Mr. Michell.

To the Neo-Platonic statement of Mr. Michell: "The ideal pattern is ready-made and comes from above. It enters the mind as archetype which takes shape as symbol, and thence it descends down the scale of human consciousness into the sphere of concrete reality. It is not invented but invoked."[8] The author replies: "The ideal pattern is constantly emerging and comes from within. It enfolds and unfolds through mind and nature in a never-ending play of form, and thence is immanent within human consciousness and the universe. It is not invented but enacted." The difference being while in the first instance the sacred order of the Isle of Avalon is a matter of maintaining union with the heavenly order, in the second instance the natural order of the Isle of Avalon IS the sacred order. Be that as it may, let us now return to the Abbey grounds.

At some point—the date is hard to determine but it is most certainly by AD 650—an earthen enclosure was made around what has become known as the ancient cemetery. This was the area directly around the original chapel. This square "Saxon" enclosure contained post holes belonging to buildings of the wattle type. The eastern bank of this enclosure, some twenty-five feet wide and ten feet high, lay close to the crossing of the existing church ruins. The evidence indicates that important burials were made in the cemetery and that some these could have been pre-Saxon. St. Patrick and King Arthur, both definitely Celtic, were always said to be buried there. If true, this suggests a date before the enclosure, closer to the mid-sixth century.

Excavations in 1954 turned up a hole fifty feet south of the Mary Chapel, exactly where the monks said they found the grave of Arthur. Slab-lined graves within it strongly suggested a burial from the earliest period had indeed been made there. Could this be the grave of King Arthur?

The story goes that after the great fire, while digging between two pyramids—mausolea—in the ancient cemetery, the monks found a massive wooden coffin. Within it were the bones of a huge man, probably slain by sword wounds to the head, and the slighter bones of a woman. Her golden hair was beautiful, but when taken up by a monk, it crumbled to dust. To confirm this really was the grave of Arthur and Guinevere the monks found a lead cross below a stone inscribed with the words: *Hic ia cet sepultus inclitus Rex Arturius in Insula Avalonia.* "Here lies buried King Arthur, in the Isle of Avalon." Debate over the authenticity of this find has raged back and forth ever since. The Latin probably does not belong to the time the monks meant it to. That is, it is thirteenth-century and not tenth or earlier. The most likely time for a historical King Arthur is between 470 and AD 540.[9]

Archaeology can really take us no further than this. The matter is complicated by the extraordinary amount of disturbance the earth of the cemetery has received over the centuries. Wherever archaeologists excavated in the ancient enclosure, graves crossed over graves and bones mixed with bones in a convoluted mix. It was said that burial alone in this "the holyest erthe" of Christendom ensured the salvation of the soul. It was this belief—and the accompanying demand—that caused the floor of the Mary Chapel to be removed in the sixteenth century and the crypt of St. Joseph to be built below. This fact, so evident to every visitor to the Abbey ruins, destroyed any remains of ancient structures on the critically important central site.

The first large stone church on the site was completed about 725 during the reign of King Ine or Ini, the Saxon king of Wessex. This lay to the east of the wooden church and was dedicated to St. Peter and St. Paul. It was Ine who gave the Abbey its charter and probably the gift of the mysterious twelve hides of land. Tradition imputes this to a King Arviragus (Avallach?) at the time of Joseph of Arimathea. William of Malmesbury also mentions the existence of an early charter granted by a king of Dumnonia in 601. The charter and the Abbey holdings developed until the remarkable situation was reached where the estates were an autonomous holding within the land of Britain. The Abbot held his own tribunal, the offices of which can still be seen in the High Street.

Whatever the date of the original charter, the strong Celtic traditions surrounding Glastonbury Abbey—especially those of St. Patrick and St. Brigit—do suggest a pre-Saxon foundation. The Saxons simply would not have permitted such traditions and especially anything to do with King Arthur. But here the matter is complicated. There are too many influences on the written documents to get to the true story. Yet this much is clear—early British Christianity stood apart from the orthodoxy created around Rome and Constantinople. The British Christians drew directly upon the old spiritual practices of the Celtic Druids. They leant heavily toward the Celtic concept of mystical communion with the realms of the plants and animals. They tended toward gnostic beliefs. The British were in the company of those who saw the Bible as providing further allegory and teaching on the ancient and universal truths. The fifth-century British monk Pelagius, for example, taught there was no "original sin." He said that creation was sacred and that through the practice of the hermetic arts and the advancement of knowledge each soul could move toward enlightenment. The Church of Rome condemned this as heresy. After the Synod of Whitby in the mid-seventh century manipulated the British secular rulers to the side of Roman orthodoxy, Celtic Christianity was no more.

During the tenth century, St. Dunstan extended the Saxon Church and instituted the Benedictine order for the monks. Dunstan was a local man of noble birth, a musician, an engineer, a blacksmith, an administrative genius, a politician, and an alchemist. He wrote a tract called the "Philosopher's Stone." It was said that his harp continued to play when he hung it upon the wall. Under his Abbotship, beginning in 943, Glastonbury led Britain as a school of learning. He and several other Glastonbury monks became Archbishops of Canterbury. Kings of England were buried in the Abbey, including Edmund Ironside. Changes followed, including the Norman conquest, but Glastonbury thrived with the great church extending ever upward and eastward from the ancient Mary Chapel.

In 1184 came the fire that destroyed everything. But the Arthurian revival was underway and the ruins allowed the monks to fashion a new mythology for themselves, a mythology that included the relics of King Arthur and Queen Guinevere. These relics eventually came to rest in a magnificent black marble tomb that lay prominently featured in the centre of the choir of the new great church.

A final piece of interesting information is that St. David visited Glastonbury early in the sixth century and claimed it as one of his foundations. An apparently genuine inscription made on brass in about 1400 was placed on a pillar just to the north of the Mary Chapel to show where David's addition to the Old Church was made. When David wished to dedicate his work, the plaque recounts the tradition that Christ appeared in a dream to remind David that he had already dedicated the church to his mother. Geoffrey Ashe has pointed out that the insistence on the part of the Abbey for an early dedication to Mary is extremely unusual. It is possible that for centuries the Old Church of Avalon stood alone with this appellation. As the "Motherchurch," the Abbey was drawing upon an ancient strand in the collective imagination that understood the isle as a sanctuary long dedicated to the Great Goddess.[10]

ENDNOTES

1. John Scott, *The Early History of Glastonbury: An Edition, Translation and Study of William of Malmesbury's*, "De Antiquitate Glastoniensis Ecclesiae," Boydell, Woodbridge, 1981, 1-2.

2. Ibid, 9.

3. Ibid, 5.

4. Philip Rahtz, *Excavations on Glastonbury Tor, Somerset, 1964-6*, R.A.I., 1971. See also "Glastonbury Tor," in Geoffrey Ashe (Ed.), *The Quest for Arthur's Britain*, Paladin, 1968.

5. Geoffrey Ashe, *The Rediscovery of King Arthur*, Anchor Press/Doubleday, 1985.

6. See also John Michell and Christine Rhone, *Twelve-Tribe Nations and the Science of Enchanting Landscapes*, London, 1990.

7. John Scott, 1981.

8. John Michell, *New Light on the Ancient Mysteries of Glastonbury*, Gothic Image Publications, Glastonbury, 1990, p. 168.

9. C.A. Raleigh Radford, "Glastonbury Abbey," in *The Quest for Arthur's Britain*, edited by Geoffrey Ashe, Paladin Books, 1968.

10. Geoffrey Ashe, *Avalonian Quest*, Fontana, 1982.

4

LATER HISTORY: THE ABBEY AND THE TOR

By the end of the thirteenth century, the Abbey owned over an eighth of the land in Somerset. Into this area the jurisdiction of the British monarch could not run. A great new church, taller, longer and more decorated than ever before, steadily grew upon the Abbey grounds. On the same hallowed site and from out of the burnt ruins of the Old Church came the St. Mary Chapel. Consecrated in 1186, the remains of this lovely chapel are still visible today.

Over the following centuries, the Abbey in the Vale of Avalon—it could no longer really be called an island—succeeded in creating an astonishing past for itself. This could hardly be called manipulation, as every age, dynasty, and institution creates the history it desires. This age was at least one built to the glory of God. The Abbey history was, in a sense, a self-fulfilling creative mechanism. As the Abbey expanded in power, wealth, influence, beauty, and form in temporal space, it needed to expand in eternal or inner space. The heavenly order had to become a mirror of the terrestrial order. The monks extended the boundaries of belief until the foundation of the Abbey went beyond Joseph of Arimathea and even the Virgin Mary, until they imputed that God in the form of Christ himself was responsible for the little church of wattle and reed.

▲ *St. Mary's Chapel, view from the southwest.*

The folk traditions of the Southwest support the tradition of Christ's coming to Avalon. Some say he came to see the homeland of his mother's mother, St. Anne. This Cornish Queen had immaculately conceived a child and her husband had cast her out from her home. Joseph of Arimathea—on one of his trips to trade for British tin—took her with him back to the Holy Land. There she gave birth to Mary. Ever since then it became the custom of the tin miners of Cornwall to cry out when smelting tin, "Joseph was in the tin trade!" Christ stopped in several places when he returned with his uncle to the home of his grandmother. He was said to have cured a leper colony at Culbone near Porlock in north Devon, to have founded the ancient churches at Godney and Christon in Somerset, and to have visited the centre of the lead and silver trade at Priddy on the Mendips overlooking Avalon. Whenever local folk wished to be adamant about something, they would say, "As sure as Christ was at Priddy!"

The great visionary William Blake immortalized the legend of Christ's coming to Avalon with the words: "And did those feet in ancient time walk upon England's mountains green." And before him and ever since, monks, mystics, priests, poets, tin miners, scholars, and ordinary folk have lent whatever credence they could to the matter. The historian E. A. Freeman put it exactly when he said, "We need not believe that the Glastonbury legends are records of facts; but the existence of those legends is a very great fact."[1] Indeed. So the people of the Age of Faith blazed with a very great fact, in which they totally believed and which created a profound impression upon their lives. Thus it came to be an irrefutable truth that a little patch of earth on the Isle of Avalon was holy.

The flaw in all this was, of course, the church. The Christian Church and the church on Avalon were temporal institutions. They came into being at one time and thus they could go out of being at any one time. This is, in fact, exactly what happened. It was impossible to push the boundaries of the Glastonbury church before the time of Christ, and fire, flood, earthquakes, and unfriendly monarchs would see to its demise. The nature of Christian faith made it impossible for many of its believers to see that the sacred tradition of the Isle of Avalon went beyond the before and beyond the after of the church.

It was hard to comprehend. The glory of god should go beyond the vicissitudes of life. The order of the monastery spread through the Vale of Avalon, put a stone church in every village, fed the poor, and cared for the sick and elderly. It reaped rich harvests from the land and created an edifice upon the holy isle of sublime and otherworldly beauty. This should not pass away. But alas, the British Church found itself in a rapidly changing world and what would not change was dashed to pieces.

THE LAST ABBOT

In 1539, envious of the power and the wealth of the Church and wishing to revive his marital fortunes, Henry VIII dissolved the monasteries of Britain. Glastonbury had been compliant to the wishes of the king and was of a good reputation. Yet the monarch found it necessary to dissolve its ancient charter, to gain its lands and to make an example of the last Abbot, the ailing, eighty-year-old Michael Whyting.

The Abbot was tried at Wells. The charge was concealing treasures of the Abbey. The verdict was a foregone conclusion. Apparently a memo found in the notebooks of the royal chancellor Thomas Cromwell said, "Arrest the Abbot of Glastonbury, find him guilty, and execute him." The king's men took Abbot Whyting back to Glastonbury. They dragged him up the Tor and hanged him—some accounts say between two of the brethren. They next quartered his body and displayed it in Wells, Bath, Bridgwater, and Ilchester. They stuck the head above the gateway to the Abbey. The ghost of Abbot Whyting is said to walk up Dod Lane to the Tor. That is, along the ecclesiastical axis of Glastonbury which runs through the naves of St. Benedict's Church and the Abbey Church, then curiously enough, across country to Stonehenge. Some say this alignment continues further to Canterbury.

The Abbey's fate was sealed, although at first it was slow. Sold by the crown, there were attempts to use the vast edifices. But at length the lead on the roof and the stone in the walls was of more value than the space within them. For generations the local people used the Abbey church, the monastery, and the Abbot's palace as a quarry. The Abbot's kitchen survived by becoming a Methodist chapel. By the eighteenth century a superstition arose that to build with the Abbey stone was unlucky and this slowed the destruction. Then in the early years of this century, the ruins came on the market and were clandestinely acquired by the Church of England. The Anglicans had to proceed cautiously as the Abbey had, naturally, always been Catholic.

FREDERICK BLIGH BOND

Under the aegis of the church once more, the ruins were stabilized and there began the long and difficult task of investigation. In 1904, the Bristol architect Frederick Bligh Bond was appointed to oversee the work. Bligh Bond was thorough and when information about where to proceed came from an unlikely source, he did not overlook it. The sources were mostly automatic handwriting by a friend of his and later from others. Within a year of the first contact—mostly with monks of the old Abbey—the trickle of information about buildings, their dimensions, location, and anecdotes about the monks themselves, became a flood. Excavation of the Loretto Chapel and the Edgar Chapel confirmed the details supplied by the sources.

In 1918, Bligh Bond published *The Gate of Remembrance*, a sample of which follows. (Braineton was Abbot of Glastonbury in the fourteenth century.)

> *As we have said, our Abbey was a message in ye stones. In ye founda-tions and ye distances be a mystery . . . All ye measures were marked plaine on ye slabbes in Mary's Chappel, and ye have destroyed them . . . There was the Body of Christ, and round him would have been the Four Ways. Two were builded and no more. In ye floor of ye Mary Chappel was ye Zodiac, that all might see and understand the mys-tery. In ye midst of ye Chapel he was laid; and the Cross of Hym who was our Example and Exemplar. Braineton, he didde much, for he was Geomancer to ye Abbey of old tyme.*

The publication of the automatic writings did not endear Bligh Bond to the church authorities. They hurried to quiet him. Eventually they dismissed him and repudiated his work. To be fair to the Church, Bligh Bond did exceed the limits of professional archaeological conduct by publicizing his subjective sources. This did not stop him from publishing further works. Eventually his research in the Abbey was validated, but not the transmissions. They access mysteries beyond the pale of the church and on into the greater Avalonian tradition. (See the section entitled "The Floor-plan of the Temple" in Chapter Five.)

THE MONASTERY ON THE TOR

To return to the beginning of the Medieval period, enough detail survives to show that a well-appointed church now stood on the summit of the Tor. It replaced the possible tenth-century chapel. Aligned with the axis of the Tor, the first church was over seventy feet long and about thirty-six feet wide. It was heavily buttressed and very likely had a narrow chancel, a wide nave, and no tower to speak of. The excavators found decorated floor tiles, some fragments of coloured plaster, and many pieces of stained glass.

To the period, 1100-1300, belongs a fragment of an altar of Purbeck marble complete with a consecration cross inscribed upon it. The excavators also found a pilgrim's badge, a tiny impression in bronze of what looks like a mother and child. The Abbey was busy promoting its "Arthurian" and "Motherchurch" image at this time, and many pilgrims attracted to Glastonbury would have climbed the Tor to visit the sanctuary of St. Michael. Then, in the middle of this prosperous age, disaster struck.

It was recorded in contemporary chronicles that on the 11th of September in the year 1275 "between the first and third hours of the day," an "earthquake" destroyed the church of St. Michael on the Tor.

All over the Tor the excavators were presented with constant difficulties by fissures in the rock of the summit. These were deep enough to swallow any material that fell into them. They also preserved the rubbish tips from the various periods of occupation. The builders of the churches blocked many with masonry, but it was this weakness—the fissuring of the summit of the Tor—that destroyed the first church.

Rebuilding soon followed, but not on the same plan as before. The second and final church on the summit was a simpler, rectangular building, much narrower than its predecessor. It consisted of only two bays—a nave and a chancel. Internally measuring fifty-two by fifteen feet, the church was richly decorated with ornamental stonework, stained glass, and coloured tile. It was likely to have had a high, decorated parapet in the local style, concealing the almost flat roof.

ST. MICHAEL'S TOWER

Later, in the fourteenth century, the existing tower was added. The plaque on the tower says in the 1360s. Though modified in later periods, it is a strongly built and fine example of Somerset architecture.

▲ *Reliefs on St. Michael's Tower: Judgement scene; St. Bridget and her cow.*

On the eastern side of the tower, a crease shows where it joined to the roof of the nave of the church. A corbel lower down, complete with a man's head, may have come from the first (eleventh-century) church. The northeast corner of the tower was rebuilt in the nineteenth century. This is shown by the new ashlars—the squared blocks of stone. There are some wonderful gargoyles—part human, part animal—above the third level.

On the western side of the tower, canopied niches for statues were inserted in the fifteenth century. Most of the statues have gone, but enough survives to show "St. Dunstan" mid-way up on the right, and below him on the left a truncated St. Michael. The identification can be positively made, as the left foot is pinning down St. Michael's traditional opponent, a dragon.

St. Michael, to whom both churches were dedicated, is a dragon slayer and protector of high places. He is prefigured in many of his attributes by the local pagan deity who preceded him, Gwythyr ap Greidyawl, a solar god, and possibly by the more widespread Celtic deity, Bel. The festival of Bel, Beli or Belinus, at the beginning of May, was an ancient fire and fertility celebration when the forces of the Underworld were banished and the light half of the year began.[2]

Beltane or the "Fire of Bel" was celebrated on hill tops during the Celtic period by the kindling of fire by a Druid. From that source all the surrounding hearth fires would be renewed. It is interesting that the Tor is oriented to sunrise in early May by the declination of its axis; that is, by a line which runs through the length of the Tor to other St. Michael and ancient ritual sites. Because of the implacable opposition to all other deities by monotheistic Christianity, Bel was eventually thrown in among the other fallen angels. He became the demon Ba'al or Belial, against whom St. Michael wields his sword of destruction.

Below him, above the arch of the doorway, is a relief of an angel watching over the weighing of a soul. The soul, seated in the scales of judgement, comes down on the side of the angel, despite the activities of the devil on the left.

Matching the scales on the other side is a carving in slightly higher relief of St. Brigit milking her cow. She can be found similarly depicted in the twelfth century ornament over the north entrance to St. Mary's Chapel in the Abbey. St. Brigit signifies the strong connection Glastonbury enjoyed with Ireland. The Irish identified Brigit with Mary and both saints have their origins in the earlier tradition of the Great Goddess. She is the patron of wells and springs, of healers, smiths, poets, and of fire. Her festival is Imbolc ("ewe's milk"), the cross-quarter day in early February. It is possible that St. Brigit is a later version of Brigantia, "High Queen," the goddess of sovereignty of Britain, who we now know as Britannia. The historical St. Brigit was said to have visited Glastonbury in AD 488 and to have rededicated the chapel of Mary Magdalene at Beckery.

Just to the west of the tower of St. Michael, the excavators uncovered a wall that marked off the sanctified ground of the church on the summit from the monastery on the shoulder below. The lower buildings included stables and several cells for the monks. There was a larger and finer structure that may have housed a resident priest. There were various rooms, one of which, by far the largest, had ovens in the corner. Was this the kitchen and refectory?

It is possible to picture the stream of pilgrims coming to St. Michael's on the Tor. Perhaps some ascend barefoot or on their knees. They pass the seven stations of the cross, which the seven main terraces on the Tor conveniently mark. They make the association with the Calvary Mount that their Saviour climbed for their redemption. Strains of exquisite chanting are caught by the wind and carry to those toiling in the fields below. No doubt indulgences and other dispensations await those who make the ascent and contribute to the coffers of the church.

We may imagine the priest hurrying up the deeply cut path on the south side of the summit—to avoid the bitter winds of winter—to enter the church by his own door. The pilgrims enter through the main door of the church on the north. Monks are busy saying prayers. Candles flicker on the altars. Laborers thankfully rest for a moment from the constant task of tending the animals that haul building materials, food, and water up the steep hill. But even with so many details, a full picture of the prosperous, late Medieval monastery could not be obtained from only the small section of the shoulder that was excavated.

The nave and chancel of the church fell into disuse and then decay after the Dissolution of the Monasteries by Henry VIII in 1539. There was the burial of one John Rawls inside what remained of the church in 1741. Now all that remains is the tower, and that is considerably repaired. The northeast corner was entirely rebuilt in the last century. In 1985, several hundred tons of hardcore and concrete were packed around the foundations of the tower, which had become exposed to a depth of several feet. On this occasion, the prayers of the laborers were answered; a helicopter was used to haul the material.

THE FAIRFIELD

A significant document confirming an early monastic tradition is the charter of Henry III granting permission in 1243 to hold an annual fair at "the Monastery of St. Michael on the Tor." One version of this prefers 1127 and Henry I, but this is unlikely.

Glastonbury, claiming to be the "Oldest Church" in Christendom, was an important and popular place of pilgrimage, and the fair, held for six days around the Feast of St. Michael—September 29—brought many to the Tor. It was a great source of news and profit. Abbot Bere, the last but one Abbot of Glastonbury, recorded in 1517 a second fair in honour of the "Blessed Virgin." This was at the beginning of September. The pilgrim's badge probably belongs to this period.

The exact location of the Fair Field is uncertain. The 1844 tithe map marks a small steep area to the west of the Tor as the site. But it is likely to have extended from there, the source of water, around the Tor to the south. Cinnamon Lane may denote an area where spices were sold. Other roads come in from the east and west. One of them, Coursing Batch, may derive from "scourse," meaning to barter or trade. "Cor" also means horn, possibly a spiral horn. Corbenic was one of the Medieval names for the Grail Castle. It is possible that Coursing Batch may retain an older Gaelic word, a "Gorsedd," a high mound that served as a Druidic meeting place.

The Tor naturally resonates with the archetypal motif of the sacred mountain, and was indubitably perceived by the many pilgrims who climbed it as a Calvary Mount. Seven-tiered mounds with labyrinthine pathways around the stations of the cross exist in other parts of Europe, but nothing quite on the scale of the Tor.

William Weston, a Jesuit writing in 1586, mentions a "very old man" who had been employed by the Abbey who scaled the Tor on his knees. The man said he could hear the lamentations of people in distress within the Tor, so "that he thought it must be a kind of approach or vestibule for souls passing into the pains of Purgatory."[3] Seven terraces and even a maze tie in well with the idea of a Calvary Mount. Labyrinths or turf mazes were

▶

Aerial view of the Tor. The concern of the builders was to "streamline" the Tor along its natural axis by creating huge, concentric terraces around it. Agricultural lynchets are smaller. The terraces in the foreground face north and west into the prevailing winds making the agricultural return on them not worth the effort of construction.

Photo by Kevin Redpath.

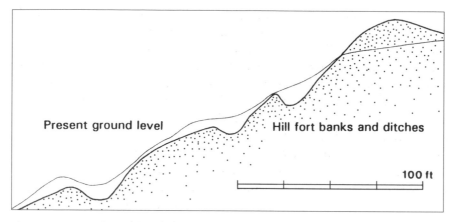

▲ *Section through the ramparts of Cadbury Castle, showing banks and ditches constructed for defensive purposes.*

vital ingredients of any Medieval fair. Their sacred purpose concerned the journey to the land of the dead and back. This is the most common purpose among labyrinth traditions alive in the world today.

About 120 years ago, the fair was removed to the town onto a field by Benedict Street, closer to the railway station. In 1988, this field became the site of a supermarket. Attempts by the public to reclaim a festival site in fields around the Tor in recent years met with an unfriendly reception from police and the town council. The Glastonbury Pilgrimage, however, an annual event of increasing popularity, sees many Catholics making the ascent up to the summit of the Tor. They are perpetuating an event of who knows what antiquity. The Protestants, however—who have a separate pilgrimage—are more wary of pagan overtones. They avoid the Tor and remain firmly in the Abbey grounds.

THE TERRACES ON THE TOR

If the terraces on the Tor were constructed for defensive purposes, what was being defended that would justify such mammoth labours? The early hill forts typically enclosed a fairly level area by means of a single ditch and bank surmounted by a timber palisade. The primary object of which was to keep out wild animals and to keep in stock. They usually enclosed an area sufficient for many homesteads; for example, the eighteen plus acres of Cadbury Castle.

The later Bronze Age and especially the Iron Age hill forts have several sets of banks and ditches and often enclose a much larger area. Examples include Hamdon Hill, Maiden Castle, Ham Hill, and Old Sarum. Maiden Castle encloses forty-five acres, Hamdon Hill nearly two hundred. They all show constructional effort equivalent to that which went into the Tor.

If the architects of the Tor built the terraces as defensive works according to the design of a Celtic hill fort, the terraces would be fewer and complete bank and ditch structures. They would have enclosed an area able to accommodate a corresponding population, which the steep slopes and the summit of the Tor plainly cannot do. It must be pointed out that such huge centres as Hamdon Hill and Maiden Castle are located in areas that provided an extremely broad and varied economic resource base. Each hill fort controlled trade routes. An equivalent centre on the island of Glastonbury would have soon found its resources depleted. Comparing the terraces on the Tor to defensive works on hill forts only serves to emphasize the differences between them and points to a totally alternative purpose.

AGRICULTURE ON THE TOR

The prehistoric and Celtic inhabitants of Britain created many field systems. Historians think that, lacking the means to farm the heavy lowlands, the early agriculturalists preferred the lighter and well drained soils of the uplands. Glastonbury Tor may fall into this category. There are, however, no examples of fields being built on such steep and exposed surfaces as the Tor. Furthermore, recent evidence points to land clearance and the use of heavy ploughs at an earlier date than was previously thought. Other sloping land was available in the Somerset area, especially along the sunny, southern slopes of the Mendips. Few terraces, if any, were made here in the prehistoric period. It can safely be assumed, however, that the lower slopes of the Tor were cultivated in historical times. A tithe map of 1844 marks an area on the eastern flanks of the Tor as the "Tor Linches." A linch or a lynchet is an artificial terrace or ridge on the face of a hill. If at all possible, they were made into a standard-sized strip called a furlong. This is a measure of land said to be that which an ox team could plough in a day.

The official interpretation of the terraces around the Tor is that they are a combination of natural slumping and Medieval strip-lynchets. Slumping, the experts say, highlighted the geological layers which underlie the Tor. The lynchets were built at a time when the Somerset Levels were

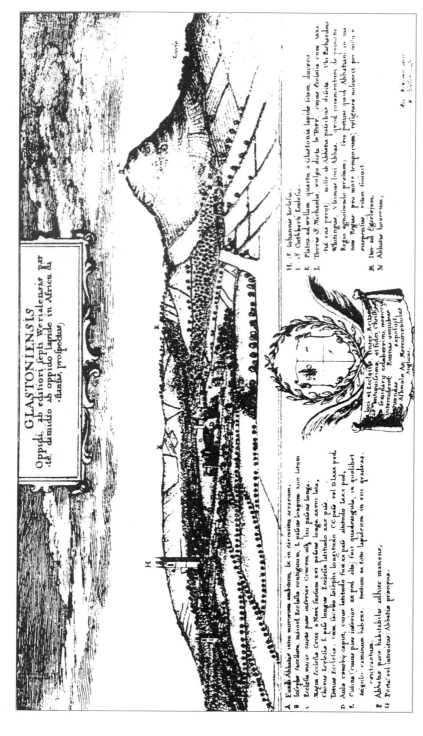

▲ Hollar's engraving of Glastonbury. In Dugdale, 1654.

undrained and it was necessary to make full use of available land for agriculture. Presumably this was during the expansion of the Abbey and the Monastery of St. Michael on the Tor in the twelfth and thirteenth centuries.

The tithe map of 1844 reveals an arrangement of strip-lynchets running quite high up around the Tor where there is a means of access from the higher ground to the east. The argument is that these lynchets, along with others on the lower slopes to the south, are all that remain of a much larger system that gradually fell out of use as the surrounding land was drained. An engraving made by Hollar in 1654 shows the arrangement of lynchets running up to the Tor. These can be seen in the tithe map and in the present day hedgerows. Several encircling terraces can also be seen higher up in Hollar's engraving, but these are on a much greater scale than any agricultural lynchet. The question is whether these were lynchets or much earlier terraces.

Land charters from the Abbey include references to "Tor fields" from as early as 1307, but they are ambiguous. They refer to land being "against the Tor," but no more. There is nothing specific relating to furlongs high on the Tor's slopes. There is no record of harvests, tithes, leases, nor of the enormous amount of labour involved in the construction of the terraces.

It is this factor that cannot be underestimated. The amount of sheer hard work necessary for the construction of these enormous terraces would have negated the return on all but the lower, broader, and sheltered south-facing slopes. If the need for cultivatable land was ever that great on the island, then it seems likely that the Abbey would have pressed other more sheltered slopes into use, for example on Chalice Hill, before it became necessary to carve out terraces on the Tor. The high, unsheltered north and west facing slopes that stand out so strongly in the photograph at the beginning of this section, are especially difficult to interpret as lynchets. The highest ones are impossible to reach with an ox team and plough.

The hillside below Stone Down to the east of the Tor preserves a fine set of lynchets. But these are dissimilar to the terraces on the Tor. They are smaller, lower, and are exactly placed to face south and east into the sun and out of the prevailing winds. They are also fairly horizontal. The terraces on the Tor, especially on the northwest flank, are so steep that level sheep paths cut across them at sharp angles. If the architects of the terraces built them for agricultural purposes they surely would have kept them level, especially as this would have allowed access from the high ground to the north. The only terraces on the Tor's upper slopes that the tithe map unequivocally shows were used for agriculture, run around to the south side of the Tor on level terrain accessed from the north. The Benedictine monks of the Abbey and the Monastery were nothing if not practical. They would have turned to land on Chalice Hill or on the north side of Bushey Combe before using higher, exposed, and less productive ground.

On the other hand, terraces would look very fine to the approaching pilgrim. They would evoke all kinds of qualities in the mind. Perhaps the monks cultivated vines on the southern slopes, and deemed it worthwhile carrying the terraces on all the way around the Tor. Before the disastrous years of 1314 to 1317 and the beginning of a long, cold period, the northern European climate was warm enough to grow vines throughout Britain. In so doing they created an image of wholeness—of a regular succession of tiers—by which the pilgrim could ascend via the stations of the cross to the monastery crowning the summit. Such Calvary Mounts were popular in Medieval Europe. They provided a symbol of the World Mountain without the pagan traditions and overtones which accompanied natural features.

The tradition recorded in the Charter of St. Patrick of the Tor being densely wooded—"I climbed with great difficulty through a dense wood to the peak of a hill which rises on the island . . . "—may have more relevance around the time it was written, that is, the thirteenth century AD, than the time of Patrick, the fifth century AD. If this was so, and the Tor was once covered with woodland, then an excavation that searched for times when trees were present or removed might throw some light on the terraces. If it can be shown that Medieval labourers cleared already terraced slopes or long-standing ancient woodland, then a step might be taken on the road toward discovering the date of the terraces. At this stage, only an excavation in a few carefully selected places on the Tor will help to date the terraces and assist in the interpretation of their purpose. And is an excavation really desirable?

THE PRESENT DAY

The Tor is in the keeping of the National Trust, who are doing all they can to preserve the landmark in a natural and unspoilt way. On some days hundreds of people climb to the summit. To many local people the Tor is a special place. They are likely to climb it for recreation or for that extra perspective on things. This is in contrast to the Abbey grounds in the centre of town, which remain relatively unused.

In the 1930s, a well known psychometrist, Olive Pixley, and the writer John Foster Forbes, visited the Tor. Ms. Pixley described a ritual from the remote past in which she saw a host of people gathering before dawn to make their way up the Tor. It was a celebration. There was drumming, singing, and chanting, freely intermixed with the cries of children and dogs. On the crest of the Tor lay a stone circle.

As the people walked the terraces, their sound and movement created a serpent-like trail of etheric energy. This became steadily brighter as more people approached the summit. As the sun rose, the raised spiral of serpent power fused with the sun's light through the agency of the stone circle. The resultant energy then shot outward through the "alignments" over the land. This was for the benefit of the plant and butterfly realms.

The key to the ritual, Ms. Pixley thought, was the vibration of sound and light. The ancients, using traditions that reached back to Atlantis, raised this energy in suitable places like the Tor for the enhancement of life.[4]

In 1945, John Foster Forbes visited the Tor in the company of another psychometrist, Iris Campbell. Her impressions also included a ritual dance, moving "sunwise" up and around the "spiral path" on the Tor. The vortex of energy so raised created an etheric canopy of a "glazed substance" through which regenerative forces could be sent, in this case, to the flower and bird life forms.

Since the idea of the Tor labyrinth was raised in the late sixties, many people have threaded its sinuous paths. (See the section on the Labyrinth in Chapter Five.) A May Day full-moon walk of the labyrinth by the Glastonbury Women's Group in 1980 culminated in a violent thunderstorm. A threading of the labyrinth by a large group at Samhain in 1984 ended at sunset with the weaving of a web of coloured threads over the summit of the Tor.

Avalonians are celebrating the old fire festivals with a bonfire on the Tor. If the weather is good, a full moon meditation may take place there. Tibetan monks are said to levitate and to be discovering the tonal keys that resonate with the Tor and allow access into the crystalline cities below! It is as natural a focus for UFOs as it is for the low-flying military jets that scream their way across the Levels and call the Tor "the nipple" on their radios. For some, more respectful, the Tor is still a Fairy Hill. For others, it is a place of healing. For yet others, it is a place that needs their healing, a place to perform rites of passage, a global power centre, a ley line centre, a galactic portal, the planetary heart chakra . . .

In the 1970s, an Italian artist and poet, Gino Gennaro, came to Glastonbury as an indigent and renewed the hermetic tradition of the

Tor. He produced a strange and remarkable book about the Tor. Called *The Phenomena of Avalon,* the discourse rambles through the fairy realm in a whimsical Blakean style. The Fairy Sophia has this to say about the Living Rock:

> *The stone by which you are sitting is the Zodiacal Stone which seals the human conscious world from its sub-conscious. During each full moon Mercury comes to lift it and release the fluids of new knowledge which, through the media of the Ley Lines, reach every earthly corner to fertilize the sterile fields of any established orthodoxy.*

Largely ignored, Mr. Gennaro is a fine representative of the latter-day Avalonian tradition. For years before his death, he insisted on the renewal of the sacred world order through the reinstatement of the yearly round of pagan festivals. This was a goal shared by many of the Travellers on the English road today and partially reinstated by the huge Summer Solstice music festival six miles from Glastonbury at Pilton.[5]

To conclude this section on academic and fabulous ideas about the Tor, (where one becomes the other it is hard to tell), mention must be made of the prolific writer on matters Atlantean and occult, Dion Fortune. She made her second home in Glastonbury in the 1930s. Her main residence was London, whose energies, she believed, were fed by the chthonian forces of Glastonbury. She lived at the foot of the Tor, beside the White Spring, on the other side of the lane to Chalice Well. In her charming book *Avalon of the Heart* she wrote:

> *The Tor is a strange hill, and it is hard to believe that its form is wholly the work of Nature. Round it winds a spiral way in three great coils, which is beyond all question a processional way... such mounts as this were always sacred to the sun.*

▲ *Dawn on Glastonbury Tor.*

THE MYSTERY OF THE TERRACES

The terraces on the Tor are not a result of natural slumping and underlying geological layers. Where slumping has occurred on the Isle of Avalon, for example on the north faces of Wearyall Hill or Bushey Combe, it is totally irregular. It does not create benches or long, level terraces. It also can be confidently said that the terraces on the northern and western flanks of the Tor were not constructed for agricultural purposes. The intention of their makers was to cut huge terraces that moulded the Tor, not lynchets.

At the same time, the lower terraces on the southern and eastern flanks do display the kind of access one would expect for arable farming. They are sunny and sheltered. The lower ones offer comparatively large and flat areas of ground. These terraces were ploughed and strip-lynchets, facing south like those on the neighbouring hill, formed out of them. Above them, however, especially on the eastern flank, are large and regular terraces like those on the north and west sides of the Tor, whose exposure and inaccessibility means they were not made for agricultural purposes. The topmost sixth terrace, most inaccessible of all, gives the game away. Though today barely perceptible because of erosion, it was never more than a few feet wide. It was not agricultural and represents a totally alternative intent.

As the situation is now, there is very little to go on in the interpretation of the terraces. There is no archaeological evidence. Working back from the most recent to the most ancient time, the monks of the monastery made some for agricultural purposes. They also may have enhanced already existing terraces to promote the idea of a Calvary Mount as a totally agricultural explanation does seem unlikely.

There is the brief period of Glastonbury's importance (in the shadow of Cadbury) in the sixth-century resistance to the Saxon tide. But the soldiers on the Tor, while they might have maintained Ponter's Ball, would have gained little from labouring on vast defensive earthworks on the Tor. The terraces, moreover, are not built for defence. They exhibit a flat contour, not one of a bank and ditch. The same is true during the period of construction of the great Celtic hill forts. No Iron Age engineer could have justified the labour of the terraces for a hill fort upon the small area offered by the summit of the Tor.

Then there is the misty border between history and prehistory. The tales in *The Mabinogion*, the Welsh poems, and local folklore give clues to a pre-Christian pagan past. They hint at a Druidic centre and an entrance-way to the Underworld. As we shall see in the following chapters, they tell of a labyrinthine journey to the land of the dead, a magical cauldron, a spiral castle, a World Tree, a World Mountain, and a seasonal struggle of great cosmic powers.

There are indications of a still deeper past in remnants of standing stones, country-wide alignments, astronomical lines of sight, and anomalies of omission. What was Ponter's Ball enclosing? It may be contemporary with the terraces. Given the large prehistoric population in the area, where was their ritual centre, as in other parts of Britain?

Looked at individually there is no strong piece of evidence that enables it to be said that the Tor's terraces were built for this specific purpose in this specific period. But looked at in context, Glastonbury Tor's intrinsic and dynamic relationship to the surrounding landscape meant it offered opportunities too attractive to miss, given its qualities, and knowing the preoccupations and the interests of the ancient Britons and their descendants. We will never know how the prehistoric people perceived the Tor. We do know it stood on a stunningly beautiful, richly wooded, and well-watered island. It formed a natural viewing point for many significant astronomical events, and the people of the Neolithic era, capable of great geomantic feats, would not have overlooked an opportunity to leave their mark upon it.

Although enthusiastic people project many far-fetched things onto Glastonbury Tor, it seems to me that none go far enough in recreating the vision of the Tor's ancient sanctity and use. The second part of this book is an attempt to go that distance. Due to the surrounding Somerset Levels, the Tor is the focus of the landscape. It is the bridge between earth, sea, and sky. It is the natural elemental temple of the area, concentrating and dispersing power. It dramatically lends itself to impression, as the monastery and terrace builders discovered. Yet, whatever the Tor was to those of the past and whatever my interpretations offer, it ultimately reflects the preoccupations of the time. So it is up to the visitor who climbs the slopes today to make up his or her own mind.

ENDNOTES

1. Quoted from Geoffrey Ashe, 1968, p. 202.

2. Beli the Great, father of Llud or Lyr, "light," the historical British king whom Shakespeare called Lear, and his daughter Creiddylad, Cordelia.

3. William Weston quotes are from Geoffrey Ashe, 1957, p. 279.

4. Olive Pixley, *Psychometry* (unpublished), courtesy of Gun Pelham, 1937.

5. Gino Gennaro, *The Phenomena of Avalon: The First Heliocentric Book for Two Thousand Years,* Cronos Publications, 1979. As for the yearly round of festivals, it is fascinating to watch the resistance of the establishment to the renewal of this tradition at Stonehenge. Police have prevented the gathering of people there at Summer Solstice—including the Druids—almost every year since 1985. The festival's content had become largely motivated by alcohol and drugs; but even as a Saturnalia, the establishment may do better than stand in the way of a deeply rooted, ancient tradition.

6. Dion Fortune, *Avalon of the Heart,* London, 1938 (revised edition, 1986).

PART
TWO

5

THE GEOMANTIC MYSTERIES: LABYRINTHS, LINES, AND ZODIACS

In 1969, John Michell described an astonishing alignment of ancient sacred sites in southern Britain. A line drawn through the axis of Glastonbury Tor passes through Burrowbridge Mump—a similarly sculpted natural hill—and when extended further in the southwest direction, passes through Brentor and St. Michael's Mount off the coast of Cornwall.[1] The alignment, extended northeastward, passes through the outer bank of Avebury Henge. This Neolithic monument is without doubt part of the most remarkable prehistoric ceremonial complex ever built in Britain. John Michell dubbed the alignment the "St. Michael Line" because of the number of hills with churches on their summit dedicated to the saint, if not exactly on the line, then not far from its route. Another name is the "May Day Line" because of its astronomical orientation, or the "Dragon Line" because wherever St. Michael goes, there goes a dragon.

Many sites on the alignment were venerated as sacred places in Neolithic times. The prehistoric people may have discovered the long, straight line of sight by lighting hilltop fires. The excavations on the Tor revealed several places where fires were regularly lit, including a foundation for what was

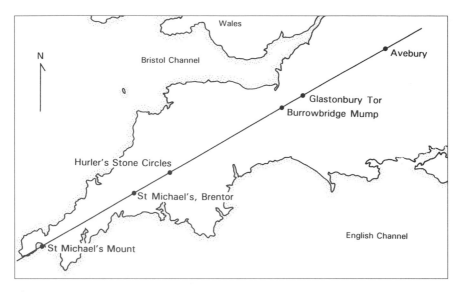

▲ *St. Michael Line Map.*

probably an elevated medieval beacon. It is interesting to note that the Tor's remaining stones, the Living Rock and the one above it on the south-west ascent route are oriented to the line. So is St Michael's church on the summit. That is, the church is aligned to the axis of the Tor, not east-west.

A feature characteristic of Neolithic sites such as the stone circles and chambered mounds is that they contain astronomical orientations. This is common in the building practices of similar cultures across the world. The ancient European agricultural communities observed the sky, then located themselves within the cosmos through the alignment of the order of their lives to the heavenly order. Stonehenge is well known for its orientation to the Summer Solstice sunrise. It also indicates the Winter Solstice sunset, the cross-quarter days, and several lunar extremes. It provides a complete calendar. The long barrow at Stoney Littleton just south of Bath is oriented to the Winter Solstice sunrise. Like Newgrange in Ireland, it admits a beam of light at dawn into its innermost chambers.

The sixty-three degree alignment of the St. Michael Line through Glastonbury Tor indicates sunrise at the beginning of May and August. These are the cross-quarter days of Beltane and Lughnasad, the calendar days midway between solstice and equinox. The alignment also indicates sunset on the remaining cross-quarter days of Samhain and Imbolc. This means, for example, that from Burrowbridge Mump on the 1st of May or

August, the sun will rise over the Tor. It also means that from Glastonbury Tor on October 31 or February 2 the sun will set over the Mump. All these days were major fire festivals in the pagan Celtic world and are likely to be part of a far older tradition.

LEY LINES

It will be helpful at this point to say something about the controversial subject of ley lines. A ley line is an alignment across the landscape between human-made sites, such as a standing stone, a mound, a temple, or a road. The line can contain natural sites, such as a hill, a spring, or a notch on the horizon. The idea that an alignment should be straight, as in a precise line of sight despite the undulations of the terrain, is held by one school of thought as the defining criteria of a ley line. An example of this will be described shortly between the Mary Chapel and the church of St. Michael's on the Tor. This example has one human-made site and two natural sites,

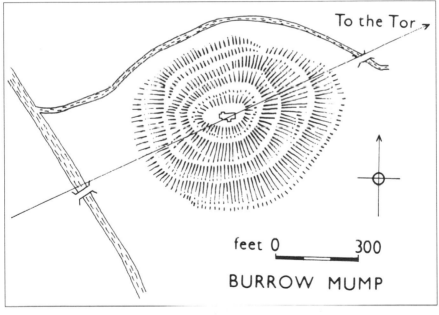

▲ *Burrowbridge Mump is an unusual conical hill dramatically situated in the middle of the Somerset Levels. At one time the hill was sculpted. With the ruins of a St. Michael's Church on the summit, it looks like a miniature version of the Tor.*

with one of those being a combination of both. Such lines may have a precise astronomical function. To be considered authentic, all sites that form the alignment should be contemporary with each other.

Another school of thought says a ley line is an "energy line" that need not necessarily be straight. Nor do the sites which compose it have to be contemporary with each other. It is valid to have a church, an Iron Age camp, and a Neolithic standing stone composing the alignment. Even if the alignment between sites is straight, the energy between them may undulate like a dragon. The St. Michael Line would fall into this category. This creates the concept of a "ley corridor" along which some kind of telluric energy travels, like light along a fibre-optic tube. This school of thought believes that at some time or another people knew all about the kind of subtle energy which moved in leys and could employ it for various purposes. The examples mentioned in the previous chapter suggest the energy was used for the maintenance of terrestrial harmony and fertility. Both groups attempt to find and measure electrical, radioactive, or some other specific quality or anomaly at the ley nodes. Astral travel or shamanic journeying along the network of earth energy leys is also suggested. The academic establishment sees the whole concept of ley lines, let alone energy lines, as anathema to serious research.[2]

One culture maintaining a living tradition which includes an idea similar to that of ley lines as energy lines is the Australian Aboriginal. The Aborigines say the landscape was crossed in the time of creation, the Dreamtime, by the creative spirit ancestors. As each ancestor, human and animal, moved over the landscape, they sang it into existence. The Aborigines call the paths of the ancestors songlines. They pass the songs of the land—and thus the right to the land—on to each generation. Artists represent songlines in their paintings as sets of concentric rings connected by lines. Each set of rings is a Dreaming site of special significance. By walking the lines, by "singing up the landscape," by visiting each site, by painting it, or by drawing it in the sand, the energies of that place and of the particular quality connected with it can be increased. The Aborigines thus participate in a reality that is at once within and without, past and present, the same and always in creation. Every part of the landscape is alive and bursting with a network of immanent, spiritual power.[3]

The maintenance of such a vital cosmography requires the presence of people to "think" it. In this cosmos, as much inner as it is outer, subtle currents of energy running over the surface of the earth certainly do exist. If such a reality once existed for the people of Europe, it does not now. They, their songs, and their cosmos are long gone. All that remains are the shadows of their world in its ruinous outer manifestation, and lines here are in dispute. Yet, it definitely is the case that the Neolithic people of Europe were interested in alignments. A visit to Dartmoor reveals long rows of stones. West Penwith in Cornwall has alignments of otherwise isolated megaliths. Carnac in Brittany has many long undulating stone rows and huge menhirs that were clearly meant to be seen over many miles. To apply the mathematical, astronomical, or even the spiritual criteria of our own age to these sites is interesting, but it will not recreate the intentions in the hearts and minds of the people who built them. Their "magical technology" may not be beyond our experiential abilities—who cannot fail to be moved by the Summer Solstice sunrise at Stonehenge?—but to understand it requires a worldview vastly different from the one which currently prevails.

Nevertheless, it is worth considering the alignments of sites in the vicinity of the Isle of Avalon. Whether they qualify as ley lines or not, whether they are ancient or modern, is uncertain. The following examples take the form of geometrical figures, lines of sight, astronomical orientations, and global great circles. On occasion, they find support by apparently being mentioned in legend. Classic ley stories, such as the arrow being fired from Old Sarum to mark the location of Salisbury cathedral and happening to coincide with an alignment to Stonehenge, do appear in the Glastonbury corpus. One favourite is that of St. Cuthbert who carried his "mother" in a wheelbarrow from Glastonbury, until the straps broke at Shipley in Sussex. At that place he founded his church. Unremarkable, you may think. But it happens that Shipley was the major seat of the Knights Templar in Britain. The Templars were a mystical order accused of practicing earth magic or geomancy. If a line is drawn from Shipley to Glastonbury, it passes through the ecclesiastical centres of Shaftesbury and Salisbury. It makes one wonder exactly what St. Cuthbert was wheeling from the "Motherchurch" of Glastonbury. Is the story an allegory of a far deeper wisdom?

Then there is Crewkerne, a rather undistinguished little town in Somerset, that over the years has maintained the legend of the coming of Joseph of Arimathea to Britain. It states that Joseph and his company—twelve in all—proceeded "in a straight line" from the coast to Avalon. As they travelled, they struck their staffs into the grassy mounds that marked the path. On arrival on Wearyall Hill, Joseph, the only member of the company who retained a staff, struck it in the ground there. The miracle of the blossoming thorn on Wearyall Hill, the sign of Pisces in the Glastonbury Zodiac, is so strong a part of the Avalonian legends that Puritans

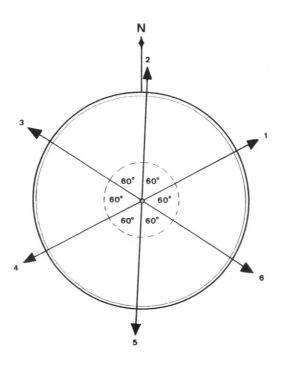

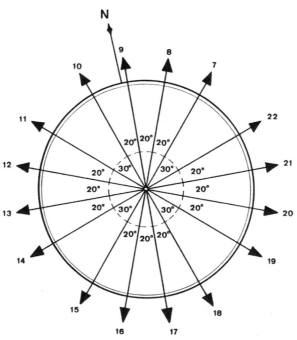

◀

The two sets of great circle alignments which pass through Glastonbury. 1. Zagorsk, Russia. 2,5. Bandiagara, Mali. 3. Chaco Canyon, USA. 4. Tiahuanacu, Bolivia and Lake Titicaca, Peru/Bolivia. 6. Lalibela, Ethiopia. 7,15. Iguazu Falls, Argentina/Brazil. 8.Ponape, Micronesia. 9. Carnac, France. 10. Callanish, Scotland. 11. Mt. Kilimanjaro, Tanzania. 12. Mecca, Saudi Arabia. 13,21. Persepolis, Iran. 14. Bali, Indonesia. 16. Fatima, Portugal. 18. Table Mountain, South Africa. 19. Filitosa, Corsica. 20. Delphi, Greece. 22. Mt. Kailas, Tibet. Most of these sites form a three-site alignment with Glastonbury. Where they form a two-site alignment it is significant only because they complete the symmetry of the geometry and because the site is significant in terms of other great circle alignments, which cannot be shown here.[5]

deemed the old tree an object of idolatry and cut it down.[4] Whether this legend describes the activating or the creation of a ley line by surveyors using sticks—"Dod men" in old English—or not is hard to say. It is as vague, and as tantalizing, as the alignment of the Abbey Church along Dod Lane to Stonehenge. The more such clues are pursued, the more Nature happily accommodates the pursuer with a glimpse of a world transfigured by a shimmering tracery of interconnected lines.

GLASTONBURY GLOBAL ALIGNMENTS

With the aid of a computer, the British scientist Terry Walsh developed a solution to one of the difficulties which plague ley line researchers, namely that of defining a straight line between sites over the curved surface of the globe. When the alignment is a line of sight there is no difficulty, but if the alignment goes over the horizon or is studied on a map, then problems arise. Maps are a projection onto a plane of the curved surface of the earth and are distorted when large distances are involved. The short distance between the Tor and Burrowbridge Mump is not affected, but when the whole distance of the St. Michael Line is considered upon a map, the curved surface of the earth produces a large deviation from apparent straightness.

On a sphere the shortest distance between two points is the great circle which passes through them. A great circle is the largest circle which it is possible to draw around a sphere. It has a centre which is always the centre of the sphere. The equator is a great circle, and, as it turns out, the sites which comprise the St. Michael Line are on a great circle. It is fascinating to extend such a line beyond the coastline and find sites of special significance in other lands upon it. With the introduction of the concept of the earth itself being a living entity, it is appealing to suggest that great circles made up of an extraordinary number of sites correspond to neural or other psycho-spiritual networks within a living body.

Using a fairly fine set of criteria (0.0015%) and a selection of widely recognized sacred sites around the planet, Mr. Walsh established eleven great circle alignments which pass through Glastonbury. The St. Michael Line, for example, passes through Zagorsk—the centre of Russian Orthodox Christianity—and Lake Titicaca, the emergence place of the Inca deity Viracocha. If the criteria are widened to embrace the concept of a ley corridor, then other sites such as Mt. Kailas in Tibet and Uluru in central Australia can be included in the line.

Mr. Walsh divides the eleven Glastonbury global alignments into two distinct groups. The first group contains three alignments arranged at approximately sixty degrees to each other. This creates a hexagonal pattern. The second group contains a total of eight alignments. This produces a four-fold pattern. This is intriguing. We shall see in the following sections that three-fold, or hexagonal, and four-fold, or octagonal, geometries are combined in both the Landscape Diamond and the dimensions of the St. Mary Chapel in the Abbey grounds. The Glastonbury great circles produce a geometrical system in keeping with the Avalonian tradition.

"ARTHUR'S HUNTING PATH"

Glastonbury Tor, Burrowbridge Mump, Hamdon Hill, and Cadbury Castle are all prominent natural hills that show signs of ancient sculpting and settlement. They possess an unusual geometrical relationship to each other. They lie in the landscape in the shape of a "diamond" or an equal-sided parallelogram known as a rhombus. The sixty-three degree St. Michael Line between Glastonbury Tor and Burrowbridge Mump forms one side of a figure whose sides all measure eleven miles.

All lines conform to this measure from the points selected with considerable accuracy. The other lines are from the summit of the Tor to Queen Anne's Well, Cadbury; Queen Anne's Well to the northern tip of Hamdon Hill's Neolithic settlement; and that point on Hamdon Hill to the east side of Burrowbridge Mump.

The diamond has some intriguing geometrical properties. The ratio between the length of the two axes is approximately four to five. The internal angles are 77.14 degrees and 102.86 degrees with a common factor of 25.71. This is a ratio of three to four. This is interesting, as 25.71 degrees is the internal angle of a seven-pointed star or heptagram. So the ruling number of the landscape figure is a seven. The diamond not only creates one of the most demanding geometrical figures, a heptagram, but it also creates a double heptagram within itself. Such dualism is in keeping with the qualities of the Avalonian Tradition.

The lines from the Tor to the Mump and from Cadbury Castle to Hamdon Hill are oriented to sunrise at Beltane and Lughnasad, and, reversed, to sunset at Samhain and Imbolc. This is the alignment of the St. Michael Line. The other pair of lines from Cadbury to the Tor and Hamdon Hill to the Mump are oriented to the northernmost setting point of the moon. This is known as the Northern Major Standstill. These lines reversed indicate the southernmost rising point of the moon—the Southern Major Standstill. We know from frequent use of this orientation at other sites, such as Stonehenge, how important these lunar alignments were to people of the Neolithic era. It is unlikely that the Neolithic inhabitants of Cadbury Castle would have missed so dramatic an event as moonset over Glastonbury Tor. Especially when it only happened every nineteen (18.61) years and indicated the time of the brightest—that is, the longest in the sky—moons.

The geometrical figure in the landscape is very striking. A remnant of its lore may have passed down in the tale of King Arthur galloping along "Arthur's Hunting Path" or "Arthur's Causeway" from Cadbury to Glastonbury on stormy winter nights. This probably meant when the moon set at its most northerly point in its 18.61 year cycle. He rides another path to Sutton Montis either on Christmas or Midsummer Eve. No one is certain. Sutton Montis is a village just to the southwest of Cadbury, on the line to Hamdon Hill. If the tradition originated from the astronomical event, then we can deduce the correct calendar time is Samhain or Imbolc sunset.

Some versions say he rode the hunting path every year, others say every seven years. Again, if the tradition arose because of the astronomical event, but became muddled as close observation of the moon ceased due to Christian disapproval, then we can conclude "Arthur" rode every 18.61 years. He may have also ridden 9.3 years later, the midpoint of the cycle, when the moon is at its opposite extreme, but there is no orientation to this time of the minor standstills.

All four sites in the diamond have a St. Michael Church nearby or upon them. Cadbury Castle has the foundation trench of a cross-shaped building that was probably a church. Otherwise there is a St. Michael

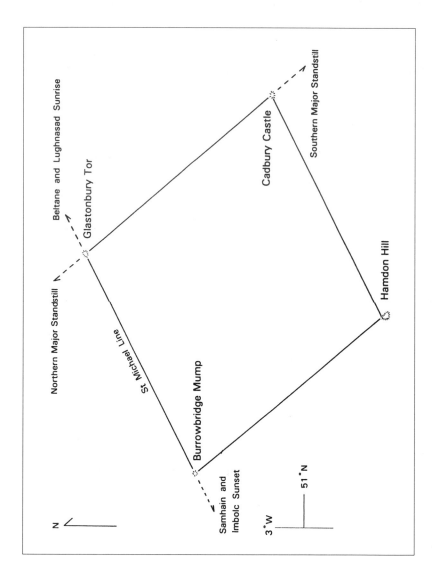

▲ *The Tor-Mump-Cadbury-Hamdon Hill Diamond.*

church at North Cadbury. Hamdon Hill has the prominent St. Michael's Hill just to the east near Montacute. This hill without its trees would reveal three distinct tiers, a shape as dramatic as the Tor. The difference being on St. Michael's Hill there was space for people to live within the walls. The ruins of a St. Michael Church stand on Burrowbridge Mump. There are no St. Michael churches within the figure. Somerton, once the Saxon capital of the Summer Country, lies close to the centre of the diamond. The exact centre of the diamond is at Ashen Cross near Midney, where a Christian cross once stood.

Grail traditions are associated with each site. It is said in some sources that Hamdon Hill is where the monks fleeing the Dissolution took and buried the Glastonbury treasure, including the Holy Grail. The quality that strikes the visitor to the hill today is the beautiful golden stone. Nearby St. Michael's Hill has its own extraordinary legend of a man who dreamed of a priceless relic being buried there. Digging at the spot shown in the dream revealed a huge black flint cross. There was also a wooden crucifix and a bell. The cross was put in a cart harnessed to twelve red and twelve white oxen. They were allowed to go where they pleased. At the place the oxen stopped, Waltham Abbey in Essex was built. Whether this was the cross given by Mary to King Arthur at Beckery cannot be determined. The bell is an emblem of St. Brigit and the red and white oxen repeat the primary Avalonian motif. The cross is in the category of objects linked with the mysteries of Britain. The Avalonian sources mention it as either under or in the pattern of the floor of the Mary Chapel.

The legends of Cadbury Castle are remarkable. The most widespread say King Arthur sleeps in a cave below the hill. He waits to come to the aid of his country in time of peril. The hill is said to be hollow. It is possible to call from the King's Well on the eastern ascent route to Queen Anne's Well on the north. The landowner recently cleared Queen Anne's Well of undergrowth, which revealed old stonework of a quality similar to the King's Well. Once a man was said to have entered the hill to find a company of sleeping warriors. On a table in their midst was a horn and a tumbled chalice. He went to pick them up, believing it would awaken the sleeping company. What took place next is described in local lore:

> Curs'd be the man
> Ever he was born
> That did not stand the chalice
> E're he blew the horn.

The horn is another of those mysterious objects linked with the mys-

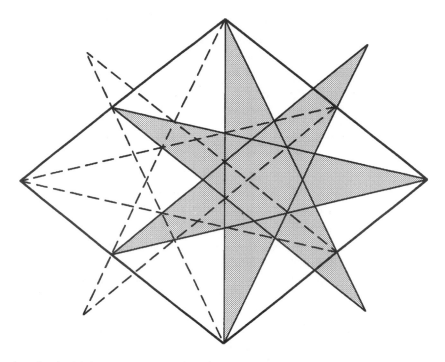

▲ *The double heptagram created by the geometry of the landscape diamond. This figure is obtained by taking a square and turning it into a rhombus until the two sets of angles are in a ratio of three to four and the two axes are in a ratio of approximately four to five (3.989 to 5). Lines are then drawn that divide the smaller angles into thirds and the larger angles into quarters. These provide all the lines necessary to create two perfect heptagrams. The mathematics and geometry of the heptagram are quite distinct, and thus the number seven stands alone from the other numbers. As a measure of the week and of the phases of the moon, seven-fold geometry is appropriate for a geomantic figure aligned to lunar extremes and the calendrical cross-quarter days.*

teries of the Matter of Britain. Apart from being an instrument of the hunt possessing obvious associations with Arthur's Hunting Path to Glastonbury, the horn is a symbol of plenty. Often depicted in spiral form, it represents the abundance of the inner world coming into outer manifestation. It is the cornucopia of the Classical tradition. It is the horn (French "cor") of the cauldron-keeper Bran of the Celtic tradition. In both cases the horn provides inexhaustible nourishment and is a symbol of the fertility of the land. Corbenic is the Grail Castle. The horn is perhaps the masculine component of the mystery that, in balance with the Grail and in service to the Goddess of Sovereignty, restores the land to health and harmony.

CHALICE HILL GEOMETRY

Another pattern in the landscape with interesting geometrical and astronomical properties centres upon Chalice Hill. If a line is drawn from the summit of Wearyall Hill to the summit of Chalice Hill, it would be found to have a distance of one mile, or 1760 yards. If this line was extended for the same distance, it would arrive at the two ancient oak trees of Gog and Magog. The distances and the alignment are very accurate. If a line is now drawn from approximately forty feet up St. Michael's tower on the summit of the Tor to the summit of Chalice Hill and then extended in the same direction for the same distance, it would be found to come to earth at the main crossing of the Abbey Church. The distance involved is 622 yards. The ratio between the distances 1760 and 622 yards is in the order of root two, being $2\sqrt{2}$, or the square root of eight.

This places Chalice Hill at the centre of an extraordinary pattern. The three sacred hills of Glastonbury form a triangle that is mirrored in two planes by the intentionally located feature of the Abbey and by the oak trees. The alignments have at their base the geodetic measure of one mile and the geometrical ratio of the square root of two.

The alignment through the summits of the Tor and Chalice Hill must have entered the considerations of the early geomancers and the founders of the Abbey. From the natural crest of the Tor through the crest of Chalice Hill, the line of sight of a tall person actually touches down on the site of the Old Church, St. Mary's Chapel. The summit of the Tor was levelled for the church, so it is possible the line of sight was originally from natural crest to crest. As far as we know, nothing was ever built on Chalice Hill. The placing of the Old Church on this alignment must be deliberate. Chalice Hill effectively hides the Tor from the Abbey Church, but any structure on the Tor would be visible. There is a good case for the foundation of the monastery on the Tor being earlier than that in the Abbey grounds. This is not all, however, for at ground level from the site of the Mary Chapel, the sun rises over the Tor, silhouetting St. Michael's tower on and around September 29—the feast day of St. Michael or Michaelmas! This is a remarkable astronomical synchronicity.[6]

The sun also rises over the Tor from the Mary Chapel on and around March 17. This is St. Patrick's Day. St. Patrick, as described in Chapter

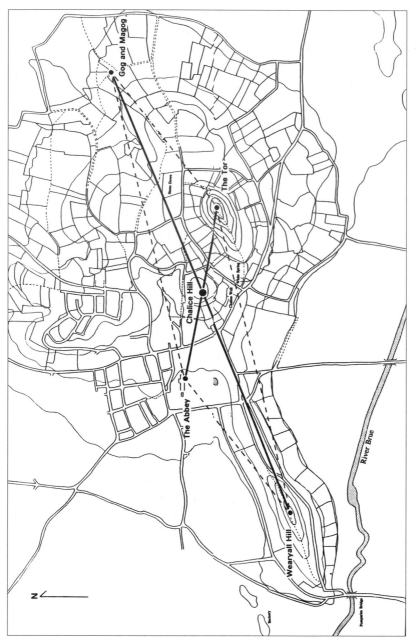

▲ *Chalice Hill Geometry.*

Three, had much to say about the Tor and is credited for the foundation of the monastery there. He is also credited with reestablishing the monastic community at the Abbey. In the Glastonbury calendar, Patrick shares his feast day with Joseph of Arimathea. Joseph is credited with the foundation of the first church in the Abbey grounds and with the bringing and burial of the Holy Grail on Chalice Hill. This solar alignment was thus triply marked with significance for the monks of Avalon. It indicated the feasts of three of their most significant patron saint's days.

Another important factor in the consideration of the location of the Old Church is the spring that comes to the surface there. Known as St. Joseph's Well, the spring lies just outside the walls of the Mary Chapel at a point where optimum observation of the Tor is possible. There is a possibility that the well shaft predates anything else on the site. Professor Rahtz thought that the well shaft might be Roman.[7] The Druidic community certainly would have known about it.

When the church of St. Michael was built, the monastery on the Tor now became visible from the centre of the new Abbey Church. The equal distances between the great crossing and Chalice Hill and from there to the Tor would have added to the ideal nature of the Abbey site. It is this measure that is in a square root ratio to the primary line between Wearyall Hill, Chalice Hill, and Gog and Magog.

We know the early architects of the Abbey employed the formulae of sacred geometry in their designs. They used the Vesica Piscis, seen in the design of the lid on Chalice Well, in the laying out of St. Mary's Chapel. The Vesica Piscis contains the proportions vital to those working in three-dimensional form—the square roots of two, three, and five. It also provides the basic construction diagram for the regular polygons, such as the pentagon, hexagon, and octagon. From these roots and figures it is possible to arrive at the ratio of the Golden Section. This governs the unfoldment of many forms in the natural world, including the spiral arrangement of many plants and shells and the proportions of the human body. It comes as little surprise to find these proportions in the establishing of the ideal location of the Abbey.

The intentional placing of Gog and Magog is impossible to establish. Records show they were only two of a wood of great oaks that covered the northern and eastern parts of the island. About seventy years ago, the two trees were spared after the public protested the felling of their giant companions—the Oaks of Avalon. The two oaks were always a traditional point of entry onto the island and the reason for their survival is that special significance was attached to them. The oaks stand beside an ancient

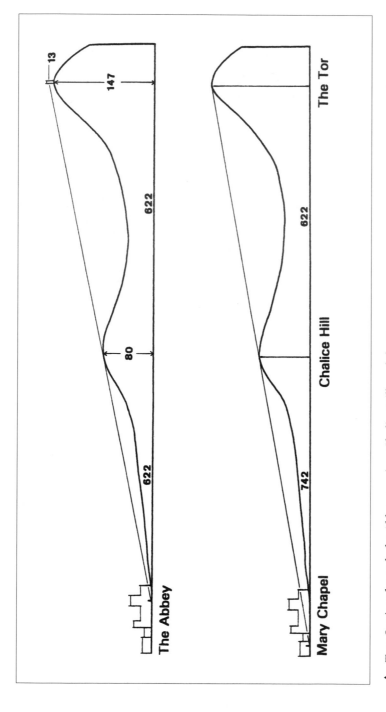

▲ Top: *Section through the Abbey crossing, Chalice Hill, and the Tor.*
Bottom: *Section through St. Mary's Chapel, Chalice Hill, and Tor.*

▲ *Tower of St. Michael's over Chalice Hill from the Mary Chapel.*

pilgrim's path, close to a holy well. If a line is drawn from them to the Tor, it indicates an azimuth close to Summer Solstice sunrise and Winter Solstice sunset. In fact, from a point on this line on the summit of Stone Down, the Winter Solstice sun sets into the notch the base of the Tor makes with the horizon. Some sources say that in the eighteenth century Gog and Magog formed a pair in a "Druidic avenue" of oak trees. Would this have run along the solstice alignment to the Tor or to Chalice Hill? Gog and Magog or Gogmagog are traditional names for giants.[8]

Whatever this geometry may reveal in its astronomy, measure, and ratio, it is not a mental scheme thrown upon the ground like a grid plan for a city. The geometry is carefully founded upon the relationship of Avalon's three most sacred hills. It subtly draws this relationship out, mirroring it and clarifying it with the placement of the Mary Chapel, the Abbey Church, and Gog and Magog. It is likely that all sites were Druidic, so the Christian architects were perpetuating an ancient tradition.

THE TOR STONES

Further evidence that Glastonbury Tor was part of a larger complex of pre-historic activity is seen in the remnants of standing stones around the Tor.

The engineer Professor Alexander Thom visited Glastonbury in the late sixties. He worked from an old Ordnance Survey map in the area enigmatically known as Stone Down. This is the high ground to the north of the Tor. In his survey, he found enough remaining stones to convince him of an alignment to the sun at Beltane and Lughnasad. This is the same alignment as the St. Michael Line. The Druid author Ross Nichols also mentions these stones. He says three menhirs stood in a north-south row upon Stone Down, with another stone to the west. However, the stones are not there now. Those that are marked on the maps are not Megalithic. They are nineteenth-century boundary stones. The map reference Professor Thom gave was ST 510390.[9]

The stones also had an alignment to the western horizon. They pointed to the Black Mountains in Wales. The builders, Thom thought, used them as sightlines for computing the movement of the moon. Like

▲ *Gog and Magog.*

▲ *The "Living Rock" on the southwest ascent path of the Tor. It marks the St. Michael Line and the entrance to the labyrinth. Some call it and its partner, slightly higher up, the "Druid's Stones." Chalice Hill is in the background.*

the Cadbury to Glastonbury line, the orientation was to the most northerly setting point of the moon. (The next Major Standstill is in 2006.)

None of these stones exist today. Only two, sometimes known as the "Druid's Stones," are evident on the Tor. They mark the St. Michael Line and the entrance to the labyrinth. The tradition surrounding the lower stone, the "Living Rock," is that it becomes energized at dawn and sunset. The stone has broken in two. The larger part lies beside the stump remaining in the ground.

Other stones do exist, however, and can be found by probing. They are particularly present on the level of the Living Rock on the southern and eastern flanks of the Tor. A stone on this level was recently seen to be close to the style on the northeast ascent route. During work on the path in 1985, segments were broken off this rock and what remains is all but hidden underground. This stone is also on the St. Michael alignment.

The 1974 Ordnance Survey map (scale 1:10,000) marks two further stones. One lies above the lynchets to the east of the Tor and another by Stone Down Lane on the St. Michael Line. The latter stone is also roughly on the line that runs up the Abbey, along Dod Lane and then to Stonehenge. These stones are not there today and were most likely boundary stones. Whether any of these stones formed part of a ring encircling the base of the Tor, or formed an astronomical observation site on Stone Down, only excavation will tell. Could they have been matched by other megaliths or a cairn on the summit? All the evidence was destroyed by the levelling that took place for the building of the Medieval church. We simply do not know.

Local builders are always hungry for stone. There is no source of good building stone on the island as the ransacked Abbey ruins well prove. Megalithic sacred sites would be the first to go on an island given over to building a monastic centre. The legend of St. Collen says the Tor was bare, but there is a popular tradition that St. Michael's on the Tor incorporated stones from a pagan monument. If this is so, and Professor Thom's rather fragmentary evidence is correct, then the Tor and the adjacent Stone Down plateau formed one of the many astronomical Megalithic complexes in Britain. The terraces would be an integral part of this system.

Despite the flimsy material evidence, the popular tradition of a stone or stones on the summit of the Tor is worth serious consideration. Those among us with psychometric abilities are able to detect the presence of a stone in the "place memory" of the Tor. I suspect—like the case of the stone chamber of Chalice Well being Druidic—there never will be actual physical evidence of ancient pagan stones. But the intuitive sense that the stones were on Avalon in ancient times, on the Tor and at Chalice Well, is correct, and absolutely correct in the greater context of the Avalonian Tradition. As we shall see in the following chapter, symbols appear in coherent groups. Where the subject of sovereignty emerges in the Celtic Tradition there tends to be a sword, a spear, a cauldron, and, always, a stone. The Lia Fal upon the Hill of Tara in Ireland emitted a high-pitched tone when touched by the rightful monarch. Similar qualities probably attended the Turoe Stone in County Galway. The Stone of Scone lies beneath the coronation chair of the British monarchs. The young Arthur drew the Sword of Sovereignty from a stone. The sword Excalibur was forged on the Isle of Avalon. It makes sense to say that the stone in which Excalibur lay was also on the Isle. It makes sense to say the stone was on the Tor. The sacred mountain and the stone able to confer sovereignty upon a king run together in the mythical imagination. Whether natural or carved, an ancient stone upon the sanctified hill of Avalon would exude a compelling and preternatural power.

THE TOR LABYRINTH

The theory that the terraces on the Tor form the remains of a three-dimensional labyrinth was thought well "worth consideration" by Professor Rahtz. Other archaeologists and historians are not so kind. The theory, first put forward in 1968 by Geoffrey Russell, is greatly explored in the Glastonbury literature. Geoffrey Ashe walked and surveyed the labyrinth in 1979. When not dismissive, most writers on the subject, including Rahtz, agree that something as large, complex, and intentionally created as a unicursal labyrinth on the Tor is very likely to be Neolithic, but as yet it is not possible to arrive at any conclusions.[10]

The path of the Tor labyrinth threads around the terraces according to a classical design found throughout the world. It appears in Spanish, Cornish, and Irish rock carvings. It appears as a traditional design motif in Arizona among the Pima, Tohono O'odham, and Hopi nations. It appears in Java, in European stone and turf mazes, and on coins and inscriptions from the ancient Mediterranean world.

The labyrinth has a variety and many layers of meaning. These include fertility, death and rebirth—the journey, and the return from the land of the dead. For the Hopi, the labyrinth represents the Sun Father, the Earth Mother, and the child in the womb. It is also a symbol of emergence, of the four directions—northeast, northwest, southeast, southwest—and of the good road to follow in life.[11] For the Tohono O'odham of southern Arizona, the labyrinth represents the path of the "Elder Brother," Iitoi, around the sacred mountain of Baboquivari. Iitoi made the maze so that the people could not follow him back into the spirit world.[12] In the Classical tradition, the labyrinth of King Minos of Crete describes the perilous journey a man can make to discover the wild and chthonian side of his nature. In this he will be aided by the maiden Ariadne (arachne = the spider), a name close to the Celtic Goddess Arianrhod, "Silver Wheel." Later European turf labyrinths

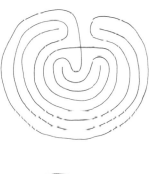

▲ *The traditional design of the Labyrinth.*

have traditions of races to catch and kiss maidens associated with them. Stone labyrinths were for prayer, meditation, and, often by the sea, for weather magic. The labyrinth on the Tor, however, is unusual, being many times larger and possessing, like the sacred mountain of Baboquivari, one more dimension than the other examples.

The terraces form seven concentric rings around the Tor that can be walked without too much difficulty, moreover, in a way that convincingly threads the proposed Classical model of a labyrinth. Where the path is obscured it is in keeping with natural erosion. Or it is where comparatively recent agriculture has ploughed out terraces and divided and fenced them off. The final turn to the summit, however, is hard to do. The slope is precipitous and there is no sign of a path. Geoffrey Ashe feels that the labyrinth enters the Tor at this point. The underlying rock is exposed, a large Tor burr or eggstone is visible, and geological surveying suggests a fracture in the layers of the Tor comes to the surface here. In recent years a custom has arisen to attach cloth prayer ties to the trees that struggle to maintain a roothold at this spot.

Stones on the southwest ascent route mark two key turning points in the labyrinth. The lower one, the "Living Rock," marks the entrance. The other is slightly higher. The outermost circuit is not passable to the north. Walking the labyrinth one way can take anything from one to five hours, and is advisable only on a dry day.

THE TOR LABYRINTH AND ITS ASTRONOMICAL ALIGNMENT

The Classical Labyrinth design for the Tor uses almost every terrace and works well due to the pear-shape of the Tor, providing a single axis and ascent way. Any other hill shape would make it harder for the labyrinth design to work.

Given the interest of the Neolithic inhabitants of Britain in astronomical alignments—for example, at Stonehenge or the local long barrows—and if it were they who shaped a labyrinth on the Tor, they might have perceived it as becoming "operative" when its axis and entrance aligned with significant astronomical events. The area was a centre of prehistoric activity. It is possible the Tor provided the focal point of ceremony, as other major monuments are lacking in the area. The people may have

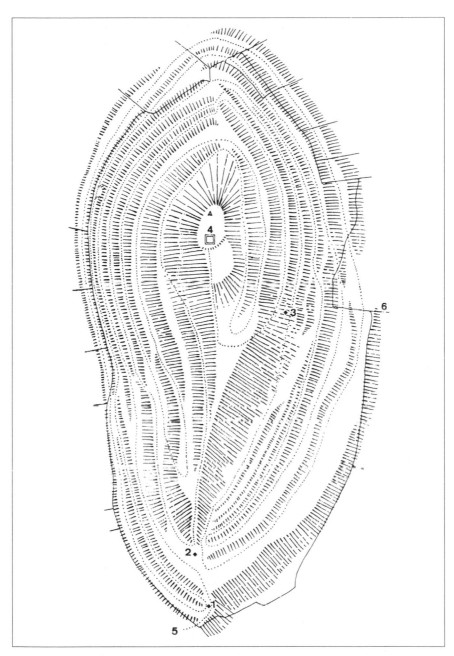

▲ *The Glastonbury Tor Labyrinth. 1. The first Druid Stone, the "Living Rock."*
2. The second Druid Stone. 3. Eggstone. 4. St. Michael's Tower. 5. Entrance to
Labyrinth. 6. Present day field boundaries.

turned to the Tor as the striking and most meaningful natural feature in the landscape and noticed its axis lay on an azimuth of sixty-three degrees.

This is a significant solar alignment. It indicates sunrise on the cross-quarter days of Beltane—May 1—and Lughnasad—August 1—and sunset on the cross-quarter days of Samhain—October 31—and Imbolc—February 2. Many Neolithic stone circles exhibit orientation to the cross-quarter days. These lie midway between the solstices and the equinoxes, dividing the year cross-wise: northeast, northwest, southeast, southwest.[13] They are important points on the agricultural and ritual calendar. From there it was an obvious step to enhance the astronomical alignment and perhaps elaborate on the other meanings of the Tor.

Perhaps the people ceremonially walked the Tor labyrinth at Samhain or at Imbolc, when its entrance upon the long ridge of the Tor pointed to the setting sun over Burrowbridge Mump. These two festivals in the Celtic tradition are particular to the Great Goddess. Samhain is the time of the Dark Goddess, Cerridwen, at the end of the year and the beginning of winter. Imbolc is the time of the Goddess Brigit, in her maiden form, at the first stirrings of spring. By threading the labyrinth at Samhain, the people may have believed they were ritually enacting the journey to the land of the dead. By threading it at Imbolc, they celebrated the return from there and the rebirth and fertility of spring.

On the other hand, they may have entered the labyrinth at Beltane and Lughnasad when the axis of the Tor pointed to where the sun rose on the eastern horizon. They lit a fire on the hilltop and saw that a line of fires extended along the pathway of the sun, through other sacred hills, and continued unerringly to the great ceremonial sanctuary at Avebury—the "mother circle" of ancient Britain.

Beltane and Lughnasad, like Samhain and Imbolc, were fire festivals in the Celtic world. Bel and Lugh or Llew, "light," were two ancient gods. It may be that "Bel's tane," Bel's fires, celebrated the energizing vitality of spring, and Lugh's fires the bounty of autumn. Bel's festival was one of orgiastic fertility, remnants of which survive in May Day celebrations. Lugh's was a time of culmination, of fairs, of making truces, giving thanks for first fruits, and preparing for the harvest. One festival sent the spark of male energy to the mother goddess at Avebury, the other received her gifts. The Celtic legend of Gwynn and Gwythyr, and eventually Arthur and Melwas, imply that the two opposing masculine forces—twins or gods—went through some kind of cosmological transition at these times upon the Tor.

This is a cosmology expressed in a geomantic pattern upon the landscape on a huge scale. We will never know if it was true in the past or not. It is only possible to make conjectures. The concepts surrounding labyrinths do, however, tie in extremely well with the traditions of the Tor. Both being entranceways to the land of the dead, the chthonic realms, or to heaven, as well as marking points of transition in the cycle of the year. Yet in the end, whether the Tor was perceived as a labyrinth in the past or as something quite different is not the matter of most significance. It will only ever be as "true" as it resonates within us today. In the words of Jeff Saward:

> The Glastonbury Tor Labyrinth most certainly is a labyrinth. The mere fact that people have pointed out the course of its pathways, defined them in print and more importantly in the mind, and furthermore have walked the pattern of the labyrinth ... confirms its existence. It exists now, and will continue to exist as long as people continue to walk its path and believe in it. A sacred site does not necessarily need an ancient history to deserve its sanctity ....[14]

THE GLASTONBURY ZODIAC

In about 1580, Dr. John Dee, scholar, astrologer, and physician to Queen Elizabeth I, visited Somerset and recorded in drawings and in notes what he called "Merlin's Secret." He wrote:

> The starres which agree with their reproductions on the ground do lye onlie on the celestial path of the Sonne, moon and planets ... all the greater starres of Sagittarius fall in the hinde quarters of the horse, while Altiar, Tarazes and Alsschain from Auilla do fall on its cheste ... thus is astrologie and astronomie carefullie and exactley married and measured in a scientific reconstruction of the heavens....

For several centuries no one was quite sure what Dr. Dee meant by any of this. He was dismissed as a maverick and a magician. Then in 1929, an artist, Kathryn Maltwood, published a book called *A Guide to Glastonbury's Temple of the Stars*. While studying the Arthurian legends, she was inspired to take the journeys of the knights literally. She took Cadbury to be the site of Camelot, for example, and if the legend said to journey west

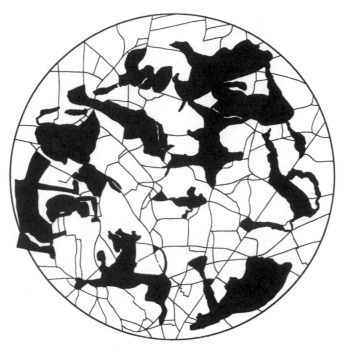

▲ *The Glastonbury Zodiac. About eleven miles across, the twelve signs formed by natural and artificial features in the landscape differ somewhat from conventional zodiacs.*

from there on horseback for a day, that is where she went. As a result of this method and with the aid of the excellent maps of the Ordance Survey and eventually aerial photographs, she began to notice a pattern of extraordinary figures upon the ground. In her book she described this pattern as a replica of the signs of the Zodiac in the sky.

The terrestrial zodiac around Glastonbury, Ms. Maltwood said, was created by the combination of natural features such as rivers, streams, hills, hollows, and contours, and intentionally located features such as field and wood boundaries, mounds, banks, and causeways. The figure of Aquarius, for example, is formed by the natural hills and boundaries of the Isle of Avalon, and perfected by the placement of earthen banks and roads. The twelve signs of the Zodiac cover an area whose circumference is thirty miles. Some figures are many miles in length. Each figure approximates the stellar configuration it represents. Occasionally it differs from the standard pattern, making a ship out of Cancer, a dove out of Libra, while some interpretations say Scorpio is an eagle and Capricorn a unicorn.

In this landscape zodiac, Aquarius is not the familiar figure of the Water Bearer. It is a bird whose form is made by the whole of the Isle of Avalon. The Tor forms the head of the figure. The connection with water is evidently made by the bird's bill reaching westward to where the White Spring and Chalice Well rise. Katherine Maltwood called the bird the Aquarian Phoenix. The phoenix of mythology renews itself through the consuming fire. This seems to perpetuate the death and rebirth themes of the Tor.

Aerial photography opened the way for other zodiacs to be found. Enthusiasts found a zodiac in Carmarthenshire in the late forties. It was centered on the village of Pumpsaint. In the seventies, investigators of this claim discovered an even larger zodiac in the landscape of Dyfed around the Prescelly Mountains. Both zodiacs repeated the patterns of the Glastonbury Zodiac. Researchers maintained that the artificial features of all of them originated in Neolithic times. Subsequent research has unearthed other places in the British landscape that yielded up zodiacs when the pattern was applied. The most documented of these are the Nuthampstead Zodiac Temple discovered by Nigel Pennick and the Kingston Zodiac Temple discovered by Mary Caine.

Although these terrestrial zodiacs are indisputably there for the perceiver, the main difficulty with them is intentionality on the part of their alleged creators. Although the symbiosis between the zodiac signs and the landscape is at times an incredible example of synchronicity, most of the time it is only credible in the mind of the beholder. Like a Rorschach test, Scorpio in the Glastonbury Zodiac differs according to the interpreter. The reflexive landscape happily accommodates all interpretations. Ponter's Ball that makes the horn of Capricorn, yes, can be seen in that light, but it also can have a perfectly mundane explanation as a defensive or boundary-marking earthwork.

But let us look at the "mind of the beholder." The mind is very powerful. To deny the existence of something because it is "only in the mind" is to deny the world-shaping power of the cosmologies that each of us carry in our minds. The mind is not a passive participant in the world. Its views, attitudes, ideas, imagination, and beliefs are tremendously powerful, and in the case of Britain, have moulded every facet of the landscape into a particular form. The social and religious views of the British have an enormous impact upon the landscape. It would be foolhardy to say that the existence of a social class system, for example, could not be read from the features of the land. Yet the British class system is merely a set of ideas, and rather dull ideas at that. Having lived in four different signs of the

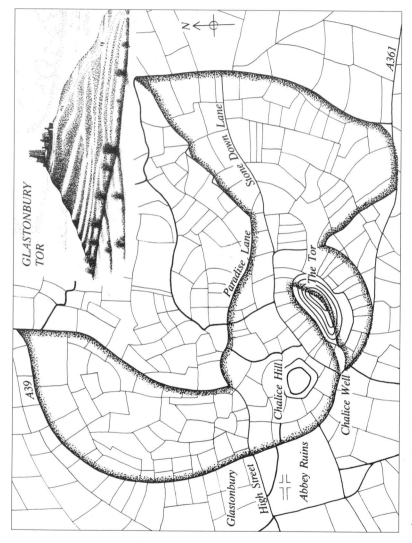

GLASTONBURY
TOR

Stone Down Lane

Paradise Lane

The Tor

A361

A39

Chalice Hill

Chalice Well

Glastonbury

High Street

Abbey Ruins

▲ *The Aquarian Phoenix.*

Zodiac for several years, I can only confirm that the profoundly imaginative idea of the Glastonbury Zodiac does exist. It informs and makes sense of the landscape. It makes it alive, intelligent, and dynamic.

A very definite sense of place arises from living within a Zodiacal constellation. The quality of each sign begins to permeate actions. Walking, driving, building, and naming places achieves resonance within a far greater context. It becomes meaningful to visit Taurus for its earthy qualities, to take a walk to the heart of Leo on a Sunday morning, to stand on the brow of Gemini, to meditate on the eye of Aries, to drink the water that gushes from the mouth of Aquarius, or to discover one's own astrological birth sign on the ground. Even people who normally do not give esoteric matters a second thought find the quality of the zodiacal giant on which they live permeating their thinking and informing their ideas.

The giant pattern of the Zodiac is as though a twelve-fold energy blueprint of the mind in resonance with and inspired by the eternal pattern of the stars is superimposed upon the natural landscape. It is exactly as John Dee described. As a result, the invisible forms of the zodiacal giants inevitably appear, gradually manifesting in the physical world what is being held in the archetypal realm. In this context it becomes superfluous to pin the existence of the terrestrial Zodiac upon the conception and labour of ancient peoples. This is an attempt to achieve a legitimation based upon antiquity for ideas and actions which need no such legitimation. It is not helpful to try to retrofit the Glastonbury Zodiac to a bygone age. It is a choice of reality pertaining to today.

Like the Tor Labyrinth, the landscape zodiacs exist to the extent that people are aware of their outlines. They exist to the extent that people make pilgrimages around them, name their houses, fields, and children after them, and above all, feel they are important to the general order of things. As their pattern is visible almost every night in the stars, the terrestrial zodiacs are classic examples of a geocentric and holistic worldview rendering meaning, relatedness, congruity, wholeness, intelligence, and dynamic order to the physical world.

Having said that, it does seem likely—at least in the poetic sense—that the Isle of Avalon as a powerful geomantic centre involved in a ritual cycle which turned the wheel of the year, would be conceived by the ancient peoples as having heavenly correspondences upon its landscape. In the following chapter, the idea of the Tor as a World Axis is explored. In such instances, the stars are generally viewed as turning around the cosmic centre, which then has about it the universe in microcosm. The landscape around the Tibetan world axis, Mount Kailas, for example, contains all the many different cosmic realms. This includes features such as the Lake of the Sun and the Lake of the Moon. It follows that a twelve-fold zodiacal pattern of the heavens is quite likely to be identified with natural features surrounding a cosmological world centre. Such an order or division superimposed upon the landscape suggests a richness far exceeding that imposed by the demands of the present material age.

Patterns with heavenly correspondences do exist in the Glastonbury landscape. The terraces on the Tor may be modelled in the image of the corona borealis or upon other circular or spiral heavenly features. Observers must have remarked upon the solar orientation of the St. Michael Line, the Tor-Chalice Hill-Abbey line, and the lunar orientation of Arthur's Hunting Path. The seven-fold geometry of the Landscape Diamond resonates with seven-fold divisions of the cosmos, such as the days of the week. And it is entirely possible that the twelve-fold division of the landscape around Avalon by the Zodiac emerges in the legendary twelve hides which formed the original grant of land to the Abbey. It is unfortunate that the exact nature of the original twelve hides is obscured by time. It would be satisfying to find in the Avalonian Tradition a place where such patterns become explicit.

THE FLOORPLAN OF THE TEMPLE

The written sources often describe the pattern embedded in the floor of the Old Church at Glastonbury. When William of Malmesbury saw the floor in 1125, he spoke of a "sacred enigma" of "triangles and squares." The strange Glastonbury prophet Melkin said the pattern included thirteen "spheres of prophecy." According to Melkin, Joseph of Arimathea "lies on a forked line (linea bifurcata) close to the southern corner of the chapel with prepared wattle above the powerful venerable Maiden, the thirteen aforesaid things occupying the place." None of which is clear, but it is infinitely suggestive. The astral monks of Bligh Bond described the Abbey after the great fire of 1184 as continuing the tradition of being "a message in ye stones." They said the "measures were marked plaine on ye slabbes in Mary's Chappel." There was the "Body of Christ," the twelve signs of the zodiac, the "Four Ways," and a cross. The goal of the Glastonbury monks was to reproduce the original foundation pattern of the Old Church in the pattern on the floor of the Mary Chapel.

When the Rev. Richard Warner saw the existing chapel in the 1820s, any evidence of the floor pattern was destroyed. The monks had dug out St. Joseph's crypt in the sixteenth century, effectively removing the area of prime archaeological interest. The Reverend described the crypt being flooded by the spring that rose there. He did, however, mention that traces of painting could still be seen on the walls of the Mary Chapel. He wrote, "traces of the suns, and moons, and stars, that covered the intervals, may still be discerned." The Reverend felt that such things were studied much more in the past than they were in his day. It would not have surprised him to find a whole compendium of esoteric and astrological science in the ruins of the Abbey.[15]

John Michell thought he could come close to reconstructing the layout of the Old Church by combining the geometric measures given by the monks with those given by the existing Mary Chapel and those given by archaeology. Michell's "New Jerusalem" diagram, so redolent with the measures and ratios of ancient temples and full of the mystical symbolism of St. John and Plato, is full of twelve-fold and, with a centre, thirteen-fold geometry. Both he and Bligh Bond thought that this geometry pointed toward the original foundation pattern of the ancient church at Avalon. The Glastonbury Tradition says this took the form of the simple wooden chapel of Joseph of Arimathea surrounded by the twelve cells of the monks. Many reconstructions of this original pattern have been attempted. What follows adds a little more to the speculation on what was actually upon the floor of the temple. The hope is that this will illuminate the Avalonian mysteries.

In Freemasonry, it is incumbent upon those who take the oaths of membership to ponder the mystery of the pattern on the floor. Perhaps more attention is paid to the decoration of the floor than to any other detail of the Masonic Lodge. The prototype for the floor pattern is said to derive from either the Temple of Solomon in Jerusalem or from the Egyptian temples. The Greek mathematician, Pythagoras, who coined the term "geometry," is reputed to have spent twenty-two years in Egypt being initiated into its science. Geometry means the "measure of the earth." In the traditions of Freemasonry, geometry—originally wielded by the hands of the Supreme Architect, or God—is the only science by which it is possible to comprehend the universe.

The triangle and the number three occupy a highly important place in the hermetic tradition of Freemasonry. Geometry is said to begin with trigonometry, which literally means "the measure of triangles." Triangles were fundamental to the builders of the pyramids, the Egyptians. The theorem attributed to Pythagoras, that the sum of the square of the hypotenuse of every right-angled triangle is equal to the sum of the squares of the other two sides, is the most important and most used of all geometrical theorems. In a Masonic allegory, the sun and moon as the two sides of a triangle beside the right-angle, represent the male and the female. They shed their light upon their product, the "Blazing Star" of the hypotenuse, or the divine child, Horus.[16] This may be represented by an equilateral triangle.

The floor in a Masonic Lodge is most likely to contain a design showing a pattern of triangles. There may be the hexagram in the form of two intersecting equilateral triangles. This is known as the "Seal of Solomon." There may be a design demonstrating the geometric principle known as the "squaring of the circle." In this the quantifiable, "rational" measures of a square are reconciled with the unquantifiable and "irrational" measures of a circle. There are a number of solutions to this problem. The Great Pyramid contains one solution where the perimeter of the square base is equal to the circumference of a circle described by the height. This quantifies the irrational number *pi.* The floor of the lodge may contain a "pentalpha" or the "Signet of Solomon." This is a pentagram or five-pointed star. Or there may be another design. Freemasonry is not a dogmatic practice and many interpretations of the canons of sacred geometry exist. But what every floor will have in common, from the least to the greatest temple, will be the chequered pattern of black and white squares.

The ancient Egyptian tradition says that when the soul leaves the body and makes the journey to the land of the dead it will enter the Great Hall of Judgement. On the floor of the hall is a pattern of black and white squares. The squares must be equal in number and they represent the life of the soul. If there are too many of either black or white, the soul cannot cross the hall and make the journey to the Otherworld. This is the earliest reference we have to a floor of this design and it set a widely followed precedent.

Nearer to Avalon we find in the Celtic Tradition the game of "gwyddbwyll." Researchers have reconstructed the game and found it similar in complexity to chess. It is played on a chequered board of black and white squares. Sometimes the black squares are replaced by red. Descriptions of the board in Irish sources suggest that a centre and four directions, representing the seat of sovereignty at Tara and the four provinces, were marked. The board is thus a microcosm of the country. The sources indicate that when gwyddbywll is played, it is invariably by powerful opponents ritually competing for the sovereignty of the land. For example, when King Arthur and Owein play in *The Mabinogion* they hold the fortune of their warriors in their hands.[17]

These examples show that in the past the chequered pattern had profound significance. It was not simply a convenient design to put on the floor. In the Gothic cathedrals, it was customary to add a further pattern to the basic background of squares. Sometimes a cross was inlaid on the floor. This has considerable Masonic and Christian hermetic significance. The cross was a sign of light and life. It represented the alchemical crucible of transformation. Cross in Latin is "crux," which is also "crucible" or cauldron. The cross represented the four elements and the death and the body of Christ. It provided a convenient pattern around which to arrange Matthew, Mark, Luke and John. Each Evangelist corresponds to a sign of the Zodiac. The other signs of the Zodiac could be arranged around a circle, as, for example, at Canterbury Cathedral. We thus find in the Western architectural tradition, as handed down through Freemasonry from Egyptian and Celtic sources, a specific set of meanings about a possible floorplan for the temple. These meanings all relate to themes belonging to the tradition of the Isle of Avalon: sovereignty; balance in polarity; the journey of the soul through life, death, the otherworldly realms, and rebirth.

Following the argument of this book, that the key to the Avalonian traditions will be found in the landscape itself, is it possible that the geomantic patterns of the surrounding topography were inlaid on the floor of the Mary Chapel? The seven-pointed star generated by the diamond of the four peculiar and distinctive hills—the Tor, the Mump, Cadbury Castle and Hamdon Hill—is the primary candidate for consideration.

The challenge is that the number seven stands alone, geometrically and mathematically. Unlike the regular polygons it cannot be generated from geometrical forms such as the Vesica Piscis. Its measures are "irrational" and do not divide, multiply, or add up to any other number. For these reasons mathematicians called seven the "Virgin" number and seventy-seven—the double heptagram—was the number of the Virgin Goddess, Athena or Minerva.[18] Could this be what Melkin meant by the "powerful venerable Maiden"? Yet seven is the measure of the week, of the notes in a scale, and it occurs frequently in esoteric symbolism. It is, for example, the traditional number of the planets and the number of the archangels, the Elohim or the "Makers of Cosmic Law." In Pythagorean symbolism, the "heptad" represents the full nature of humanity. It combines the three-fold spiritual body with the four-fold material form. It is the task of the geometer to reconcile the distinctive properties of seven with the numbers around it, especially the entirely "rational" properties of the numbers six and eight.

The endlessly unfolding heptagram demonstrates why the number seven is often taken to represent eternity. It is the point beyond the six "knowable" dimensions of this world. It represents the completion of this life as well as the seed that can pass through the portal into the next. The seven is the point in the centre of a six-faced cube around which all turns and through which all things have their end. It is the point in the centre of a six-pointed star. The number eight is the beginning of the next octave, and thus eight represents the step beyond. Eight appears on its side as the symbol for infinity.

As a symbol of the Virgin Goddess represented in the Christian tradition by the Virgin Mary—the "Maiden"—and as a symbol of the gateway between the worlds, the seven-pointed star fulfills the criteria of the Avalonian tradition. It is tempting to speculate that the heptagram was represented in the floorplan of its most elaborate temple, especially a temple which exuded such sanctity that burial within or nearby was a guarantee of the salvation of the soul.

If the seven-pointed star from the landscape around Glastonbury was to be placed in the floor of the Mary Chapel, it would have the benefit of providing a cross by virtue of the four-square diamond upon which it is based. This diamond is also divided into two equal triangles that have the unusual ability of being extremely close to the proportions necessary to fulfill the geometer's task of "squaring the circle." With base angles of 51°25' they are only 26' short of the angle of the Great Pyramid. In other words, a circle whose diameter was equal to the breadth of the diamond would have a circumference equal to four times its height.

On the other hand, the geometry surrounding Chalice Hill may have entered the design of the Old Church. The line of sight from the summit of the Tor through the summit of Chalice Hill touches down to earth between the centre of the chapel and the likely location of the original altar. As the Abbey church grew eastward, the centre of the great crossing formed a ratio to the other measures that passed through Chalice Hill in the order of $\sqrt{2}$. This ratio is geometrically obtained by drawing the Vesica Piscis using no more than a compass and a straight edge. The ratios of $\sqrt{3}$ and $\sqrt{5}$ are also obtained from this figure. Bligh Bond was certain these ratios were used throughout the Abbey. The Mary Chapel, for example, is theoretically contained in a $\sqrt{3}$ rectangle. In his publications, Bligh Bond demonstrated how the theoretical or ideal dimensions of the Mary Chapel may be drawn within a hexagon or hexagram.

John Michell presents an alternative analysis which reveals how the ratios of the Mary Chapel can be contained within an octagon. This is closer to the actual measures of the Chapel.[19] On the following pages are diagrams that illustrate how the hexagon and the octagon can be combined in the dimensions of the Mary Chapel to create a heptagram. This suggests a possible design for the pattern on the floor of the Chapel. Given that the heptagram has its own unique geometry and given that the geometer's task is to resolve the meanings which six-fold, seven-fold and eight-fold figures represent, this appears to provide a happy solution to the problem.

Whatever the pattern on the floor of the Old Church and the Mary Chapel may have been—whether it contained a zodiac or originated in Egypt or Jerusalem; whether it was based on three-, four-, five-, six-, seven-, twelve- or thirteen-fold geometry, or was rooted in the geomantic proportions of the Avalonian landscape itself—it is highly conceivable that the pattern was set in a chequered floor and that its meaning was about the journey of the soul through the lands of the living and the dead. From the evidence which remains, the tiles on the floor of Glastonbury Abbey were not black and white but red and white. This was partly because that was the colour of the local clay, a brick red. Yet it is satisfying to think that the monks were perpetuating the ancient colour dyad of the isle in their church, thus maintaining the death and rebirth themes of the Isle of Avalon.

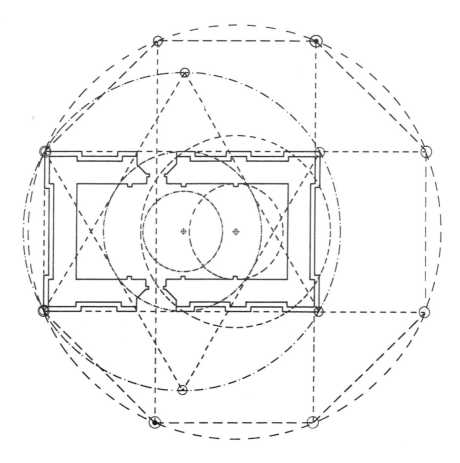

▲ *The dimensions of the St. Mary Chapel, deriving from both hexagonal and octagonal geometry.*

The Mary Chapel was constructed after 1184 when fire destroyed the "Old Church." The Old Church enclosed the ancient wooden chapel said to be built by Joseph of Arimathea. The St. Mary Chapel is supposed to retain the dimensions of these original features.

The $\sqrt{3}$ geometry of the hexagon and its internal hexagram or six-pointed star create a rectangle that defines the ideal outer dimensions of the Chapel. The ideal width—given by Bligh Bond—is 39.6 feet. The ideal length is 68.6 feet. These measures are only true when taken from the outer footings, not the wall surface.[20]

$$39.6 \times \sqrt{3} \ (1.732) = 68.589$$

This length can only be discovered theoretically, as the eastern end of the chapel was removed to connect it to the main church. The diameter of the circle of the hexagon is 79.2 feet. In the centre of the hexagram is drawn a circle of half this measure, 39.6 feet, equal to the external width of the Chapel. A circle half that measure again is drawn in the centre of the Chapel.

Lines drawn through the points of an octagon also define the outer dimensions of the Chapel. They create a length that is a foot shorter than the hexagon. This is in fact the actual length of the Chapel measured from surface wall to wall, 67 feet. The width of the octagon is 95.04 feet, and, as with the hexagon, a circle whose diameter is half that and another half that again are drawn. It can be seen that the inner circle of the octagon defines the internal width between the wall columns of the ground level and the width between the walls of the upper level, 23.76 feet.

One sixtieth the diameter of the hexagon is 1.32 feet. Thirty of this measure make the ideal width of the chapel. Six of them make the total thickness of each wall, 7.92 feet. There are seventy-two of the measure in the width of the octagon, 72 x 1.32 = 95.04. The hexagon and octagon are thus in a five to six relationship and 1.32 feet is the measure used throughout. 1.32 x 40 is equal to the internal length of the chapel, 52.8 feet. This length is divided into four bays of 13.2 feet each. The central bay defines the centre of the hexagon and another the centre of the octagon. The middle of the third bay is bisected by an internal line of the octagon and marks the doorways. Each bay is one third the outer width of the chapel if the ideal measures of the hexagon are employed, 3 x 13.2 = 39.6. Thus the inner length is in a four to three relation to the outer width, or in a two to three relation to the hexagon.

Black dots show two points of the octagon that lie on sites of great archaeological interest. The upper right point is the "St. David" pillar placed to mark the line where the Old Church ended and additions began. The lower left point is the site of a mausolea or "pyramid" below which King Arthur was said to be buried.

The measures of the hexagon and octagon combine to create many numerological and geometrical ratios. The pattern of interlocking circles is the dominant theme in the decoration of the walls of the chapel. The figure shows that the intersection of the two sets of circles, created by the hexagon and octagon, coincide with measures in the chapel's design. Could they have also played a role in the design of the pattern on the floor? Is it possible to find in the proportions of the chapel the, so far, missing five to four ratio that is found in the geomantic diamond?

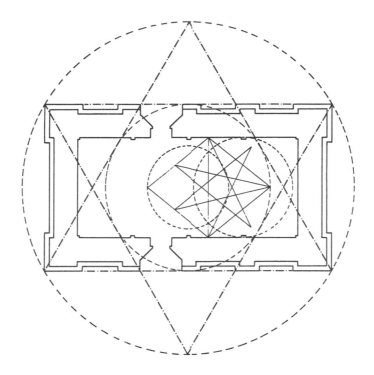

▲ *The heptagram created by the geometry of the St. Mary Chapel.*

The two inner circles of the hexagon and the octagon, each being one quarter of their diameters, intersect to create a vesica of unequal proportion. A vertical line is drawn through the points of intersection of the vesica to the walls of the chapel. A diamond is created by lines drawn from these points to points on the central axis of the chapel defined by the internal ratios of the hexagon. This diamond has a four to five relationship between its axes. As can be seen, the vertical axis is one quarter the width of the octagon, 95.04 x 1/4 = 23.76 feet. The horizontal axis is three eighths the width of the hexagon, 79.2 x 3/8 = 29.7 feet.

Their common factor is 5.94 (which is 4.5 x 1.32).

4 x 5.94 = 23.76 and 5 x 5.94 = 29.7

From this diamond, which is present in the geometry of the landscape around Glastonbury, it is possible to draw a heptagram. The four to five ratio produces angles of 102° 40' and 77° 20' as compared to the 102° 51' and 77° 9' angles of a heptagram. This is an insignificant difference. Located between the doorways and the altar, the seven-pointed star lies within the chapel at the point most likely to be the centre of the pattern on the floor. The heptagram is produced through the synthesis of the six-fold and eight-fold geometry which determines the dimensions of the St. Mary Chapel. It represents the number of the "Virgin Goddess," eternity, and the gateway into the dimensions of the unknown—the entry to Annwn.

▲ *A conjectural restoration of the pattern on the floor of the St. Mary Chapel. This restoration includes most of the elements hinted at in the sources: the "triangles and squares" of William of Malmesbury, the Cross, the "Four Ways" and the Zodiac of the monks who communicated with Bligh Bond, the thirteen "spheres of prophecy" of Melkin, and the Glastonbury foundation pattern of the central wattle chapel surrounded by the twelve cells of the monks. It is possible to imagine representations of the signs of the Zodiac in the twelve circles. The man, Matthew—Aquarius; the lion, Mark—Leo; the bull, Luke—Taurus; and the eagle, John—Scorpio, of the Evangelists lying in the arms of the cross. The unusual lines of the diamond and the "virgin" heptagram may even provide clues to the mysterious "bifurcated line" and the "venerable Maiden" of Melkin. The pattern is arrived at by reducing the size of the heptagram in the previous illustration by a factor of five to four. The length of the Landscape Diamond is now equal to the width of the chapel. To the geometer it is possible to recreate from this pattern the hexagon and the octagon in the relationship to each other as described in the previous illustrations. Thus all the ratios of the St. Mary Chapel may be obtained from this floor pattern, which gains its proportions from the Landscape Diamond. Each large tile of the chequered floor is about a foot across and was probably decorated. An altar would have stood at the eastern end of the Chapel. The sources mention tombs elsewhere. The arrangement of the twelve circles is determined by the heptagram and may be studied in greater detail in the work of John Michell.*

ENDNOTES

1. John Michell, *The View Over Atlantis*, Sago Press, 1969. Fully revised edition: *The New View Over Atlantis*, Thames and Hudson, 1983.

2. For a reasonable assessment of ley lines, it is worth reading the work of Ronald Hutton, *The Pagan Religions of the Ancient British Isles*, 1991, pp. 121-130. For the diametrically opposite mystical perspective, try Grace Cook, *The Light in Britain.*

3. For an excellent description of Aboriginal culture, see Robert Lawlor, *Voices of the First Day*, Inner Traditions, 1991.

4. E.J. Watson, "The Legend of Crewkerne," in Anthony Roberts, Glastonbury: *Ancient Avalon, New Jerusalem*, Rider, 1978, p. 28.

5. I am grateful to Terry Walsh for the use of his material. Most of what is used here is in *Global Sacred Alignments* by Terry Walsh, University of Avalon Press, Glastonbury, 1993.

6. I would like to thank Sig Lonegren for checking the astronomical calulations on site. His knowledge and instruments allowed a degree of accuracy I could not have obtained. Taking an angle of elevation from the Mary Chapel to the Tower/crest of Chalice Hill to be 6.5° (obtained from trigonometry using a 1:25000 map and confirmed on the ground), the predicted angle of sunrise at this latitude for Michaelmas, September 29 in 1990, is 101°43'. The actual orientation is, in fact, extremely close to 100 degrees. Adjusting for this gives September 27 and March 17 as the optimum days. Given the width of the solar diameter and the unknown factors, such as the original height of Tor, first glimpse of sun, or full diameter, a deviation of up to 2 degrees is fully tolerable. However when the date of observation is altered to AD 35, the predicted angle is 100° 38' for full sunrise. Even allowing for a foundation date of AD 700 this would seem to clinch the matter.

7. Philip Rahtz, *Glastonbury*, London, 1993, pp. 84-87.

8. For more on giants, see Nicholas R. Mann and Marcia Sutton, *The Giants of Gaia*, Brotherhood of Life, Albuquerque, 1994.

9. Mary Williams (ed.), *Glastonbury: A Study in Patterns*, RILKO, 1969.

10. Rahtz, 1968 and 1993. Geoffrey Ashe, *The Glastonbury Tor Maze*, Gothic Image, 1979. *Caerdroia 14*, 1984.

11. White Bear (O. Fredericks), personal communication, Sedona, April 1989.

12. Jeff Saward, "The House of Iitoi," *Caerdroia*, 1989.

13. A. Thom, *Megalithic Sites in Britain*, Oxford, 1967, p. 102.

14. Jeff Saward, *Caerdroia 14*, 1984.

15. Rev. Richard Warner, *An History of the Abbey of Glaston*, Bath, 1826. The Reverend may have been influenced by Thomas Hearne, as much of what he was reporting was copied directly from Hearne, who wrote *The History and Antiquities of Glastonbury* in 1722. It seems that before the age of copyright laws it was common practice to repeat verbatim what had been previously written. While this has the effect of preserving information remarkably well it also has the effect of preserving attitudes, errors, and hampering new research. A cynicism under the guise of healthy "scientific" skepticism toward the Glastonbury legends, for example, is to be found in all accounts, and innaccurate measurements of the Mary Chapel are inherited from author to author rather than the writers actually taking measures on the ground.

16. Albert Pike, *Morals and Dogma (of the Ancient and Accepted Scottish Rite of Freemasonry)*, Southern Jurisdiction of the United States, 1925.

17. *The Dream of Rhonabwy*. In Ireland the game was called brandubh.

18. John Michell, *The Dimensions of Paradise*, Thames and Hudson, 1988, p. 78-9.

19. John Michell, 1990, p. 132-33.

20. Frederick Bligh Bond, (1) *The Architectural Handbook of Glastonbury Abbey*, Glastonbury, 1909. (2) *The Gate of Remembrance*, Oxford, 1918, p. 150-51.

6

MYTH AND LEGEND: CAVE, CAULDRON, MOUNTAIN, AND TREE

The Avalonian legend central to our quest is that the Tor is the abode of Gwynn ap Nudd, King of the Welsh fairy race, the Tylwyth Teg. Gwynn is the leader of the Wild Hunt and Lord of Annwn. Nudd is pronounced "Neeth" and means "night" or "black," Annwn or Annwvyn is pronounced "An-noo-in." It is the name of the Celtic Underworld. "Ap" simply means "son of." Nudd is an ancient British deity of the Underworld. He is also known as Nodens and has an aspect which embodies the serpent spirit of the nearby River Severn. There was a temple of Nodens at Lydney in Gloucestershire. Nudd or Nodens is closely related to Woden of Germany and to Nuada, the great king of the Irish fairy race, the Tuatha de Danaan.

Gwynn ap Nudd, "White Son of Night," appears often in Celtic lore. He is a deity or a semidivine hero. He is associated with the Western Paradise of the Celts, the Avalon of the Britons, and the fairy mounds or hills—the Sidhe—of the Tuatha de Danaan. As a descendant of the Children of Llyr, the "Sea," Gwynn is kin to the giant Bran, keeper of a cauldron of rebirth.

As leader of the Wild Hunt, Gwynn is also related to the British Horned God, Herne the Hunter, rider of a great black horse. In northern parts of Britain, Gwynn rides with King Arthur in the Wild Hunt. In Scotland, Gwynn ap Nudd and King Arthur become the same. They both assume the mantle of the archetypal hero or king asleep in a cave under a mound. In the Welsh legends, Gwynn helps Arthur hunt a great boar, Twrch Trwyth, which ravages the land. In Germany and Scandinavia, the Wild Hunt is known as Odin's or Woden's Hunt or the "Herlethingus" the "troop of Herle." In Somerset, the Wild Hunt on their spectral horses are said to emerge from the Tor at Samhain or at any dark and stormy time. The riders are accompanied by the Cwm Annwn, the white-bodied, red-eyed "hounds of hell." In Devonshire, the hounds of the hunt are called the Wish Hounds and inspired Sir Arthur Conan Doyle's Hound of the Baskervilles. The tradition of all these places say the Hunt seeks the souls of the dying or the deceased to take into Annwn, the Celtic Underworld.

An account of Gwynn ap Nudd and his abode upon the Tor is given in a Life of St Collen—pronounced "cothlen"—a Welsh saint who came to Glastonbury in the seventh century.

One day St Collen, ex-abbot of Glastonbury, having taken up a hermitage beside a spring at the foot of the Tor, overheard two peasants talking about the castle of Gwynn ap Nudd. They said it was concealed within the Tor. The King of Faery held court there, and welcomed folk to its shining towers. But strange things would occur. A person could enter the castle for what they thought was but a night and a day and not return for many years, if he or she returned at all!

The saint dismissed this talk as superstition. In fact, he said it was the work of the Devil. The men were perturbed by this. They warned Collen that Gwynn was upset by lesser things than that and he might well have to answer for it.

Sure enough, that very day a messenger appeared at Collen's door. He was human but not quite human. He carried an invitation from Gwynn for the saint to visit the castle on the Tor that night. The saint refused. The same thing happened the next day. But when the invitation came for the third time Collen, knew he had to go. He filled a phial with holy water and made his way along the paths that led up the Tor.

He passed through strange mists. Somewhere near the summit he was conducted through an entranceway and into the shining castle of Gwynn ap Nudd. It was the fairest castle he had ever seen. It had the best appointed hosts and many musicians with every kind of instrumental and string music. It had horses with boys on their backs, the fairest in the world, and girls of noble aspect, lively activity, light footed, lightly dressed, in the flower of young age. It had every dignity that was known to the court of a powerful king. Collen was taken into a great hall where a feast was in progress, music played and the finely dressed fairy folk enjoyed themselves. All the fairies wore red and white, the livery of Annwn.[1]

At the end of the great hall Gwynn sat on a golden throne. He greeted St Collen cordially enough, asking him if he would eat. But the saint knew full well the danger of eating fairy food and so declined, saying "I do not eat the leaves of a tree!"

Gwynn then grew angry and asked, "What was the matter? Have you not seen such fine food before? Have you not seen folk clad in such finely coloured clothes?"

To this Collen replied, "Although the food and the manner of dressing is very fine, red is the colour of fire and white is the colour of frost and cold." He then took out the phial of holy water and scattered it all around. Slowly, Gwynn, the fairies and the castle vanished into the mists. Finally there was only the Saint, the wind, and tumps of grass on the lonely Tor top.[2]

Gwynn ap Nudd is the guardian of the gates and a Lord of Annwn. He shares the latter role with Bran, Pwyll, Pryderi, and Arawn. The female Underworld rulers tend to appear in the sources as hags, generally in triple or nine-fold form, but the queen Rhiannon has a full character. It is Pwyll, Rhiannon, and their son Pryderi who imprison Gwydion in Annwn. Gwydion is the leader of their opponents, the Children of Don, the "Sky" or the Overworld.

Gwynn is a chthonic deity of ancient origin presiding over the Underworld and the dark half of the year. He is an Earth God, who Robert Graves calls the "Serpent Son." His symbol, despite his name, seems to be the red dragon—emblem of Somerset and of Wales. As a Dark God of the chthonian realms and as a hunter, Gwynn ap Nudd is closely connected to the antlered deity Herne or his European equivalent Cernunnos.

In the following episodes from the Welsh text, *The Mabinogion*, Gwynn has a counterpart, a twin, Gwythyr ap Greidyawl—the spirit of the light half of the year—with whom he is locked in a perpetual cosmic dance.

Creiddylad, daughter of Llud Silver Hand, the most majestic woman ever in Britain or the three islands; for her Gwythyr son of Greidyawl and Gwynn son of Nudd fight every May Day until the Judgement ....

Gwynn son of Nudd, in whom God has set the energy of the demons of Annwn, in order to prevent the destruction of this world, and Gwynn cannot be let loose ....

Creiddylad daughter of Llud Silver Hand had gone to Gwythyr son of Greidyawl, but before he could sleep with her Gwynn came and carried her off by force. Gwythyr collected an army and went to fight Gwynn, but Gwynn conquered ... When Arthur heard of this he went into the north and called on Gwynn ... and peace was made between Gwynn and Gwythyr. Creiddylad was left in the house of her father undisturbed by either side, and every May Day the two men would fight, and the one who conquered on the Day of Doom would keep her.[3]

Gwythyr ap Greidyawl's name can be taken to mean "Victor son of Scorcher." He appears to have a solar or even a stellar origin. He would be of the Children of Don—many of whom name the constellations. Robert Graves calls Gwythyr the "Star Son." Creiddylad emerges as a Persephone figure journeying around the solar cycle of the year. Llud Silver Hand may be the great Irish king Nuada Silver Hand who has solar connections, but the name points toward Llyr, god of the sea.

Gwynn and Gwythyr circle around the female figure. They divide the cycle of the year and the cosmos into two parts, an upper and a lower. They repeat a division or struggle between the deities of the Underworld and the Overworld that can be found throughout the Celtic Tradition. The Children of Don: Gwydion, Govannon, Amaethon, Arianrhod and their allies, struggle against the Children of Llyr: Bran, Manannan and their allies, the Underworld rulers Arawn and Pwyll. A struggle between the sky and sea. Arianrhod herself perpetuates the cosmic division by giving birth to the great hero Lugh or Llew, "light," and the dark sea deity, Dylan. Eventually this theme emerges in the Arthurian material with King Lot (Llud) marrying Arthur's sister to produce the dark brother Medrawt or Mordred and the exemplary good brother, Gawain.

Several islands off the western coasts of France, Britain, and Ireland, such as Mont-Saint-Michel and the Scilly Isles, claim to be the "Isles of the Dead," or the "Land of the Blessed," or "Tir na mBam," the Land of Women. The latter means the place where the regenerative power of the Great Goddess prevails. But if Ynis Witrin, the Isle of Avalon, was also held as being where the souls of the deceased went for rest and reincarnation, then there is an extremely strong case for understanding how the place was perceived by the ancient peoples of Britain. With the entranceway to the Underworld localised on the Tor and with the two springs, one red and one white—the colours of the Underworld—flowing out from under it, ample reasons are provided for the Celtic peoples of Britain to revere the island.

Such a view may at least help us understand the purpose of Ponter's Ball. The builders did not create the massive earthwork as a defensive structure for a non-existent settlement upon the island. They built it as a ritual boundary marking off the outside world from the sanctuary within. Upon the island rites of initiation were performed, involving the most sacred mysteries of them all, the relation between the living and the ancestral dead.

CARADOC AND KING ARTHUR

Let us now return to Caradoc's story of Melwas, King of the Summer Land and the imprisonment on the Tor of Guinevere and the ensuing struggle there with King Arthur. Similarities appear when this story is compared with the rivalry between Gwynn and Gwythyr for Creiddylad as described in *The Mabinogion*. Gwynn tackles Gwythyr on the Tor for Creiddylad in exactly the same way as Arthur tackles Melwas on the Tor for Guinevere. Mediation is effected by King Arthur in the first case and by the monk Gildas and the Abbot in the second. Structurally the two stories are the same, only the names change.

The synchronistic quality of the whole increases when it emerges that Melwas is the Cornish equivalent of the Welsh Gwynn ap Nudd, that the Summer Land is a name for the Otherworld, and that both Creiddylad and Guinevere are daughters of a solar king. Llud Silver Hand, father of Creiddylad, while closely identified with the sea god Llyr, also has a solar character. As the Irish Lludd or Nuada he has characteristics that embrace both Underworld and Overworld. Shakespeare later made him King Lear and Creiddylad became his daughter Cordelia. In a Welsh tradition, one of the "three fathers" of Guinevere is said to be none other than Gwythyr ap Greidyawl. He appears as a solar king. In the Medieval tradition, King Leodogranz—identified with Leo in the Zodiac—is the father of Guinevere. He gave as her dowry a solar symbol, the Round Table. Scratching the surface even deeper we find that in the Celtic tradition the sun was a goddess. It was only at the hands of later patriarchal transcribers that her powers were given to her "father."[4]

The description of Gwynn and Gwythyr in *The Mabinogion* provides further layers of meaning to the whole story. Gwynn ap Nudd, "in whom God has set the energy of the demons of Annwn," is a chthonic deity ruling over the dark half of the year. He may even be a Horned God of Death. He was a hellish anathema to the incoming Christians, who duly banished him from his home. Melwas receives similar treatment in his story. He is a dark, shadowy villain, servant to his lusts and abductor of the queen. Gwythyr ap Greidyawl, on the other hand, like King Arthur, is a hero. He triumphs over the dark half of the year—presumably at May Day—and ushers in the light. Gwynn and Gwythyr are paralleled in the Egyptian tradition by Set, the Spirit of the Waning Year and Osiris, the Spirit of the Waxing Year.

The version of the story in *The Mabinogion* makes it clear that both characters are necessary to the whole conception of male deity. It is implied that if one finally triumphed over the other in this cosmic scheme of things, the "Day of Doom" would follow. The twin light and dark gods complement each other to constellate the full aspect of the God. The God, by virtue of his transformations, is then able to make the round of the year in companionship with the omnipresent Goddess. The exquisite art on the first-century Gundestrup Cauldron suggests such a dual division of the masculine deity. The Horned Earth God Cernunnos is matched by the Sky God Taranis. The emblem of Taranis, the "Thunderer," is the wheel, and elsewhere, a hammer. The different scenes on the cauldron tell the story of the two deities replacing each other in turn as lover of the Goddess.[5]

The Christians had no such cosmological concern. They were ushering in a new, transcendent and monotheistic era. Gwythyr was a "serpent" killer and a heavenly deity of light. He eventually became identified with St. Michael and was made the patron of the Tor and other high places. As an intermediary step, King Arthur, who mediated in the original story, becomes Gwynn's twin, his polar opposite. It is Arthur as the "good" British king who defeats the wicked abductor Melwas in the second story. Instead of mediating the two forces within his sovereign being, Arthur has become the classic Apollonian sky deity taking on, like Gwydion, the powers of the Underworld.

The Solar Goddess has almost sunk out of the picture as Queen Guinevere, but we need only a glimpse of her shining golden hair in the mythology to restore her previous glory. This is provided in the Avalonian tradition by the golden hair that greeted the monks who excavated her grave. As mentioned above, we also find in a Welsh Triad that Gwenhwy-far—"white phantom"—is considered to be a daughter of Gwythyr ap

Greidyawl, a solar god. Finally, in another Arthurian episode the queen marries her abductor Yder or Edern, the son of Gwynn ap Nudd, god of the Underworld! Although Guinevere—Persephone-like—only enters the Underworld through her "abductions," she is able to fulfill the role of the Solar Goddess. The ancient cosmic dance of the deities around the cycle of the year cannot be concealed.[6]

▲ *The Glastonbury Cauldron. A bronzed bowl from the Lake Village, circa 200 BC. The bowl incorporates unusual three-fold patterns in its design.*

Either Caradoc is modernizing or rather Christianizing an earlier pagan legend of two rivals or twin gods turning around the yearly cycle in partnership with the solar goddess—a mythical form found all over the world and deeply embedded in the Celtic tradition—or there is a remarkable coincidence at work.[7] We are either looking at Christian history based upon a myth from the ancient past, or we are looking at the ancient past through the myth of Christian history. Where one becomes the other it is hard to tell. If the Arthurian story is an update of the Celtic legend of Gwynn, Gwythyr, and Creiddylad, then we have a glimpse from an early literary source into ancient beliefs about the sacred nature of the Tor. Caradoc clearly had good reasons for locating the struggle on the Tor and the legend of St. Collen reveals that at least Gwynn was to be found there.

We may speculate that the Tor was the scene of some great fertility ritual at the beginning of May, when the powers of the Overworld and the Underworld struck a balance to ensure the blessings of the Solar Goddess and the continuation of the cycle of the year. Conversely, at Samhain, the beginning of the dark half of the year, the Underworld deity Gwynn prevailed. The gates of Annwn stood open, the Wild Hunt rode forth, and the dead were gathered in. The cosmic drama of light and dark, the living and the dead, day and night, summer and winter, continued on its cycle.

Whatever the Christian traditions conceal they also reveal why a youthful transcendental religion with no place for a dark side, which saw death as the antithesis and not as a part of life and whose doctrine could not allow reincarnation, needed to rid the Tor of a ancient deity of the Underworld and rebirth by means of an exorcism. In this religion's worldview it was necessary to permanently establish a church of St. Michael, the dragon killer, upon the heights of the Tor. As for the Solar Goddess, she maintained herself on Avalon as Mary and her Son.

MORGAN LE FAY

In early Welsh literature a "Ynis Avallach," the Isle of Apples, appears. It is the home of the mythical ancestor Afallach or Avallach. He is the father of Modron, who is the mother of the great hero Owein. The Isle is described as the seat of one of the "Three Perpetual Harmonies of the Island of Britain."[8] It is an earthly paradise also known as the "Fortunate Isle" whose inhabitants live for hundreds of years on the fruits of the trees that grow there. They neither know old age or disease. The Isle remains in the era, common in world mythology, known as the Golden Age. It seems reasonable to connect Avallach to the origin of the name Avalon, especially as in old Welsh "aballon" means apple.

In Geoffrey of Monmouth's *Life of Merlin,* the bard Taliesin is made to say that the island is ruled by nine sisters or seers, whose chief was the enchantress Morgan. Her epithet le Fay either means "of the Fairies" or le Faye, "the fate." In 1193, Giraldus Cambrensis wrote "the place which is now Glaston was in ancient times called the Isle of Avalon . . . and Morgan, a noble matron and the ruler and lady of those parts, and kin by blood to King Arthur, carried him away to the island . . . that she might heal his wounds." In later Grail literature, a king called Avallach or Evalake is given as the father of Morgan le Fay, whose home is the Isle of Avalon. Geoffrey of Monmouth describes Arthur's sword Excalibur as being forged there.

Excalibur, a symbol of Celtic sovereignty, was given to Arthur through the hands of a woman identified only as the "Lady of the Lake." Could this be Morgan? As dweller upon the Isle of Avalon and kin to King Arthur, she represents the rightful sovereignty of Britain after the Roman withdrawal. The emphasis upon descent through women in the British sources indicates such things were reckoned matrilineally. Through these connections we are led to assume that the sovereign spirit of the land of

Britain was envisaged as having lain dormant for three and a half centuries in the hands of the goddess who dwelt in the landscape, wells, and sacred groves of the Isle of Avalon. All the legends turn on the sword of sovereignty being given to the rightful monarch after the Roman withdrawal from either a stone or from the "lake." Both are symbols of the feminine and sovereign spirit of the land. In the Celtic tradition, this aspect of the Goddess was preeminent. In the Grail tradition, not only was the dying Arthur brought to Morgan's home at Avalon—and where else would it be more appropriate for a monarch to pass over than at the gates of Annwn?—but Excalibur was returned to the Lady of the Lake by Sir Bedivere at Pomparles Bridge ("Pont Perilous") at the foot of Wearyall Hill.

The name Morgan can be traced through Irish mythology to Morrighu, "Great Queen," a dark and sovereign goddess associated with water and often represented, like King Arthur, as a raven. She may be an aspect of a primeval chthonic deity and triple war goddess, the Badhbh. Eventually she and her ilk were identified with the fairy folk of Ireland, the Tuatha de Danaan and went to inhabit the Sidhe, the fairy mounds or hills. In other words, the magical and sovereign ancestors of the land went to live within the earth. In Welsh, Modron or Morgan simply means "mother." In the Breton tradition, Morgan is Queen of the Otherworld. She is a great healer and keeper of the holy springs, who lives on an enchanted island.

If via Morgan le Fay an ancient Great Mother cult can be conclusively associated with Avalon, then the long and persistent dedication of the "Mother Church" at Glastonbury to St. Mary makes perfect sense. The isle was a focus for the energies of the Universal Feminine, or the Great Goddess, who embodied the spirit of the land. She is represented in the archetypal realm by such symbols as the stone, the throne, the spiral, the cup or the cauldron, blood, and water. Closely associated with these symbols in the Celtic tradition is the achieving of rebirth through the cauldron—that is, the womb of the Earth Goddess—and of the renewal of sovereignty through the giving of its talismans, especially the sword. The means of access to these mysteries indisputably lies upon the Isle of Avalon. For rebirth, one entered the Underworld. Its entrance lay upon the Tor, guarded by the Horned God and the Wild Hunt. For sovereignty, one sought the sword of Avalon, Excalibur. The cauldron could be found in the Castle of Bron or Bran, the Fisher King on Wearyall Hill, or in the spiral castle of the Tor or the swollen belly of Chalice Hill. Everything indicates that the ancient tradition surrounding the cauldron of plenty, of nourishment, of rebirth, of inspiration and poetry is the precedent for those of the

Holy Grail. Everything indicates that within the later Grail legends there is concealed an allegory of the ancient worship of the Goddess of the Land and Sovereignty and of her companions, the Twin Gods.[9]

THE GODDESS AT BECKERY

There are two stories, one ancient and one modern, about Avalon being sacred to the Goddess which concern the Isle of Beckery. This is, or it was before engineers drained the Somerset Levels, a tiny island off the tip of Wearyall Hill. Beckery has long been sacred to Mary Magdalene. The Glastonbury monks said St. Brigit built the chapel at Beckery in the late fifth century. The chapel contained Brigit's relics and her bell. It was subsequently visited by so many Irish it became known as "Little Ireland"—beck Eire.[10] Excavations in 1887 and 1967 could not rule out an early foundation date for an eremetic site there, possibly even a Celtic one, but the most likely date of foundation was after AD 700.

The first story is about King Arthur. According to the fourteenth century monk John of Glastonbury, the King was resting on Wearyall Hill. He was directed in a dream to visit the chapel of the Magdalene at Beckery at dawn. As is often typical of Arthur, he would not go and sent a servant. When the servant was slain for violating the site, Arthur was persuaded to go. He made his way to the chapel but could not enter as two flashing swords barred his way. He fell to his knees and the swords parted. Upon entering the chapel, he witnessed a priest conducting Mass at the altar. The priest was assisted by the "Blessed and Glorious Mother of God, carrying her Son in her arms." When the priest asked for the host—the body and blood of Christ—she presented the child as a sacrifice. As the body and blood were consumed the child miraculously remained unharmed. When the Mass was over, Mary picked up the crystal cross from the altar, came down the aisle, and gave it to King Arthur. In turn he presented the cross to the Abbot of Glastonbury, who placed it above the high altar of the Abbey Church. As a result of this vision Arthur dropped the old coat of arms that showed three red lions on a background of silver (or according to another account, a red and a white dragon), in favour of one that showed the Virgin and Child over the right arm of a cross. [11]

This legend is found in a slightly different—and earlier—form in the anonymous French romance *Perlesvaus.* Here Arthur's kingdom is in chaos. Arthur wanders through the wasteland created by his own failures. The Grail keeper, the Fisher King, lies grievously wounded in his castle. He has received a wound in the "thigh" by a spear. King Arthur finally comes to a small chapel on the "Isle of Avalon" by the "Moors Adventurous" and has a vision of the Lady offering her Son as the host in the Mass. The episode is accompanied by a mysterious flame. He sees the Grail pass through various transformations until finally it becomes a chalice. Thereafter, the Fisher King is healed, Arthur's fortunes are restored, and joy returns to the court.[12] It is said that because of this episode and under the new coat of arms he was able to win the strategic battle against the Saxons at Mount Badon.

As many commentators on the Arthurian Legends have pointed out, the reason for the collapse of the Round Table and the creation of the blighted land appears to lie in Arthur's inability to unite with his queen Guinevere.[13] Not only does she elope with Lancelot, but she is constantly being abducted. In the Glastonbury legends her abductor is Melwas, who, like Gwynn ap Nudd and his son Yder, takes the radiant lady into the Tor, that is, the Underworld. Guinevere and Melwas represent something which is always slipping away from Arthur. The quest of the Knights of the Round Table is as much a search for a solution to this mystery as it is for the Grail.

The Fisher King represents Arthur's condition. He has the Grail, but carries a wound in the genitals inflicted by a spear. He spends his time futilely fishing on the waters of the lake. The Fisher King is unable to enter the domain of the feminine. He is unable to consummate union with his whole self. In Arthur's case, this means the inability to carry out the sacred marriage of the king with the queen, the champion of the land with sovereignty. Arthur is separated from his chthonian nature. As a result of the introduction of a transcendental cosmology, King Arthur no longer knows his elemental, physical, deeply sexual, otherworldly, or subconscious side. He is magically and symbolically impotent. In these circumstances, the abductor, King Melwas, represents Arthur's sexual "other" self. [14]

Arthur and Guinevere are unable to have children. Guinevere, a solar goddess, is asexual. She is an ideal of loveliness, a spiritual being, not a fertile one. To enter the Underworld she has to be abducted. The one child Arthur does have, Mordred, results from union either with his half-sister Morgan le Fay, Queen of Avalon, or, more likely, with his other half-sister, Morgause. Queen Morgause is wife of Loth or Lot, a king both of the North and the Underworld. As "sisters" of Arthur, Morgan and Morgause fulfill the traditional requirements of magical sovereignty, but at the cost of being labelled "evil" by the new dualistic cosmology. They are both Queens of the Underworld, dark, seductive, and highly sexual women.

Mordred may in fact be King Arthur's whole self, born of the magical union of a king and queen of the land. Mordred is the true heir to sovereignty. He is traditionally born at Beltane, May 1, the day the Lord of the Waxing Year, conceived at the Winter Solstice, comes into his own. Mordred is finally the destroyer of the Arthur. He mortally wounds the king at the battle of Camlamn, at the same time meeting his death. Mordred, his mother, the Goddess of the Land, and King Arthur represent a sacred world and a mystery tradition that cannot, yet, come to be.

In the legends of the chapel it is significant that Arthur has again returned to Avalon and tries to reconnect with the forces to be found there. This is an attempt to restore the order of the kingdom. In the earlier episode of the Lady of the Lake, Arthur had to recover the sword of sovereignty, Excalibur, which he had broken. It was through the drawing of Excalibur from a stone that Arthur's right to the sovereign power was originally recognized. In Eschenbach's version of the Grail legends, *Parzifal,* the mysterious token of divine presence on earth is represented as a stone. The Grail as stone expresses the realization that spirit is not separate from the creation, the creation being the domain of the chthonian, sexual, and watery Great Mother.

All the sources agree that the sword Excalibur was forged on the Isle of Avalon. It was in the keeping of the Lady of the Lake, otherwise known as the Goddess of the Wells or Springs. It had extraordinary powers. *The Mabinogion* gives Arthur's sword this description:

> With a design of two serpents on the golden hilt; when the sword was unsheathed what was seen from the mouths of the serpents was like two flames of fire, so dreadful that it was not easy for anyone to look.[15]

The sword had much more than a simple practical function in Celtic society. As well as being an object of prestige, conferring power and status on its owner, it was vested with symbolic significance. Swords were exchanged as gifts of allegiance or when treaties were made. No doubt swords were inherited and used in rites of initiation. They became charged with meaning. Many swords are found in lakes and rivers. They were deposited as votive offerings to the deities and spirits of place. Extensive rites, prayers, and other ceremonial acts accompanied the deposition. There is evidence of swords being used to decapitate bodies. The head—the source of wisdom and the seat of the spirit—was then placed beside or in a well or shaft. It is possible that with the Roman conquest, a sword or swords that had come to represent lineage and over which treaties and other oaths were made, was cast into the waters of the land. The thought being that the Goddess of the Waters, of the sovereign spirit of the land, would ensure its safety and eventual renewal.

The Arthurian legends say that Excalibur was eventually returned to the waters of Avalon at Pomparles Bridge, the "Perilous Bridge." This is barely half a mile from the chapel at Beckery. The Perilous Bridge is the narrow way the knights had to cross to enter the Grail Castle. It is highly synchronous that from ancient times a narrow trackway between the tip of Wearyall Hill and the mainland, where Street is today, lay at this location, the entrance to the Castle of the Fisher King. It was elevated above the tides and floods that periodically rushed through the narrow strait. If the floods were high then this trackway was immersed, making passage across it truly perilous.[16]

As the goddess Brigit was the keeper of the wells, it seems straightforward to suggest she is a candidate for the "Lady of the Lake." As the goddess Brigantia or Britannia of the northern Celtic tribes, she embodies the sovereign spirit of the land. The sword, the grail, the stone, the cross, the well-springs of the land are all her symbols. All these things are in some way or at some time buried below the surface of the land and of consciousness. She is also the Goddess of Fire. This may have a connection with the flame and flashing swords of Arthur's vision at her chapel on Beckery.

The Irish identify Brigit with Mary. As the Christian Mary could hardly contain the powers of the original Brigit, it is significant that the island of Beckery was always dedicated to Mary Magdalene. Between the two Marys, the asexual Virgin (Guinevere?) and the transparently sexual Magdalene (Morgan?), it was possible for the Goddess at Beckery to constellate the powers which moved through the waters as the primal and sovereign spirit of the land. We may imagine the ancient Britons visiting the low-lying isle, completely surrounded by the glassy waters, and invoking her spirit at auspicious times. In Medieval Glastonbury, some kind of balance was always remembered through the strong tradition of the Magdalene. A lovely chapel dedicated to her can still be found on Magdalene Street.

The associations are tenuous but it seems likely that another sanctuary of the ancient British goddess of fire, water, sexuality, and sovereignty was at the hot spring to the north of Glastonbury at Bath. The Romans dedicated the spring to the goddess Sulis Minerva. Her name means the "Solar Goddess of Wisdom," or more broadly, "the fire goddess in the waters of the earth." The hot springs gush from out of a steaming, red-stained, vaginal cleft. Sulis Minerva was probably the name given to the older, resident British deity.

After and because of his vision into the power of the sources welling up from the earth in Avalon, Arthur has the symbols of sovereignty restored to him by the "Lady of the Lake." He receives a crystal cross and a sword from the hands of the Great Goddess herself. These talismans allow him to revive his kingdom. The stone or crystal represent the deepest powers of the Universal Feminine, deeper even than the cross or sword. When Arthur returns to Avalon for the third and final time, he seeks healing for his wounds from the hands of Morgan le Fay. He passes on, but the mystery of the Sovereignty-granting Goddess and the balance of the Twin Gods remains.[17]

BRIDE'S WELL

Throughout all the episodes described above, the symbols involved—the cup or cauldron, the cross, the sword, the spear, the stone or crystal, the blood or fire, the waters—go straight to the heart of an ancient magical mystery. The goal of this mystery is the union of the masculine spirit of the king with the female spirit of the sovereignty of the land. This goal is still mythically potent, and remains in the dreams of the British today as the second story of Beckery will illustrate. This is not the official version of the story, but is how the story is told around town. The two versions are not so very different.

Shortly after the turn of the century, Wellesley Tudor Pole—founder of Chalice Well Gardens and instigator of the nationwide daily "Silent Minute" of meditation and prayer during the Second World War—dreamt that a precious relic was hidden in Brigit's or Bride's Well at Beckery. This could only be recovered if a young maiden "pure in heart" went to the well at dawn. It just so happened—as it always does in a good story—that Tudor Pole had two young friends who qualified. They went to Glastonbury and searched the waters of Bride's Well. The well, which supplied the water for the monks of the monastery at Beckery, was still there at that time. About to give up the search, they at last summoned up the courage to get in the shallow water. A foot struck against a hard object. They cleaned off the mud and found they held an ornately decorated blue glass bowl.

Tudor Pole was naturally delighted. This was a fulfillment of his mystical inclinations. But this was not all. A certain doctor, John Goodchild, came forward and said he was guided to place the bowl in the well a few years before. He had found the bowl in Italy in the 1880s and believed it to be, if not the cup of the Master, Jesus, then an important component of the second coming of the Christ. Goodchild was a friend of Fiona Macleod whose literary work made much of the Celtic queens and of the Celtic goddess Bride. They saw Bride or Brigit as the returning deity who would usher in a new era of feminine-inspired spirituality.[18]

A gathering of experts were invited to inspect the little bowl and the result was surprising. It was either a bowl of a sort popular among aristocratic Romans in the Near East around the middle of the first century, or it was a nineteenth-century Venetian copy of that period and style. As a result of the controversy, a second symposium was convened, which, regrettably, could be no more conclusive than the first. By now, of course, the press was on the case and references to the Holy Grail were flying around. Everyone started backing away from the furore amid accusations of occultism. Finally, and we are now in the 1990s, the conclusion came through: it was a mid-nineteenth century, Italian glass bowl. There was a sigh of relief. The bowl, however, whatever its origin, is now charged with psychic significance. Although once regularly used by those inspired by the work of Tudor Pole, Fiona Macleod, and Goodchild—who, incidentally, insisted it remain only in the care of women—the blue glass bowl is now securely locked away.

Nothing but a slight rise where the monastery and chapel of rest stood can be seen today at Beckery. The worst kind of industrial development threatens the site. It is worth hunting for the stone that marked the site of Bride's Well. It has been moved from its original location to the side of the River Brue. Divining for the site of the well has proved inconclusive. Any hole three feet deep would fill with water. As for the glass bowl, it did inspire a renaissance of feminine spirituality, but perhaps not in the way the original participants in the drama perceived it or would have wanted it to be. They saw it in the terms of Christian mysticism; while today in Avalon, and indeed around the world, goddess and women-centered spirituality is largely finding itself in far older and earth-oriented symbolic themes.

THE LANDSCAPE GODDESS

When viewed from the south, the Isle of Avalon resembles a reclining figure of a pregnant woman. The Tor is a breast, Chalice Hill the pregnant belly, Wearyall Hill a slightly raised knee, and Stonedown a head falling down abruptly into the Levels. This idea is explored and developed by Geoffrey Ashe and Kathy Jones.[19] It was, however, the parapsychologist Serena Roney-Dougal who first pointed out to me that the two springs gushing out from under the breast of this landscape giantess are in the same place as the wounds in the side of Christ.

If Avalon was ever conceived as being in the image of a huge goddess with the Red and White Springs in her side representing—cornucopia like—the waters of an Earth Mother perpetually giving birth, then a newly arrived and a radically different conception of the nature of spiritual power would, by necessity, be compelled to walk the path taken by the Church at Glastonbury. There would have to have been a transition from chthonic deity to transcendent deity. A transition from a world where power came from below to one in which power came from above. This transition can be read from the change in motifs of a symbolic or mythological nature in the Glastonbury legends. Although the discovery that a pagan stone of sovereignty on the summit of the Tor—where it formed the nipple of the breast of the landscape giantess—was replaced by a cross and then by a church, would move the evidence into the realm of fact.

The first motif of transition is the Divine Mother with a child in her arms. She replaces the Goddess and the Twin Gods. The mother and son symbol speaks for itself. The all-pervading, sexual, omnipotent, and often ominous Goddess births a new age identified with the Divine Child. She in turn becomes a Lady, a virgin no less, "redeemed" by the child she carries. Her ominous, dark, and sexual character disappears. Whatever one may think of this, the motif is present throughout the later Avalonian traditions. Arthur saw the Lady and Child in his vision at Beckery. The Old Church was dedicated to St. Mary from time immemorial. Even the screen behind the high altar of the great Abbey Church of St. Peter and St. Paul featured Mary and Child in the central position in all their glory. The Benedictines were famous for their Mariolatry, and Glastonbury was always being promoted as the "Motherchurch" of Britain. As for the other god, the Dark God of the waning year, he went the way of the Dark Goddess. There is little evidence of either appearing in the later Glastonbury traditions.

The second motif would be concerned with the transition from the "wounds" of the figure in the Avalonian landscape to the wounds of Christ. This is not to say that dealing with the figure of the landscape giantess was ever consciously on anyone's mind—although it may have been, she is too obvious to miss—but there is a natural sympathy between the red and white waters gushing from the body of the isle and the fluids issuing from the body of Christ. The story of Joseph of Arimathea provided exactly the kind of symbols the monks of Glastonbury needed to comprehend this mystery in terms of their own cosmology. Joseph, according to Biblical tradition, provided the tomb for Christ. He was around for the deposition from the cross and was the most likely candidate for the collection of the blood and lymphatic fluid from Christ's wounds. Joseph may have provided the upper room for the Last Supper, or was at least wealthy enough to provide the utensils. When the authors of the tradition made the Holy Grail into the cup used by Christ at the Last Supper—a connection the romancers probably made in the thirteenth century—Joseph was the obvious candidate for being the recipient of the cup. One tradition has Joseph cast into prison without food or water, and sustained for forty years by the miraculous appearance of the Grail. The Glastonbury tradition however starts off with the two cruets and for a very long time, perhaps centuries, there is no mention of the Grail. The myth was in the making.

The third and final motif is, then, the Grail. The creative, nourishing, and rejuvenating cauldrons of the Celtic Otherworld, exemplified on the Isle of Avalon by the land formations and by the birth waters of the womb of the Earth Mother—Cerridwen, Arianrhod, Brigit, Morgan, whoever she may have been—made the transition to an equivalent creative source in the Christian cosmos. The cup used by Christ at the Last Supper could accomplish this transition, as the Gospels describe the cup as the source of "everlasting life." Although the source of divine outpouring is, strictly speaking, the wine transformed into the blood of Christ, the words in the Bible make it sound as though the source is, in fact, the vessel in which the miracle of transformation takes place. This was convenient as the cup was an actual, tangible thing—which it was possible to quest for—remaining in the world as a token from God of proof of a divine presence on earth. The cup of transformation became the Holy Grail, replacing the cauldron or womb of the Earth Mother. From here it is easy to see why many of the Grail romancers when asked the question "What is the Grail?" replied "Mary."[20] The springs gushing from the womb of the Avalon Earth Mother actually come closer to the mystery of the redeeming blood of Christ than the Grail, by virtue of their being the contents of the cup. On the one hand there is the clear water of the White Spring, bubbling from its pagan sanctuary. On the other hand there is the water of the Red Spring, transformed into the blood of Christ by the blessing of St. Joseph, emerging from Chalice Hill.

The Celtic tradition surrounding the Cauldron of Plenty overlaps frequently with Christian tradition. Many more motifs of transition appear. The spear, for example, another of the four talismans of the Tuatha de Danaan, appears as an instrument in the passion of Christ. The spear was responsible for the wound of the Fisher King. In the older European Mystery Tradition, the spear, with its derivation in the dawn of human origins, was the symbol for the integrated and directed masculine power and sexual energy.[21] The spear eventually became the wand in the Tarot, the crozier of the Bishops, clubs in the suits of cards, and a vital emblem of the monks of Glastonbury. Many bodies in the graves of the cemetery of the Old Church had staffs accompanying them. It was Joseph's staff on Wearyall Hill which planted the seeds of the Glastonbury foundation. The two other talismans, the sword and the stone, find their way into the Arthurian traditions of Avalon and even into the esoteric Christian traditions. We should expect a recrudescence of all these earlier motifs in the Christian traditions of Avalon, and it is in this context that the above stories of Beckery make perfect sense.

THE HOLLOW HILL

A set of cohesive legends, though of uncertain origin, take the form of passages into the earth of Avalon. There is either a tunnel running from the Abbey to the Tor, a hollow space within the Tor, a crystal cave, or an underground Druidic temple and other strange and mysterious subterranean spaces.

In a text by the fourteenth-century John of Glastonbury, supposedly recording the fifth- or sixth-century Glastonbury prophet called Melkin, "The Isle of Avalon," meaning Glastonbury, is described as being "greedy for the death of pagans, above others in the world." This no doubt refers to the tradition that Avalon, the Isle of Glass, was the "Blessed Isle in the West" containing the entranceway to Annwn. Here the soul of the Celt went to await reincarnation. Melkin may be the highly respected Welsh bard, Maelgwn of Gwynedd, who died about AD 547. Melkin via John goes on to say that Avalon was "decorated at the burial place of all of them with vatincinatory (chanting?) little spheres of prophecy." Among the "pagans" buried there was Joseph of Arimathea:

He lies on a forked line (linea bifurcata) close to the southern corner of the chapel with prepared wattle above the powerful venerable Maiden, the thirteen aforesaid sphered things occupying the place. For Joseph has with him in the tomb two white and silver vessels filled with blood and sweat of the prophet Jesus. When his tomb is found . . . neither water nor heavenly dew will be able to be lacking for those who inhabit the most holy island.[22]

Understood literally, along with all the other legends of things contained within or buried under the floor of the Mary Chapel, the implication is that powerful forces can be unleashed from within the earth of Avalon. It is also easy to see how the tradition of Gwynn ap Nudd localized on the Tor and guarding the entrance to Annwn could lead to the idea of the Tor being hollow. It comes as no surprise to find many tales of disappearances into the Tor, usually in the form of people entering through some secret passageway and, if returning at all, then returning mad.

In one of these stories, thirty monks engaged in chanting in the Abbey grounds find a tunnel opening before them. They bravely go inside and advance toward the Tor. However, some disaster befalls them and the full story could never be obtained from the three—two insane and one struck dumb—who return. There is a similar story from about forty years ago when two local lads entered the cave and returned stricken with fear. They were quite incapable of describing what they had encountered.

As for the Druidic temple, the closest we can get is the Welsh Triad that describes the Isle of Afallach (Glastonbury), Caer Garadawg (Stonehenge?), and Bangor (Bangor Is-coed in South Wales) as places which kept a "perpetual choir." One hundred choristers chanted in turn each hour around the clock. The poem seems to imply that this was a continuation of a Druidic tradition. If so, then Glastonbury has a claim to being one of the twelve legendary Druidic colleges in Britain. Although little archaeological evidence of the other nine colleges has ever been found, all three mentioned sites possess a major ecclesiastical foundation, bear indications of earlier use, and furthermore, fall on the arc of a circle at intervals which divide it into twelve equal parts. This has led to speculation on the existence of a huge geomantic figure crossing the face of Britain known as the "Circle of the Perpetual Choirs."[23]

There was certainly much upon the island favoured by the Druids. An oak avenue from Gog and Magog, a grove of sacred yew trees in the valley between Chalice Hill and the Tor, and a Druidic initiation by water ritual at the two springs are suggested by various authors. The initiation either takes the form of entry into stalactite caves via the White Spring under the Tor, or a death and resuscitation in the unusual five-sided underground chamber of Chalice Well.

One version of the Tor labyrinth has it completing its final revolution inside the Tor. That is, the labyrinth formed a processional way to the summit and disappeared into a tunnel on the southeast flank before winding its way into the Tor's depths. There is a story that in the nineteenth century a hole appeared on the summit of the Tor down which things were dropped and heard to fall for a long way. Then there was a set of steps, which were only uncovered for a short way before being filled up again. The excavators of the summit of the Tor recorded nothing but deep fissures. The tradition of an entranceway on the Tor persists, and only recently could it be heard around town that the flagstone in the tower concealed a deep well.

All the stories of the hollow hill are strongly figurative and symbolic images that are difficult to substantiate in fact. The spiral castle, the chanting voices, the mysterious tunnel, the crystal cave, the shining castle, the test by drowning, the cauldron of rebirth, are all images of the subconscious mind and find their meaning and reality there. There is, however, the fact that the springs which rise under the Tor have cut tunnels and chambers in the more solid areas of rock. This is something water diviners have confirmed. A spring would be capable of cutting tunnels through the soft limestone and provide the potential for sizeable chambers to form. A natural chamber over two hundred feet back in the hill side is located at the foot of Well House Lane. At the same time the calcium carbonate in the limestone will crystallize in the right conditions and has undoubtedly formed beautiful stalagmite and stalactite formations under the Tor.

A large part of the hollow hill motif may arise from the association of Gwynn ap Nudd with the Tor. Gwynn is closely related to the Irish Tuatha de Danaan, who, when banished by the Celtic Milesians, went to live underground in the fairy mounds. Here they, and the mounds, became known as the Sidhe (shee). Gwynn may be a son of Nuada, the great Irish king of the Tuatha de Danaan. The Welsh tradition makes much of the capture of Gwydion by the Underworld ruler Pwyll and his son Pryderi. Gwydion was imprisoned in the Castle of Arianrhod upon the island known as Caer Sidi. It was here that Gwydion received the gift of poetic inspiration from the Cauldron of Annwn. This must be the same brew that Cerridwen prepared in her cauldron. The name Caer Sidi, "Revolving Castle," is often applied to the mounds of the Sidhe. The Tuatha de Danaan are said in Irish tradition to have built the megalithic chambered mounds.

These Neolithic monuments took the form of huge cairns of stone or earthen mounds with a stone-lined entrance passageway and an inner chamber. The classic example, Newgrange in County Meath, has an entranceway that is astronomically oriented to the Winter Solstice sunrise. The mounds were left alone by the Irish for millennia, as not only did they belong to the fairy folk but were the abode of the dead. Gwynn ap Nudd as the son of Nuada, as the "King of Faery" and possibly as a "Lord of Death" is as much associated with these hollow hills, the "Fairy Hills of the Sidhe," as he is with Glastonbury Tor. They are all sacred mounts, entrances to the Underworld, and it is easy to see how the attributes of one could be carried over to the other.

The identification of Gwynn ap Nudd with King Arthur is also suggestive of the hollow hill motif. King Arthur is the archetypal "sleeping hero" who will awaken to champion his land in time of need. His tradition states that he rests in a high hill—such as Cadbury Castle—which therefore contains a cave. As Gwynn and Arthur are the leading figures in the Wild Hunt—along with Herne the Hunter—then Glastonbury Tor must contain a cave. Before Christian demonization of the Wild Hunt occurred, could it be that the Tor was seen as a place from where a retinue of powerful warriors rode forth as champions of the sovereignty of the land?

Lastly, the coherence of the hollow hill motif may arise from the meanings constellated by the archetype of the Great Mother. There is sufficient evidence to maintain that the Isle of Avalon was her sanctuary long before the Christians came and dedicated the first church to her. The section above points out the island even looks like her and the cup or cauldron is her symbol par excellence.

From the work of C. G. Jung, we know that the mother archetype appears consistently throughout the history of human experience. According to Jung, symbols of the mother include the many forms of the goddess as well as things arousing our devotion or awe, such as the ocean, the earth, the moon, or the heavenly city—for example, the New Jerusalem. She models the form of the perfect city on earth. She is, in the microcosm of the city, the palace or the sacred isle, the mirror of the celestial order. She represents fertility and can be associated with "a rock, a cave, a tree, a spring, a deep well, or various vessels . . . Hollow objects . . . and, of course, the uterus, yoni, and anything of a like shape."[24] These things can have a positive or negative countenance or meaning. The deep well, for example, can be the source of nourishment or an abysmal pit. She can mean death as well as birth—exactly the themes of Avalon.

Finally, Jung states that the "place of magical transformation and rebirth, together with the underworld and its inhabitants, are presided over by the mother."[25] In this psychological context, the Isle of Avalon as entryway to the Underworld and place of rebirth must of necessity present itself to human consciousness as containing a hollow cave, a receptacle, a vessel, a womb—even a woman's form—in which these magical processes of transformation and rebirth can take place.

THE WORLD AXIS

In the following extracts from the extraordinary poem, *Preiddeu Annwn*, "The Spoils of Annwn," attributed to the sixth-century bard Taliesin, there are several interesting references to a place that could be Glastonbury Tor.

> *Complete was the prison of Gwair in Caer Sidi*
> *Through the spite of Pwyll and Pryderi.*
> *No one before him went into it;*
> *A heavy blue chain firmly held the youth,*
> *And for the spoils of Annwn gloomily he sings,*
> *And til doom shall he continue his lay . . .*
> *Thrice the fullness of Prydwen we went into it;*
> *Except seven, none returned from Caer Sidi.*
>
> *In Caer Pedryvan forever revolving,*
> *The first word from the cauldron, when was it spoken?*
> *By the breath of nine damsels gently it is heated.*
> *Is it not the cauldron of the Lord of Annwn, in its fashion*
> *With a ridge around its edge of pearls?*
>
> *It will not boil the food of a coward or one forsworn,*
> *A bright sword flashing was thrust into it,*
> *And left in the hand of Lleminawg,*
> *And before the portals of the cold place the horns of light shall be burning.*
> *And we went with Arthur in his splendid labours,*
> *Except seven, none returned from Caer Vediwed.*
>
> *Three times twenty hundred men stood on the wall of Caer Wydr.*
> *It was difficult to converse with their sentinel.*
> *Three times the fullness of Prydwen, we went with Arthur,*
> *Except seven, none returned from Caer Colur.*

Caer Sidi is the Castle of Arianrhod, who is the sky aspect of Cerridwen. Robert Graves comments that to be in her castle was "to await reincarnation." Gwynn's task was to conduct souls to her. Gwair is an archetypal youthful prisoner in the Castle—an imprisonment that Gwydion sought to become a poet. The "heavy blue chain" is water. Prydwen was Arthur's ship, and Lleminawg was later to become Sir Bedivere. Caer Wydr, the "Glass Castle," is Ynis Witrin, the Isle of Glass or Avalon. Caer Vediwed, Caer Colur, and Caer Wydr are all synonyms for Caer Sidi, the "revolving castle" of Arianrhod. In Welsh, Arianrhod means "silver wheel." Her name was given to the Corona Borealis, the Northern Crown, while that of her brother Gwydion was given to the Milky Way. The image is of a huge, ethereal, slowly revolving, shining castle of glass or crystal, surrounded by water and reached only by means of a special vehicle.

Arianrhod either mated with her brother Gwydion or with a sky god called Nwyvre, "Space," to produce twin gods of light and darkness, Lleu and Dylan. Here we can recognize the polarity of Gwynn and Gwythyr, Melwas and Arthur.

Graves suggests that Caer Arianrhod should not be so much conceived as revolving but that all—the cycle of the year, the earth and sky, or the Zodiac—revolves around it. In this sense, the castle lies beyond the world. It can only be reached through an Otherworldly or shamanistic journey. Like the Pole Star in the sky, it forms the *axis mundi* or world axis. Can we get from here to the spectral and otherworldly castle of Gwynn, or to the terraces that encircle the Tor? The "spoils" being sought from the siege of Caer Sidi are, of course, the Celtic Cauldron of Plenty, Poetry, and Rebirth, the later Christian Grail.

Every spiritual tradition creates a map of the universe or a cosmography. This invariably divides the universe into three areas: the sky, the earth, and the underworld. In the Christian tradition, these are heaven, earth, and hell. The Nordic tradition calls these regions Asgard, Mitgard, and Utgard. They are respectively the home of the divine, the human, and the elemental beings. In the Native American tradition, the cosmos has two classes of spirit beings, "Those Above" and "Those Below." Among most tribes these are represented by the animal powers, for example, the Thunderbirds and the Underwater Serpents. The ubiquitous Plumed Serpent deity is the classic example of mediation between the Above and the Below and the Middle World, which is where the humans live. In all these traditions; the three levels are connected by an axis. The axis may take the form of a ladder, a tree, a pyramid, or a mountain. This is in the centre. The axis makes movement between the three realms possible. According to

Mircea Eliade, the researcher into comparative religion, this axis is conceived as passing through an "opening." It is through this opening or "hole" that the people can pass on their spiritual migrations. Or it is through this opening that the soul of a human passes, either at birth, death, or during some kind of journey, such as shamanic ecstasy.[26]

The traditions surrounding the Isle of Avalon are directly related to this sacred topography. The Christians saw the island as both the entrance to the underworld and to heaven. Avalon was at once "hungry for the death of pagans" and the "most holiest erthe"—in which burial alone secured salvation. The Christian imagination saw many openings in the earth here, from the reports of "tunnels," to subterranean tombs and castles. Even Arthur's vision at Beckery, when he looked through an opening guarded by flashing swords, can be seen as a glimpse into this otherworldly topography. It is significant that he returned with a crystal cross, the element usually associated with the realms of the underworld.

From what evidence remains of the ideas of the pre-Christian Britons, it is clear that the Avalonian tradition provides ample illustration of the centre, the connecting axis, the three cosmic regions, and the opening between them. Avalon was the entrance to Annwn, the Underworld. It was the place of departure and rebirth of the soul. It featured the opposition of the Sky God with the Earth God. It was—if our reasoning is correct—the dwelling place of the Goddess of the Underworld, of Rebirth, of the Wells, of the Sun, Stars and, ultimately, of the Sovereignty of the Land. If Caer Sidi, "Revolving Castle"—so closely associated with Annwn—and Caer Arianrhod, "Silver Wheel" or Northern Crown, can be shown to be associated with the Tor, then we are extremely close to a widely held conception of the world axis—that of a mound or mountain with the heavens turning around its summit. Sometimes the Pole Star is envisaged as fastened to its summit. In East Indian cosmology, for example, Polaris shines directly above the "Centre of the World," which is Mount Meru.[27]

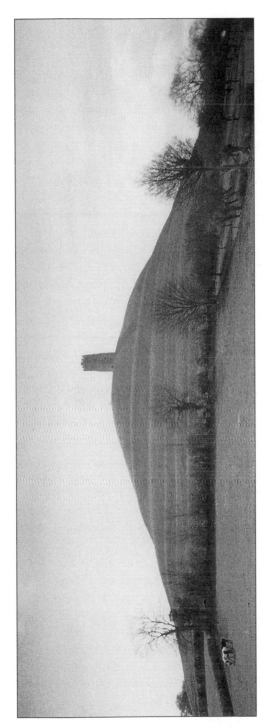

▲ *Glastonbury Tor seen from the north.*

THE WORLD MOUNTAIN
AND TREE

Two symbols consistently associated with the World Axis are the World Mountain and the World Tree. They give form to the abstract principles of centre, movement, and axis. The shamans of the Siberian Tatars and the Yakut climb a mountain with seven levels when they make their otherworldly journeys. The mountain is at the centre of the world and at the top is the Pole Star.[28] If no actual mountain is available to represent the Cosmic Axis, then one is built. Mound or pyramid building was the custom of nearly all the cultures of North and Meso-America. Many ziggurats of ancient Mesopotamia had seven levels. Silbury Hill was built with seven distinct layers. The mountain, mound, or representation of is the "World Navel," or "Omphalos." It is the meeting place of the directions, the centre, the above and the below. On the summit of the World Mountain is the sky opening. Below it is the Underworld opening. From here it is not hard to draw a parallel between the sacred mountains of the world and the seven-tiered slopes of Glastonbury Tor.

Seven is the number characteristic of sacred mountains. The number must be conceived as a descending as well as an ascending sequence. The seven notes of the musical scale ascend and descend until they pass into the next octave. There are seven steps, seven veils, seven seals or portals to the dimension that lies beyond the one in which we live. There are seven circuits to the traditional labyrinth design that the Tohono O'odham see encircling the sacred mountain of Baboquivari. The Nordic tradition conceived the cosmic regions as being connected by a seven-coloured "Rainbow Bridge." Seven is also traditionally associated with space and time by being the number of the planets and the days of the week.

The path up and around the World Axis or Mountain finds definition by passing through gateways and crossing thresholds. These are marked with a path or by wayside features such as columns, statues, or shrines. The movement of the pilgrim along and through these features induces an experience of the dimensions of the sacred. All architectural space employs the themes of entry, path, and shrine. In Medieval Europe, this culminated in the portal, nave, and apse of the cathedrals, such as Glastonbury Abbey. Back on the Tor, the pilgrim wound his or her way ever upward, toward the light-filled sky. Shrines and gates marking the path provided a sense of movement into progressively more sacred realms and exalted states of being. Each step along the spiral path became a metaphor of the steps through life. The plain stretching away on every side provided an overview of the cosmos and of what was being left behind. Eventually, the summit was obtained. As the home of the Sky, Solar, and Stellar Gods and Goddesses, the Elemental Spirits such as the Thunder, Lightning, and Rainbow, the pilgrim was literally transported to the Otherworld. Then came the return journey.

The complement of the World Mountain is the cave. In most cosmological traditions, the realm of the spirit beings is attained through journeys into the earth as well as into the sky. Many Australian Aboriginal Dreamtime ancestors, for example, are present in the sky or live there for a while, but all have specific places of emergence and homes within the earth. The most significant source of prophecy and wisdom for the ancient Greeks did not come from the heights of Olympus, but from the Delphic Oracle. This was a "pythoness" or priestess who spoke while suspended over a fissure in the earth. Whenever a British hero such as Peredur or Gawain arrives at a mound, not only is the scene set for an encounter with an otherworldly being, such as the Black Oppressor or the Green Knight, but it is made clear that his opponent draws his power from within the mound. In the ancient and traditional worldview, the source of wisdom and psychic potential lies within the earth. We saw above how any encounter with the archetype of the Great Mother is always accompanied by the powerful image of the cave of rebirth.

The World Tree develops the theme further. A tree has invisible roots that reach down and spread into every corner of the Underworld. The roots access the deep earth wisdom. The tree concentrates itself on the middle plane of earth, presenting its trunk as axis. The branches reach into the sky, touch the celestial regions, and provide fruit. The shaman makes a drum from the trunk of the tree, hollowing it out to create the "opening" between the worlds. The Nordic tradition knew the World Tree as Yggdrasil. The Nordic God Woden, who gained his wisdom—and the runes—by being suspended from a tree, is matched in the British pantheon by the ash god Gwydion. His opponent was the alder god Bran. In the well-developed tree symbolism of the British Isles, the ash and the alder represent the sky and the sea. Mircea Eliade describes the symbolism of the World Tree in detail. He writes:

> *In a number of archaic traditions the Cosmic Tree, expressing the sacrality of the world, its fertility and perenniality, is related to the ideas of creation, fecundity, and initiation, and finally to the idea of absolute reality and immortality. Thus the World Tree becomes*

a Tree of Life and Immortality. Enriched by innumerable mythical doublets and complementary symbols: Woman, the Wellspring, Milk, Animals, Fruits, etc., the Cosmic Tree always presents itself as the very reservoir of life and the master of destinies. [29]

Motifs of the World Tree include souls waiting to be born among its branches and a World Serpent coiled around its base. Both motifs are associated with the Tor. The Tor acts as a reservoir of souls awaiting rebirth, enclosed by a spiral dragon embodied by the terraces. The shamans upon the Isle of Avalon journeyed to the base or the summit of the tree to find wisdom, or to retrieve, heal, or discover the destiny of a soul.

Given that these "archaic traditions" are very likely to provide insights into the nature of the Avalonian Tradition, it would not be surprising to find vestiges of tree veneration on the Isle of Avalon. The archetype of the sacred mountain is in plain evidence from the the Tor itself and its traditions of the underworld and rebirth. The symbolism of the World Tree is to be seen in the legends of the Apples of Avalon and the Holy Thorn. The apple is associated with rebirth and immortality and the thorn with the theme of perpetual regeneration. The "leaves of the tree" also crop up quite inexplicably in the legend of St. Collen. They are the food of the fairies. This makes perfect sense when the context of Gwynn ap Nudd is kept in mind. He is a representative of the Underworld forces in the struggle with the Overworld, a struggle symbolically depicted in the British Tradition by the "Battle of the Trees." Then there is the tradition of the oak forest covering the island; the two remaining venerated giants, Gog and Magog; and the possibility of the perennial yew tree grove beside the two springs. Finally, the great Abbot Dunstan had a dream in which a tree emerged from Glastonbury and covered Britain with its branches. He saw the cowls of monks upon it.

We may conclude from the literary, topographical, and physical evidence that the British Celts and their Druids—quite likely the equivalent of shamans—held the Isle of Avalon to be the place of the World Axis, with its attendant caves, pathways, openings, World Mountain, and World Tree. It is likely there was a tree or specific trees where certain rituals were conducted or journeys undertaken. The Tor—whether or not its terraces were carved during prehistory—is the prototypical sacred and spiral mountain. It provides the steps to the above. The springs provide the means of egress from and the means of access to the magical realm of the spirit beings below. The cave at the White Spring is the emergence place of the psychic potential that lies at once within the world and within consciousness.

Here, the sources of prophecy, wisdom, poetry, sovereignty, sexuality, healing, rebirth, immortality, and abundance are actualized and become visible. The physical topography of the island provides an exact mirror of the sacred. It is the cosmogony in microcosm. The Isle of Avalon contains the cosmos and thus is the point of connection—and of journeying—between the worlds.

ENDNOTES

1. In the extant versions of the story of St. Collen, the colours of the clothes are given as red and blue. My investigations have persuaded me that this should read red and white. This is not only because these are the traditional colours of Annwn, but because I have seen sources which describe the White Spring water as "blue-white." I think the white was dropped in transcription. Both blue and white are associated with cold.

2. For this story and other descriptions of Gwynn ap Nudd see Charles Squire, *Celtic Myth and Legend,* London, 1905. Also S. Baring-Gould and J. Fisher, "Life of St. Collen," *Lives of the British Saints,* 4 volumes, London, 1907-13. The story is from the Welsh.

3. *The Mabinogion,* trans. J. Gantz, 1976, pp. 148, 159, 168.

4. Janet McCrickard, *Eclipse of the Sun: An Investigation into Sun and Moon Myths,* Gothic Image, Glastonbury, 1989.

5. Jean-Jaques Hatt, *Celts and Gallo-Romans,* translation by J. Hogarth, London, 1970.

6. (1) *Triad 56.* (2) "Yder," in R.S. Loomis, *Arthurian Tradition and Chretien de Troyes,* New York, 1949. (3) Yder becomes Edern ap Nudd, "Eternal Son of Night," in the story of Gereint and Enid in *The Mabinogion.* Edern is a challenger and potential abductor of Guinevere. He continues his father's cosmic role but in the garb of a knight. His exploits take place in the vicinity of the Summer Land. (4) It is also possible that Nudd, Nodens, Nuada and Llyr, Lear, and Llud (Silver Hand) are one and the same. There is a sense in which Gwynn ap Nudd becomes a father to Creiddylad, giving rise to the "winter sun."

7. For further examples of the mythic pattern of contest between "The Bright and the Dark" over an Otherwordly woman in the Celtic tradition, see Caitlín Matthews, *Arthur and the Sovereignty of Britain,* Arkana, 1989.

8. *Trioedd Ynys Prydein* (The Welsh Triads), edited by Rachel Bromwich, Cardiff, 1961. Triad 90: The Three Perpetual Harmonies of the Island of Britain:

> *One was at the Island of Afallach*
> *and the second at Caer Garadawg (Salisbury?)*
> *and the third at Bangor (Is-coed in Flint).*

In each of these places were 2,400 religious men; of these 100 in turn continued each hour of the twenty-four hours of the day and night in prayer and service to God, ceaselessly and without rest forever.

9. See Caitlín Matthews (1989) for a thorough study of the Goddess of Sovereignty in British mythology.

10. This could be a false etymology. "Beckery" in Old English may refer to a place where bees were kept.

11. John of Glastonbury, trans. by James P. Carley, *John of Glastonbury's "Chronica,"* Oxford, 1978, 77ff. Also given in Philip Rahtz and S. Hirst, *Beckery Chapel, Glastonbury, 1967-68* (Archaeological Report), Glastonbury, 1974.

12. *Perlesvaus (High Book of the Grail)*, trans., N. Bryant, Cambridge, 1978.

13. For example, Gareth Knight, *The Secret Tradition in Arthurian Romance*, Wellingborough, Aquarian Press, 1983.

14. Such transcendentalism is depicted in accounts of the Grail quest. Instead of the Grail or Cauldron being the source of life, later accounts—including modern films—depict it as being external to life, a source of externalised spirit. Sir Galahad, for example, when he finds the Grail, achieves his own apotheosis and so never returns with the Grail. It is only Sir Bors, who after finding the Grail, fulfills its promise by living a peaceful life on the land with his wife.

15. *The Dream of Rhonabwy.*

16. The bridge is mentioned by Leland, circa 1570.

17. One other symbol of the sovereignty-granting goddess is the mare. In the Celtic tradition the king united with a mare, who may have been pregnant, in some ritualistic form. One account has him bathing in and imbibing a broth made from the meat. This may have happened at Lughnasad. As far as I can tell, the horse only appears in the Avalonian Tradition as part of the Wild Hunt. If evidence of a horse cult were to emerge upon the isle, it would add to the evidence for Avalon being linked with the sources of sovereignty.

18. For the full account of the bowl and subsequent events in early to mid-twentieth century Avalon, see Patrick Benham, *The Avalonians,* Glastonbury, 1993.

19. *The Goddess in Glastonbury,* Kathy Jones, Glastonbury, 1990.

20. Welsh poets often punned or rhymed off Mair, "Mary" and Pair, "Cauldron."

21. See my arguments in *His Story: Masculinity in the Post-Patriarchal World,* Chapter Five (Llewellyn Publications, 1995).

22. James P. Carley, *John of Glastonbury's "Chronica,"* Oxford, 1978.

23. The circle centres on the probable Druidic site, Whiteleafed Oak in the Malvern Hills. The only prehistoric archaeological confirmation of such a huge geomantic figure comes from Durrington Walls, north of Amesbury and about two miles from Stonehenge. Here enormous circular buildings capable of accommodating a choir of hundreds once stood. Durrington Walls, a henge, is contemporary with Stonehenge, as is the Devil's Ring Finger standing stone in Staffordshire. The stone lies on the topmost point of the twelve-fold circle. All these features are late Neolithic, not Druidic. See John Michell, *City of Revelation,* London, 1972, p. 84.

24. C.G. Jung, *The Archetypes and the Collective Unconscious,* Bollingen Series XX, Princeton University Press, 1959, p. 81-82.

25. Ibid.

26. Mircea Eliade, *Shamanism: Archaic Techniques of Ecstasy,* trans. Willard R. Trask, Bollingen Series LXXVI, Princeton University Press, 1964.

27. Ibid, Chapter 8.

28. Ibid.

29. Ibid.

7

THE UNDERWORLD:
RED SPRING AND
WHITE SPRING

Between Chalice Hill and the Tor there once existed an exquisite little valley, full of trees, into which flowed and blended two
very distinctive springs. Southerly facing, with the land shelv-
ing down to the water's edge, well-watered by a swiftly flowing
stream, the valley was the natural gathering place for those
visiting the isle.

One of the springs, on the side of Chalice Hill, flowed
through a grove of yew trees. It echoed the colour and sap of
the trees, for everything the water touched it covered with a
blood-red deposit. The other spring, on the side of the Tor,
emerged from a cave in a small and verdant combe. Its flowing
water coated everything it touched with a white deposit.
Because of their colour the waters were known as the Blood
Spring and the White Spring, and their symbolism and sacred
nature has ceaselessly resonated throughout the traditions and
myths of the ancient Isles of Britain.

Today, the Blood Spring is restored and its water flows
through a decorous succession of pools and gardens. The
name "Blood Well" appears on maps earlier this century. The
name "Blood Spring" appears on papers referring to the prop-
erty going back to at least the mid-eighteenth century. There

155

▲ *A recent view of the crowded base of the valley between Chalice Hill and the Tor. Chalice Well and the White Spring lie behind the high wall and up Well House Lane on the right.*

is a slight possibility that it was also known then as St. Joseph's Well. This name appears in accounts of the brief period when the spring became a popular place of healing. The documentary sources are, however, not clear on the matter. They could be referring to other springs. The much older name Chalcwell (AD 1256) or Chalkwell (1306) is preferred. This presents a problem as the Blood Spring is not chalk, but iron. The sources could be referring to the spectacular limestone deposits of the White Spring.[1] Whatever the case, the Blood Spring is known today as Chalice Well, the first mention of which appears in this century. The chalice is associated with St. Joseph, however, and in 1750 the chalice appeared on the seal of the bottled water taken from the spring. Since 1958, the spring has been in the care of Chalice Well Trust. The Trust was founded by Wellesley Tudor Pole with the object "of preserving the well and surrounding land so that it would continue as a sacred shrine for all to visit and receive nourishment."

The White Spring is not so fortunate. Its setting was destroyed and is now encumbered by a stone reservoir. This was built by the Water Board in the 1870s to supply water to the town of Glastonbury. A wall and a road, Well House Lane, divide the two springs and prevent their waters from flowing together—as they must once have done—in a single stream.

THE CHALICE WELL

A complex subterranean system of unknown size and depth in the overlying sandstone and the limestone substratum of the area provides the water which rises in the spring at Chalice Well. The water could originate from under the Mendip Hills to the north or, far less likely, from the Black Hills in South Wales. If the Mendips are the source then the water may be returning to the surface after a long period underground, perhaps several decades. Judging by the high chalybeate (iron) content, the constant temperature of fifty-two degrees Fahrenheit (eleven degrees Celsius) and the steady rate of flow of approximately one thousand gallons an hour, the spring is not affected by surface water fluctuations and is of an old, deep, and extensive origin. However, the possibility cannot be excluded that the water does in fact originate in the complex geological layers which form the upper part of the Isle of Avalon. As described in Chapter One, the sandstone of the Tor is all that remains of a vast sandstone layer laid down upon an ocean floor. Iron subsequently leached into a section of this, hardening it and making it able to resist erosion. As the rest of the layer eroded away, the Tor was formed. The iron-rich sandstone hill acts as a sponge for rainwater with the level terraces facilitating water absorption. Water is then slowly and regularly released from the spring at its foot.

After the founding of Chalice Well Trust and before the gardens were established, the Trust sponsored archaeological excavations. These began in 1960. Before this time a Catholic Seminary, a women's community, and a boy's school occupied the site. The restoration process began by removing the four-story building that stood at the bottom of the gardens and entirely dominated this part of Chilkwell Street. A Regency house on the site of the current car park, once the Anchor Inn, was accidentally struck in the process and consequently also had to be removed. The excavation trenches yielded surprisingly little. They gave evidence of prehistoric and Roman use of the site and showed that the yew trees which are present throughout the garden had always grown there. One stump of yew, eleven feet underground, dated to the Roman period (AD 43 to 410). The valley floor has risen considerably over the years and the challenges this presented and the small area examined may have been responsible for the slight amount of evidence obtained.

The presence of the yew trees is intriguing. The Celtic, Classical, and Christian traditions associate this tree with death and rebirth. It is possible for a yew to reach extreme old age, to have the greatest longevity of any European tree, and to achieve a massive girth. I have seen trees in Surrey

▲ *The Chalice Well.*

over forty feet around. It is also possible for the yew to become hollow, and, when the time is right, either to send new shoots upward from the hollow core or for new seeds to take root within it. Yew berries are red and somewhat toxic. Observation of these qualities was probably responsible for the original association of the tree with death and rebirth. Whatever the case, the tradition is to plant a yew tree in every graveyard. In Brittany, the churchyard yew sends "a root to the mouth of every corpse." The implication is hope of resurrection. Carpenters used the wood for coffins and for weapons, especially the English longbow. The bark is red and if struck the tree will bleed copious quantities of red sap, hardening—like blood—to black.

In the ancient Classical world, every sacrifice to Hecate, the Death Goddess, was made with a wreath of yew around the animal's neck. The yew in the lore and the tree calendar of the Celts marked the Winter Solstice, the time of death and rebirth.[2] Finally, when the archaeoastronomer Sir Norman Lockyer visited the Chalice Well in the early part of this century, he said the well was oriented to the Winter Solstice. It is hard to know what he actually meant by this, apart from the fact the valley generally looks in the direction of sunset at this time of year.

▲ *Yew trees at the foot of Chalice Well Gardens.*

If we can assume that the yew was always present around the Blood Spring—and the evidence shows it was—then it is likely that the affinities between the trees and the rubeate waters of the spring were noted, if not deliberately cultivated. The suggestion has even been made, I am not quite sure by whom, that the Druids used pairs of yew trees beside the waters of the Blood Spring as a processional pathway. Given the lack of evidence for a full picture, this avenue is suggested by the magnificent pair of yew trees which stand in the lower part of the gardens. It may safely be assumed that before the spring was diverted or otherwise channelled, its water flowed in a red-coated stream bed beside these two trees, one of which is likely to be at least three hundred years old.

A further, although probably similarly apocryphal, attribution to Chalice Well concerns the underground well head and the chamber beside it. The well head itself was originally a free-standing stone structure with a corbelled roof that became buried as the valley silted up. The silting happened quite rapidly after the woods on Chalice Hill and the Tor were removed—in the thirteenth century? The present well lid is set in the roof of this stone structure. The adjacent chamber is unusually constructed, having five sides. It has a ten thousand gallon capacity and can be drained and then refilled. It takes ten hours to fill and can be emptied much faster. Some say that the chamber was used for a Druidic initiation ritual involving death by drowning followed by resuscitation. Two metal rings set into the wall of the chamber at shoulder height are cited in support of this suggestion. These rings are not there today. The sides of the well head are built from very large blocks of stone apparently laid without mortar, a style of construction that has baffled attempts to date it. It was most likely built around AD 1200 using stones from the Abbey Church. This burnt down in 1184 and a great deal of reconstruction took place shortly after. The brick vault of the pentagonal chamber suggests a much later—mid-eighteenth century, perhaps—date of construction, although lower stones appear similar to those of the well head.

It certainly would be hazardous to propose so ancient a time as the Druids for the construction of the chamber, especially when we know the Druids relied solely on natural settings for their rituals. In fact, Druidic construction at Chalice Well can be entirely ruled out. What the story does reveal, though, is the persistent association of the spring with the theme of death and rebirth. The story is a reminder from "folk memory" or deep intuition that the two springs of Avalon were once the scene of extraordinary rites of initiation.

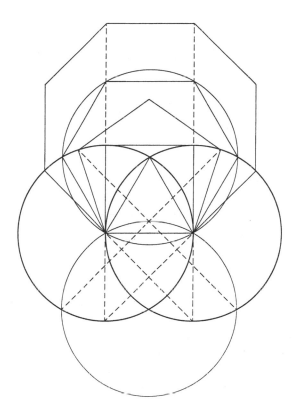

▲ *Succession of Polygons, generated by the Vesica Piscis.*

THE VESICA PISCIS

During this century, the geometrical form known as the Vesica Piscis came into Chalice Well Gardens. Its two interlocking circles are present in the stone of the pool in the lower part of the garden. This was built in the 1970s. The flow form which pours water into the pool was added in 1993. The Vesica Piscis is (inaccurately) wrought in iron over the entrance to King Arthur's Courtyard in the central part of the garden and it is present on the lid which covers the well head. Frederick Bligh Bond designed this lid in 1919 as a thanks offering after the Great War. Bligh Bond, as architect in charge of the restoration of the Abbey, found that the proportions generated by the Vesica Piscis were present throughout the Abbey, especially the Mary Chapel. Bligh Bond was a friend of Alice Buckton, who owned Chalice Well from 1912 to her death in 1944. It was she who proposed the idea for Chalice Well Trust. Alice Buckton was part of the alter-

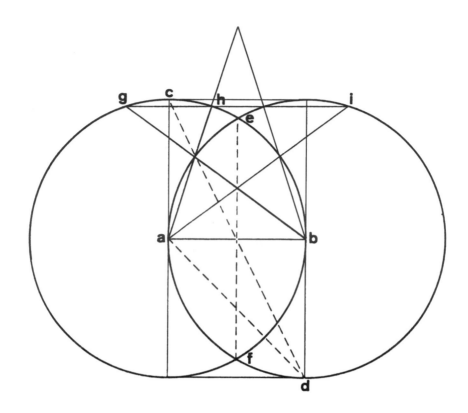

▲ *The lines of a pentacle divide each other so that the length of a short section, gh, is in the same proportion to the remaining section, hi, as hi is to the whole line, gi. These are the ratios of the Golden Section. When ab = 1, ad = √2, ef = √3 and cd = √5.*

native, more native, feminine, and mystical spirituality which was developing at that time. The intertwining circles on the lid of the well were spoken of by her circle as representing the blending of spirit and matter.

From the Vesica Piscis it is possible to generate a succession of exact polygons: the equilateral triangle, square, pentagon, hexagon, octagon, decagon, and dodecagon. An exact heptagram or seven-sided figure cannot be produced. The Vesica Piscis also contains proportions within itself that are in the order of the square roots of 2, 3, and 5. If 1 represents the original unity, then root 2 ($\sqrt{2}$) governs its expansion (or its division) in a two dimensional plane, and root 3 ($\sqrt{3}$) governs its expansion in three dimensional volume. The square root of 5 ($\sqrt{5}$) leads to the Golden Proportion or *phi* (Φ) that governs an analogous progression of forms, numbers and volumes. This proportion or ratio is visible in the natural world where growing forms such as trees, plants, and shells replicate themselves so that the new growth is in the same proportion to the original as the original is to the new form (original plus new growth), or B:A::A:(A+B). Although it is unsatisfactory to do this, as it is a ratio not a number, phi can be expressed as 1 to 1.618 or 1 to 0.618. The Golden Proportion or Mean finds expression in the spiral nautilus shell, in the proportions of the human body, and is used extensively in the proportions of sacred architecture.

The Vesica Piscis is a powerful symbol of the creation and generation of forms in the natural world. Given the long and successive use of the site of the two springs as a place of death and reembodiment, it is not surprising that this generative symbol should appear there. It is possible to imagine the progression created by the Vesica Piscis endlessly unfolding into the inner dimensions of the Otherworld as much as it unfolds into the outer dimensions of the external world. The progressive sets of relationships created by the two overlapping circles present an allegory of the situation where the ideal proportions of the inner world of divine potential unfold into visible manifestation.

THE TOR SPRINGS

In times of drought, the waters of Chalice Well are of great benefit to Glastonbury. When the Well House Lane reservoir was supplying water for the town, water from Chalice Well could be diverted into it for a nominal payment to the owners.

To the south of the Tor are several places where water rises. They are directly subject to rainfall and do not have the mineral content of the Blood or the White Spring. Just south of the main road below Ashwell Lane is a spring known as St. Dunstan's Well. There is also a small pond. Until recently, a barn stood close by and was said to be built from the remnants of a pilgrim's chapel dedicated to the abbot.

Further to the east lies a large, open reservoir built at the end of the last century. It is filled with water piped in from West Compton. From there the water is filtered and pumped up to a reservoir on the Tor's northeast flank. This was built in 1949 to supply Windmill Hill. It has two chambers with a fifty thousand gallon capacity. It is easy to hear the water flowing into the reservoir below the steel door, and people often wonder where the water comes from. It does not come from the Tor. A well has been suggested on the summit of the Tor but not found. A trial pit in the tower struck immovable masonry over a fissure that runs immediately below.

Water diviners, while saying the Tor is extremely difficult to dowse because of the many different kinds of subtle energy, confirm the Water Board's analysis of a spring rising in the permeable blue lias strata of the Tor. The stratification is a complex mixture of limestone and clays, capped by the hard Midford Sandstone. As the strata slope to the south and west, it is easy to see how the water finds its way below the sandstone to the White Spring. Whatever the source of the water, whether from rain or from an artesian system, the White Spring and its partner Chalice Well are part of a remarkable system capable of gathering huge amounts of quite separate and distinct water which then emerge side by side on the surface.

Diviners have also suggested a correspondence between the terraces of the Tor and the radiating patterns of energy that flowing water generates. The two synchronize and resonate with each other to produce a "cone of aurically interpenetrating sheafs."[3] These are said to assume seven-fold forms. Some schools of thought, such as that inspired by the work of Rudolph Steiner, say that water is a medium capable of being "encoded" by subtle energies. Through flowing vigorously in certain patterns, water can carry the imprint of the cosmic forces then prevailing. Ideas like this are behind the flow form at the bottom of Chalice Well Gardens. In terms of the Chinese geomantic art of Feng Shui, the Tor is a place where the earth and sky currents, the yin white tiger and the yang blue dragon, concentrate as a result of the watery level plain and the towering hill, and meet in a dynamic which is at once harmonious, challenging, and invigorating.

THE WHITE SPRING

When I first visited Glastonbury in 1977, there was little evidence that a second spring rose in the valley beside Chalice Well. A walk past the reservoir at the bottom of Well House Lane revealed a gaping, ragged hole in the stone facade from out of which emerged distant sounds of dripping and running water. It was a dark and chilling place. This had not, however, deterred jazz and other musicians in the sixties from exploring its interesting acoustical properties.

It was only later, when I made my home in Glastonbury, that I learnt a spring rose there. Piecing together the information that it was as unique as Chalice Well and flowed from out of a cave system under the Tor—the entrance to the Underworld—it seemed extraordinary that there was absolutely no public knowledge of the spring and that no mention of it was made in the traditions. It seemed as though the spring was cloaked in a conspiracy of silence.[4]

I then discovered that when the building of the reservoir was proposed in 1872, local antiquarians raised an outcry about destruction of a site steeped in historical and mythological interest. It was a popular beauty spot much frequented by locals. The antiquarians said that stone foundations could be seen on one side of the little combe which were possibly the remnants of monk's cells. They mentioned that the waters of the spring coated stones as well as any branches or leaves which dipped into the water with a heavy, white mineral deposit. In 1896, George Wright wrote this description of the White Spring in his recollections of the previous forty years:

> *And what was Glastonbury like then? One thing that clings to me was the beautiful Well House Lane of those days, before it had been spoilt by the erection of the reservoir. There was a small copse of bushes on the right hand running up the hill, and through it could be, not seen, but heard, the rush of running water, which made itself visible as it poured into the lane. But the lane itself was beautiful, for the whole bank was a series of fairy dropping wells—little caverns clothed with moss and verdure, and each small twig and leaf was a medium for the water to flow, drop, drop, drop, into a small basin below. This water contained lime, and pieces of wood or leaves subject to this dropping became encrusted with a covering of lime. For a long time I attended those pretty caverns with affectionate care, and Well House Lane was an object of interest to all our visitors.[5]*

The antiquarians, including George Wright, said the place had many traditions associated with it, that it was popularly known as the White Spring, and that the public strongly protested its destruction. What had happened in one hundred years to change this?

The area was suffering from cholera outbreaks at the time and the town council, under pressure from a government inspector, deemed it necessary to secure a safe source of water. So despite the protests, during the 1870s, construction of the reservoir went ahead. The stone reservoir was placed to fill the little combe, a heading was built behind, and the area above it was back-filled.

I have seen no photographs of how it once must have looked. But from descriptions and the remaining evidence it is possible to conclude that the combe sloped upward quite steeply on the north and east sides and lay open to the southwest. A fair amount of blue lias stone lay close to the surface covered by a profusion of growth. There were overhanging trees, abundant ferns, mosses, lichens, ivy, shade-loving flowers and grasses, and a huge calcsinterous accretion of limestone and vegetative deposit. As George Wright described, organic debris became encrusted by lime to form basins and "little caverns." When the organic matter decayed—or in some cases, became fossilized—the white stone or tufa came to resemble a sponge, full of tiny holes. The whole may have had a feminine bulbous shape, characteristic of spring or stream deposits with a high lime content. Underground flows of such water characteristically create flowstone formations, stalactites or stalagmites.

The spring, or as we shall see, the springs, dramatically emerged out of an opening about half way up the back wall of the combe, above the tufa or limestone formations. This would be about ninety feet from the present lane and twenty feet above it. A rock-lined grotto must have once existed there. We can be certain that at one time or another the opening in the back wall of the grotto was quite large, even cavernous due to the volume of water. Its size altered due to surrounding growth, the accumulation of flowstone, the shifting and erosion of the soft rocks, and the concerns and attitudes of the people of different times.

In order to maintain the flow and quality of water, the builders of the reservoir dug out the natural caves at the back of the combe and installed a low, brick-lined tunnel. For the last part of the tunnel, for we are now some forty feet below the present ground level, they must have worked entirely underground. At just over one hundred feet back from the original opening, they ended the tunnel in a cave. This natural cave in the blue lias of the area can hold up to a dozen people. Subjected to what is evidently a relatively recent collapse of the ceiling, further access into the cave system is not possible.

After completing the tunnel back to the cave, the builders constructed a collection chamber, finished the reservoir, and built a pumphouse on top of it to create the pressure necessary to supply water to the town. Study of the flow of water into the collection chamber reveals that the builders also tapped into other springs apart from the White Spring. Judging from the high iron content of one of these springs, it appears that a small offshoot of water from Chalice Well finds its way under Well House Lane to emerge beside the White Spring. This offshoot flows slowly and

▲ *The reservoir built in 1872 at the foot of Well House Lane for the waters of the White Spring.*

intermittently, depositing a high concentration of iron. Sometimes it stops altogether. It could either be natural or the leaking remnant of the system designed to introduce Chalice Well water into the reservoir during times of drought. The other springs are also intermittent and every indication points to their being surface water from the Tor.

If a picture of the White Spring were to be drawn, it would show that it was joined in its richly foliated little combe by several other water sources. The White Spring, emerging from a cave, covered the stones and plants with a thick white deposit which built up appreciably over the centuries to form attractive flowstone formations—the "fairy dropping wells" of George Wright. Other sources periodically flowed with rain water and so contributed to the overall lushness of the scene. After falling over rocky, moss and mineral covered ledges, all joined in one stream that ran down the combe, mixed with the waters of Chalice Well, and ended up first in the marshes down below and subsequently in the River Brue.

The White Spring itself has a high calciferous or calcium carbonate content. This originates from the limestone which underlies the area. In the right conditions, calcium carbonate or calcite will crystallize into a variety of forms or create flowstone formations. Examples of these can be seen at the quarry in nearby Dulcote Hill or in the spectacular cave at Wookey Hole. It is insoluble and will precipitate rapidly to calcify any surface it contacts. This fact was discovered very quickly after the water of the reservoir came on line and began to clog the pipes of the town. By the end of the nineteenth century, water was piped in from West Compton to supply Glastonbury.

We can be certain that water-worn caves do exist in the limestone under the Tor. The legends imply that they are there. We may conjecture that calcite crystalline formations are present in the caves, but this is not as likely as deposits in the form of stalactites and stalagmites. The water finds lateral pathways through the limestone strata before emerging at the surface just below the level of the sandstone.

According to the Water Board, the White Spring "rises in the Midford Sands overlying the upper lias beds" on the Tor and "flows from the heading in Tor Hill." The rate of flow of the White Spring fluctuates considerably. It can range from a minimum of a few thousand gallons a day to a maximum of over thirty thousand gallons a day. It has an average closer to fifteen thousand gallons a day. To this can be added the water of the other springs, which more or less doubles the rate of flow. The Water Board calls the spring "Tor Springs" or "Well House Spring." The source of the water may be the Tor itself, or an artesian system. The total volume of all spring water, including the Chalice Well—which rises about twenty feet lower—does conform to the amount of rain water falling on the surface area above the springs. If the springs are surface water, it is then hard to explain the striking difference in mineral content between the two main springs or the constant rate of flow of the Chalice Well.[6]

THE UNDERWORLD

White Spring water is pure and pleasant to the taste. It shares with Chalice Well a similar but totally distinct subterranean origin, indicating that the Isle of Avalon lies over complex geological system capable of holding two quite different aquifers alongside each other. The high mineral content of the White Spring water indicates a fairly lengthy period underground, but perhaps not as long as Chalice Well water. While Chalice Well water is likely to have obtained its colour by flowing through geological strata into which have leached tremendous quantities of iron, White Spring water just picks up the minerals present in limestone.

What is so unusual is that two quite distinct springs should rise within a couple of hundred feet of each other with only a small catchment area above them. The terraces on the Tor soak up water like a sponge and convey it through the fissures in the sandstone to the limestone strata below. Somewhere in this there is a geological formation capable of holding water, impregnating it with minerals, and then—at least in the case of Chalice Well—releasing it at a constant rate of flow regardless of fluctuations in rainfall. A large bed of sand would have this ability. While this may help explain the instability of the Tor, it does not fully account for the high mineral content of the water. Water which flows through sand tends to be very clean. This suggests the possibility of an artesian well with water from a distant source. On the other hand, Chalice Well does behave like water from a sandstone bed, while the fluctuations of the White Spring suggests a cavernous system, capable of filling and emptying more quickly. The limestone beds however may fold into the sandstone at some point, making pockets, even lakes of water, creating exactly the kind of mysterious subterranean realms which the Avalonian legends have always implied.

All this suggests unusual underground conditions that we should expect to find in other places nearby. The Mendips, for example, are famous for their caverns, and a world cave-diving record was set at Wookey Hole. The powerful springs at Wells, just six miles away, gave the place its name. We should also expect to find in an area of such aquatic anomaly places where the water is heated by the fire of the inner earth. We do indeed find this twenty miles away at Bath, where, practically unique in Britain, water is heated to high temperature and emerges as a hot spring.

The hot springs at Bath, however, are exactly where we expect to find them, in a valley beside a river, not hundreds of feet above the surrounding land. Though both places attracted considerable pagan veneration, it is the uniqueness of Avalon's situation which suggests to the imagination that it opened to the depths of a vast inner world. The waters at Glastonbury imply an underworld realm where access to mysterious dimensions is possible—exactly what the legends tell us! We may also expect similar legends associated with the sinkholes on the summit and the springs that rise at the foot of the Mendip Hills. Wookey Hole is traditionally seen as the opening to the realm of the Underworld Goddess—otherwise known as the Wise Woman or the Witch of Wookey Hole. But nothing quite as unusual as two elevated and adjacent springs, one red and one white, is to be found there.

The main piece of historical evidence for the entrance to the Underworld being located on the Tor is the story of the Welsh St. Collen. He was said to be Abbot of the monastery in the late seventh century. He then retired for a life of contemplation beside a spring at the foot of the Tor. The story of his encounter with Gwynn ap Nudd is given in Chapter Four.

Apart from firmly locating Gwynn and the Underworld entrance on the Tor, the legend reveals the attitude adopted by the Christians to the earlier Celtic tradition. The actions of St. Collen amount to an exorcism of the Underworld realm. Eventually, the building of the church of St. Michael on the Tor indicates that the wish was to completely do away with the chthonic Underworld forces instead of honouring them as the older Avalonian traditions appeared to do.

THE WHITE SPRING
TO THE PRESENT DAY

If Collen's dwelling place was beside the calcerous caves of the White Spring, where better could he have obtained access to the Underworld realm of Annwn? And though it is tempting to speculate with the gentleman antiquarians that the stones still visible in 1872 were the remains of St. Collen's cell, it is more likely that they came from the medieval period when the Monastery of St. Michael on the Tor was flourishing and some system was necessary to make water available to the many pilgrims and their animals. On the other hand, a sacred purpose is possible. St. Brigit was a patron saint of Glastonbury—she can be seen with her cow on St. Michael's tower on the Tor—and as the traditional protector of wells and water sources, a shrine or a small chapel may have been built for her beside the spring.

The Glastonbury fair held for six days around the Feast of St Michael, September 29, attracted many thousands of people. A tiny field on the corner of Well House Lane and Chilkwell Street is called the Fair Field on old maps. Once the Fair Field was much bigger and extended around the southern flanks of the Tor. The fair was thus held near the springs, and a system that reinforced the banks of the stream and made the waters available for every kind of need would have been a necessity. Subsequent building in the area has removed the opportunity for discovering this system.

Indeed, it is unfortunate that the area around the White Spring is so spoilt. Not only the reservoir, but the busy road into town from Shepton Mallet and the houses crammed up against it, all detract from what once was a lovely scene. Chilkwell Street was built in an era without motorized traffic and the houses with their fronts right on the street can no longer function in the old community way. Without the vision of those who saw what the Blood Spring could become and the subsequent creation of Chalice Well, we would have nothing at all of the area's former beauty.

Over one hundred years ago, the White Spring was taken from the people over their objections and used for a short while. Then in the mid 1980s, after lying derelict for many years, the Water Board sold the White Spring without considering the responsibility it had for restoring what was originally a public water source. The sale was not as well publicized nor as open as it could have been. The purchaser of the spring obtained it for a pittance over the longstanding requests of others to be informed of the sale. The Town Council or other bodies did not seem aware of or interested in the restoration of a historical landmark.

The purchaser of the spring converted and sold the pumphouse as a dwelling. At the time of writing, the water is being bottled and sold. An attempt is being made to lease a rather dank cafe inside the reservoir. Although an entrepreneurial spirit is being shown here, it goes against the general public feeling that the waters of the White Spring should flow freely once more. The capital investment is quite contrary to the vision of a restored sacred landscape, which is, after all, Glastonbury's greatest asset.

There is a great deal at issue here. On the one hand, the present owner of the spring, with permission from the appropriate authorities, is doing what he sees fit in the current economic and spiritual climate. It would require a considerable amount of money—many times more than the original purchase price—to remove the cafe, the old pumphouse, the reservoir, and then restore the spring. On the other hand, this restoration would be a great contribution to Avalon's sacred and beautiful landscape. It would add to the experience of the increasing numbers of visitors who climb the Tor on one side of the White Spring and visit Chalice Well on the other.

On another level, a restoration would result in the flowing and blending of two springs that were, to people of all previous ages, symbolic forces—two telluric streams—which underpinned the sacred and mythical dimensions of Britain's ancient land. It would be a shame to keep these forces suppressed in an age where cultural strengths are again being recognized as lying in symbols and values which arise from and honour the natural environment. What is the nature of these two "telluric streams" and how are they relevant to us today?

ENDNOTES

1. Greek: *chalkos*—copper, *chalybeis*—iron/steel. Both pronounced "k," i.e. kalkos, kalybeis. (Greek *chalazios*—precious stone). Latin: *calc*—chalc, *caix*—lime. *Webster's Dictionary.*

2. Something should be said of the Celtic Tree Calendar here. Attempts by different authors to recreate the arrangement of trees around the calendrical cycle of the year depart from each other. The version given by Robert Graves in *The White Goddess* is widely followed, but is, on his own admission, only a step toward a full picture. This may not be obtainable. For the time being, the reader is advised to be aware that in the indigenous tradition of the British Isles each tree hosts a constellation of symbolic, alphabetical, mythical, and practical meanings. An analogy might be provided by the stations of the Medicine Wheel.

3. Stanley Messenger, personal communication, 1984.

4. The silence around the White Spring is unnerving. Our local historian Geoffrey Ashe hardly makes mention of it, although living directly beside it! Dion Fortune wrote practically above it and says not a word. The many characters associated with Chalice Well in this century are silent about their neighbouring spring. The excavators of the Chalice Well and the Tor, Raleigh Radford and Philip Rahtz, even in their most recent publications complete with reconstruction drawings (Rahtz,

1993) say nothing. As far as I can tell, only the Druid, Ross Nichols, has appreciated the importance of the two adjacent springs. Philip Ross Nichols, *The Book of Druidry*, 1975.

5. G.W. Wright, "The History of Glastonbury During the Last Forty Years," in *Bulleids of Glastonbury*, Armynell Goodall, Taunton, 1984, p. 37.

6. In the spring of 1994, after a wet winter, the White Spring was flowing at 22,000 gallons per day. Total flow from all springs was approximately 50,000 gpd. Taking average rainfall for Glastonbury to be twenty-six inches per year and assuming the catchment area of the White Spring to be the Tor, or about one-sixth of a square mile, then, after allowing one-half loss for evaporation and one-fifth loss through run-off, the volume of water to be expected emerging from the Tor is in the region of 50,000 gpd. If the catchment area was extended to include all of Chalice Hill and more of Stonedown, then the rate of flow could be reasonably expected to be in the order of 60,000 gpd. This amount does not exceed the average volume of Chalice Well, 25,000 gpd, plus the average volume of the White and other springs, 30,000 gpd.

8

THE MATTER OF BRITAIN: DRAGONS, BLOOD, AND HEAVENLY DEW

There is possibly no place in the British Isles other than the Isle of Avalon that so embodies in its tradition and natural forms that which pertains to the esoteric subject known as the "Matter of Britain." Such a claim will, of course, be hotly disputed.

The Matter of Britain is the corpus of myth, legend, history, and symbolism that provides the people of Britain with a charter for their nature, their spirituality, their sovereignty, and ultimately, for their destiny. It is itself a branch of the tree of the Western Mystery Tradition that for millennia has pursued the Great Work of human development. It has frequently been compelled to do this in a veiled form. The Arthurian material is central to the subject and gains its weight from the fact that it has its derivation in the exceedingly remote history of the land. The rich vein of lore that constitutes the Matter of Britain has its roots firstly in the pre-Roman and pre-Christian British Tradition, and secondly in the renaissance of that native tradition in the period immediately following the Roman withdrawal at the beginning of the fifth century. This is the time of King Arthur.

Although it contains many later interpolations, the old Welsh text *The Mabinogion* is full of the colourful characters who come to fill the court of King Arthur in later legends. Arthur himself is a hero in the fantastic, exaggerated, and preternatural Celtic mode. Queen Guinevere began life as Gwenhwyvar, Sir Kai as the Celtic hero Kei, Sir Bedivere as Bedwyr, Sir Percival as Peredur, Merlin as Myrddin, the sword Excalibur as Caledvwlch, and so on. As we have seen, magical cauldrons are a feature of this tradition and provide the qualities that we later come to expect from their successor in the High Histories of the Holy Grail.

All these characters and symbols figure strongly in the Avalonian Tradition. The historical reality of some of them is borne out by the excavations at nearby Cadbury Castle. The excavations show that in all likelihood Cadbury was a royal seat from which its sovereign combated the Saxons at the time of a historical King Arthur. The tradition says that Arthur and Guinevere are buried in the Abbey grounds. The tradition says that Excalibur was made in Avalon and returned to the waters there by Sir Bedivere at Pomparles Bridge. The Grail ended up in Chalice Hill or beside the Red Spring, transforming its waters into the blood of Christ. The Castle of the Fisher King, where Percival finally asked the three questions of the Grail Quest, is upon Wearyall Hill. But it is to a theme which repeats itself several times in the ancient literature, that of two dragons, one red and one white, that we now must turn in order to grasp the subject at hand.

THE RED AND THE WHITE DRAGONS

In Geoffrey of Monmouth's *History of the Kings of Britain,* the aspirant to the throne of Britain, Vortigern, is persuaded by his magicians to build a stronghold after his collusion in a massacre of other British leaders.[1] This is during the period of turmoil after the Roman withdrawal when the Saxons are invading from the east and the issue of sovereignty—dormant for so long—is reopened. Vortigern is foiled in his attempt to gain the throne because two dragons, one white and one red, are in conflict below the foundations of his castle. This is revealed to him by the Archdruid Merlin, who also prophesies his death.

The Mabinogion draws a similar picture when three plagues ravage the land during the time of the rule by Lludd. King Lludd finds no solution until his brother Llevelys tells him to overcome two struggling dragons and bury them "within the strongest place you know of in the island."

▲ *View of the Tor with the pilgrim's path on the southwest ridge.*

It is the same two dragons who appear later under Vortigern's castle. At stake in these situations is the sovereignty and health of the land. The reason the dragons shake down Vortigern's castle is that his actions render him unfit to rule.

We can only assume that the two dragons or serpents represent the earth spirit. As polar forces, they bring the inner and the outer worlds into manifestation and hold them in a dynamic balance. They are the primary forces of creation. The symbol of two serpents or their equivalent occurs in many traditions. Two flame-spitting serpents decorate the sword of British sovereignty, Excalibur. In the Tibetan Buddhist tradition, two dragon-like essences, one red and one white, combine as our parent's sperm and ovum to draw in our individual consciousness. There is the famous yin-yang symbol of the East. In Chinese art, two dragons are often shown encircling a radiant disc or pearl, a symbol of the Sun. It is said that when the forces the serpents represent are balanced, the state of abundance, health, and harmony in life prevails.

This cosmic polarity is also evident in the legends of Gwynn ap Nudd "in whom God has set the energy of the demons of Annwn." As described in Chapter Four, Gwynn is locked in a perpetual struggle with his twin, Gwythyr ap Greidyawl. They compete for the hand of the Solar Goddess, Creiddylad. This early legend matches the later Arthurian one, where Melwas, the King of the Summer Country, holds Queen Guinevere on the Tor until Arthur secures her release.

The two stories are structurally identical. Both take place on the Tor and reveal a cosmic drama where two protagonists, one identified with the Underworld and one with the Overworld—a Sky God and an Earth God—turn around a yearly cycle in companionship with the Celtic Goddess of the Sun, the Land, and Sovereignty.[2] The time of transition seems to be May Day and Halloween. If one of the protagonists were to conquer, it would be the "Day of Doom." The Goddess possesses both a chthonic and a solar nature. Guinevere is a heavenly queen who is nevertheless "imprisoned" in the Underworld. An equivalent story in Greek mythology is that of Persephone, who spends half the year in the Underworld and half the year in the Overworld. In Egyptian mythology, the equivalent story is of the Goddess Isis and the struggle between Osiris and Set. In Hopi and Southwestern mythology, the story is of the ancestral, founding goddess— sometimes known as Spiderwoman—and the Twin War Gods who engage in a world-shaping ball game.

Although we must be careful not to read too much into the symbols, when so little actual evidence exists for pre-Christian beliefs, May Day in the Celtic tradition is the festival of Beltane that ushers in the light half of the year. Six months later, Samhain or Halloween ushers in the dark half of the year. Gwynn, or in the later legend, Melwas, is the Dark King of Winter and Gwythyr, or Arthur, is the Bright King of Summer. They are the Lords of the Waxing and Waning Year. They enact their drama in the world whose many elements are provided by the abundant cauldron of the Goddess. The geomythical pattern is confirmed when we note that the countrywide alignment created by Glastonbury Tor, Burrowbridge Mump, Avebury stone circle, St. Michael's Mount, and other sites points to the rising sun at May Day and Lughnasad and to the setting sun at Halloween and Imbolc. As the festival days of the Gods Bel and Lugh are indicated by these dates, they too appear as Lords of the Waxing and Waning Year.

Through Gwynn and Gwythyr's journey around the solar cycle of the year and the greater cycle of birth and death—the Underworld and the Overworld—a balance is maintained. Each gives way to the other at the appropriate time. This pattern is repeated throughout the Celtic Tradition with the struggle between the Children of Don, the Sky, and the Children of Llyr, the Sea. This theme of cosmic polarity finds expression in the rich symbolism of the tree. Folklore preserves accounts of the Holly King and the Oak King replacing each other as Lords of Winter and Summer. The Celtic arboreal tradition culminates, some would say, in the Welsh poem known as *Câd Goddeu*, the "Battle of the Trees." Here the Ash God Gwydion leads the Overworld in a seasonal struggle against the Alder God Bran, King of the Underworld. The tree is universally recognized as the symbol of life connecting every region of the cosmos and figures prominently in European and Middle Eastern creation myths.

It is important to recognize that the forces of the opposed powers do not permanently defeat each other—as St. Michael does the Devil—but through their perpetual dynamic, they sustain the sacred order. If one were to triumph over the other, it would indeed be the "Day of Doom." The killing of the dragon—spatially present in the lines across the landscape—was an important part of the ritual turning of the wheel of the year throughout all the ancient European traditions. But the dragon of the solar year, like a snake shedding its skin and the tree its leaves, always renewed itself and returned.

THE BLOOD MYSTERIES OF AVALON

Gwynn ap Nudd is associated with the dark, chthonic, underworld realm, with horns, serpents, and, paradoxically, with the colour white. His name means the "White Son of Night." His symbolism evidently includes the white face of the moon. But Annwn, the Celtic Underworld, is as much red as it is white, and red is traditionally the colour of earth. The colour of the Earth Goddess—who by definition is chthonic—is red, deepening to black. White, the colour of spirits, is likely to be a reference to Gwynn's death-dealing power. This is an aspect of the masculine mysteries where men are to the realm of death as women are to the realm of life. While women's wombs make them the givers of life, men's powerful limbs and large hands make them the ideal hunters and fighters—in short, the takers of life.

In the legend of Gwynn and the Wild Hunt, we may be hearing distant echoes of the rites of male initiation that took place upon the Isle of Avalon. Men were taught to face their fears and their killing powers in rituals around the taking of a life—human or animal—and thus they learnt the reciprocation necessary for a death and the responsibility which went with it. In this way the vital but potentially disruptive warrior energy was harnessed and directed so the men could become the champions of the Goddess of the Land.

In this context, we may ponder the meaning of a "little death" in reference to the release of white semen in male orgasm. There is the wound in the genitals received by the Fisher King. There is an association between the white lance dripping red blood—one of the four talismans of the Grail Quest—which wounded the Fisher King and the penis. In the original hunter-gatherer culture, the spear in the hands of the man was the evident connection between the death of the animal and thus the continuation of the life of the people on the one hand, and the skill, prowess, and the virility of the male hunter on the other. The life of the tribe, the death of an animal, a man's spear drawing red blood, his penis emitting white sperm, were all bound together in a web of reciprocal relationships.[3]

The qualities of Gwythyr ap Greidyawl are bright, solar, and although in theory white, they are, in fact, red. His solar nature is a complement to the lunar earthiness of Gwynn. Between the two gods the rites of initiation upon the Isle of Avalon taught men to balance the energies of the masculine. The complementary polarities, the balance of powers, and the reversals between them are a feature of the primary dyad of red and white. This dyad is found in the symbology of creation mythologies across

▲ *The pelican feeding its young with blood from its own breast depicted over the east gateway of the Abbey.*

the world. The symbols are part of a cosmological order where traffic between the terrestrial and the otherworldly realms is always possible. The blood mysteries are central to this order, as people everywhere believed—until the discovery of genes—that the blood was responsible for the transmission across the dimensions of ancestral and spiritual qualities. The ancient Mayan people believed that by lancing the penis with sting ray spines, the proper respect was shown to the spirit realm. Sharing blood binds people together as "brothers." On some level—strongly present in the Christian mysteries—most people still believe that blood enjoys a subtle communion with the spirit world.

The people of ancient Europe—going back to at least the time of the great Paleolithic cave art—used powdered red ochre during burial rites. White ochre was used in rites of origin and birth. Ghosts or spirits were invariably depicted as white. Red blood indicated the presence of life. The same is true in many Native American and Australian Aboriginal traditions. Several Aboriginal tribes of Arnhem Land represent the first Creative Spirit Ancestor with patterns of concentric red and white rings. They display these in a ceremonial ground painting at the place where the First Ancestor emerged from the earth in the Dreamtime. The Dreamtime, or the Dreaming, is the creative epoch when the potentials held in the energy of the inner world are actualized in the external. The red for the ceremony comes from the blood of initiated men. The Aborigines paint red and white rings on a heavy wooden pole that is rhythmically raised and lowered at the centre of the ground painting during the ceremony. The alternating red and white colours represent the primary cosmic duality that nature makes so manifestly obvious in the sexes.[4]

As an example of this primary dyad at work in the process of cognition, anthropologists found that among isolated tribal peoples there may exist no names for colours apart from red or white. Things are either red or they are white. There may be many names for shades of red or white, but all colours belong to either category. If something is neither red nor white, then it is black, a non-colour. This ties in with the qualities, discussed in Chapter One, attributed to semen and blood. The ambiguity about them finds resolution in what may be called the "black"—the invisible realm of inspiration and dreams. This is the place of all potential, akin to the Aboriginal concept of the Dreamtime.

In his profound work *The Tibetan Book of Living and Dying*, Rinpoche Sogyal writes: "During the development of the fetus, our father's essence, a nucleus that is . . . 'white and blissful,' rests in the chakra at the crown of our head at the top of the central channel. The mother's essence, a nucleus that is 'red and hot,' rests in the chakra . . . located four finger-widths below the navel." The white and red essences are contained within the subtle energy channels of the body which account for all the functions of the "psycho-physical system." Rinpoche goes on to say that at the close of life the white essence descends the central channel toward the heart, inducing an experience of "whiteness." The corresponding ascent of the mother's essence induces an experience of "redness." When the essences meet in the heart, there is an experience of "blackness." The mind is at last free of thoughts and there dawns what is called the "Full Attainment." According to the Dalai Lama: "This consciousness is the innermost subtle mind. We call it the buddha nature, the real source of all consciousness."[5]

The implication is that through dying or through inner or shamanic journeying, it is possible to reach profound states of consciousness in which the primal colours of red and white are synomynous with tremendously potent experiences. These inner states are presumably true for all people, not just for Tibetans. I myself have attained a meditative state where I encountered a fundamental polarity which I experienced as red and white forces. I intuitively knew these forces signified the joining of my parent's sperm and ovum. I also knew that I could "go between" them, separating them, and so journey on into the next world. This would have meant death to my body. Or I could have chosen to allow these creative forces to remain in their dance of polarity and I would return to this life. Obviously, I chose to return.

In the Mystical European Tradition, the Alchemists sought to discover the process whereby a "base metal" or the soul could be refined into something of more value or transmuted into a finer state. Through their art, the Alchemists could achieve that which nature needed aeons to accomplish. They sought the secret of creation. The process always involved a stage of death and "putrefaction." Only when the compound in the alchemical crucible became black—the "toad"—could it be further refined by the Universal Solvent. This was also known as the Philosopher's Stone. In most instances the Alchemists describe the solvent or the stone as two-fold. It is the Red Elixir and the White Elixir, or the Red Mercury and the White Mercury. The red was of the nature of the sun and gold. It was the "water of heaven." The white was of the nature of the moon and silver. It was the "water of earth."[6]

By working with what we know of the Western Mystery Tradition, from comparison with other indigenous initiatory traditions and from the remnants of the Avalonian Tradition, we may imagine the Isle of Avalon as the principal location for the most important rituals of initiation and rites of passage for the ancient Britons. Inextricably tied in with this were the rituals of the year and the rituals which reenacted the stories of creation. As a whole, the rituals created a context in which the people could experience their relationship to the cosmic order. Through constantly establishing and reliving this relationship, they could find congruency and thus meaning.

Young men and women came to the Isle at the onset of puberty and were taught the spiritual significance of their new powers. This involved long and complex rituals of story-telling, costuming, dance, and song. Perhaps when the young women finally entered the yew tree grove and approached the waters of the Red Spring, they apprehended the sympathetic resonance between the blood of their own menstrual flow and that of the body of the earth. It is possible that before they were able to do this a terrifying aspect of the Earth Goddess appeared. This apparition subjected them to some bloody and even cruel ritual of menstrual blood. C.G. Jung records instances where the maiden figure of Persephone or Kore was was made to drink blood and bathe in it at the hands of the Earth Mother.[7] The archetype of the Great Mother presented itself as the devourer or the hag. By making this aspect of the Goddess conscious through the means of dramatic initiation, the fragmented, denied or projected aspects of the self were integrated. The Earth Mother hag who appeared at the initiation of young women was terrible, but not traumatizing. She was whole-making. Even as she doused the girls in blood—reproducing the blood of their mother that crowned them at birth—or pierced their hymen, or immersed them in the blood spring, she held them or they were held in the arms of the older women.

When the young men came to the springs, the shamans or elders taught them the mystery of their right relationship to the inner world and to the earth. Confronted by the waters in a context where ritual wounds were inflicted upon their bodies—possibly directly upon their penis—the young men had to integrate their fears and childhood traumas. As a potent representation of the unconscious, the medium of water—blood-red, white, abundant, scarce, cleansing, freezing, consumed or consuming, poured from and into cauldrons—took them into the mythic realm. There, the stories, songs, dramatic acts, prayers, and the presence of the shamans facilitated the making of the whole self. Through these processes men learnt the balance of their killing and inseminating powers. Women, in a sense, were already in their power because of the innate, and often bloody, transformations of their own bodies.

Later in life these initiatic mysteries changed. The fierce, warrior energies of the young male had matured. He had faced death in ritual, in the hunt, and possibly in the arts of war. Any false pride was replaced by the true qualities that came from experience. He had learnt, like a woman, to bleed. He had learnt to commune with and give to the spirit of the animal that gave itself to his spear. Perhaps he had learnt what it meant to take the life of a human, or give up the life of a friend. We know that the Druids arranged considerable debt exchanges between the killer and the kin of the killed, even in the circumstances of war. Through these practices, the man became fully "enculturated" and his energies focused and directed. He now had to learn the blood mysteries of the heart. The latter part of his life turned in this direction.

The women, on the other hand, received their initiations not so much from cultural practices, but from nature.[8] Responding to the changes within their bodies and with the feelings that accompanied these changes, they already knew the blood mysteries of the body and of the heart. They had chosen the men they wanted to be their lovers. They had given birth to children with whom they shared the intimacy of love, the alchemy of the breast, and the ties of blood. When the women fulfilled this part of their lives, they turned to the other mysteries. Those mysteries today may be termed "masculine." The men turned to those we would call "feminine." The initiatory processes for men and women were very different.

Other initiations were received later in life. The Avalonian Tradition implies these always involved the mysteries of death and rebirth. Ecstatic sexual rites were also likely, probably at Beltane. We may imagine rites around the birthing and the "enspiriting" of a child. Cross-cultural comparison suggests this involved the recognition of the spirit of the child, its clan and personal totems, and probably its name. It was, after all, a reincarnating spirit. Evocations of being in the womb may have returned memory to the first experience of "redness." Birth and the encounter with direct light may have recalled the first experience of "whiteness." Throughout all these initiatory processes, the rites performed reenacted the myths of creation. The repetition of the acts of the world-shaping creatures and deities sustained the world in the image of the cosmic order.

THE TWICE BORN

The ultimate initiation was for the very few. Through a ritual death by means of a trance state induced by drugs, drumming, bodily control, fasting, or even by suffocation, the initiate journeyed to the Otherworld. Perhaps this was accomplished on the horses of the Wild Hunt. In the Otherworld, the journeyer obtained a vision and a token of power. Then they voluntarily returned—or were resuscitated—to the land of the living.

The value the Celts placed upon the head—it was the repository of words, songs, spiritual wisdom, and vision—suggests that the highest initiations for men involved "opening" the centres of subtle perception which lay there. Remnants of these practices may be visible in the archaic images of foliage gushing from the head of the Green Man, or the antlers sprouting from the head of the Horned God. The Celtic description of the Otherworld being red and white, having red and white creatures, and so on, suggests an "attainment" or "enlightenment" experience close to that described in the Tibetan Tradition. An inner journey which led to the experience of the "white and blissful" masculine essence —the "semen in the head"—would be tremendously invigorating for men. Pursuing the Otherworldly goddess—usually depicted upon a horse and possessing solar qualities—might be analogous to the Tibetan description of the "red and hot" feminine essence. While for men, she was unattainable, for women, the reverse was true. An inner journey to the realm of the red, chthonian, always pregnant Earth Mother allowed women to be renewed and invigorated by their experience of the feminine essence.

We know from their poetry that the ancient Britons conceived of reincarnation or metempsychosis as the reappearance of a specific personality or soul in a sequence of human or animal bodies. They also may have identified a life with a collective ancestral energy, such as the spirit of a clan or of a mythologized ancestor. Yet it is to the meaning of the idea of reincarnation as a total transformation or rebirth during a single lifetime which occupies our attention here. This meaning is at the heart of all the initiatic traditions that have come down to us through the ages, including the Tibetan and the Christian.

The "virgin birth" of Christ did not mean an impossible transcendence of the genetic principle, it meant a second birth in his lifetime. This was accomplished through the introduction of a spiritual energy that our culture acknowledges in the appointment of a godmother. The resurrection of Christ, in the cave or the womb of the earth, again illustrates this principle of a spiritual rebirth. This time it is through the godmother as Earth Mother. Indeed, the alchemical processes of soul death, rebirth, and utter transformation of the being find parallels in almost every tradition. This is usually through initiatic processes involving immersion in earth, fire, water, or blood. In Christian cultures, this has become the rite of baptism. In shamanic cultures, healing, prophetic, or other powers are not obtained until the initiate "dies before they die." This involved long training and arduous ordeals.

There is some evidence that the Druids practiced initiatory ritual sacrifice to the four elements. The initiate was buried in earth, immersed in water, suspended over fire, and deprived of air—or possibly flung from a cliff. Although death was the result in some cases, in other cases the initiate returned by having induced a cataleptic trance, by being revived, or—most frequently—by the initiators holding back at the last possible moment. The point being the initiates were shrived of their vanities and fear of death. The knights in the Arthurian legends met a similar challenge when they bent their necks to receive the reciprocal blow of their giant opponent. Only through the facing and thus the integration of fear is the journey to the Otherworld possible. There is the suggestion that the unusual chamber of Chalice Well was used for ritual drowning, although it cannot possibly be of the age of the Druids.

The Red and the White Springs of Avalon deal in the occult side of alchemy and the magical arts that involve the initiations of death, transmutation, and rebirth through the powers of water, blood, milk, and semen. These mysteries are necessarily hidden as they imply a sacred content to creation and to sexuality. They also imply self-actualized spiritual development, reincarnation, the honouring of the "dark," the unconscious, and the opening of subtle energy centres in the body. As the present established order is dominated by Christianity, even in countries founded upon freedom of belief, these ideas are all frowned upon.

Although these mysteries can only be cursorily mentioned here, let it be said that any facets of the human psyche that are repressed, denied, or otherwise rejected will inevitably reappear in a pathological or destructive form. Fear has always been understood as the great initiator. It is only through going into places where fear is strongest that wholeness is achieved. It is the complete lack of understanding of the initiatic practices of the Western Tradition that dramatically displayed death, the dark, fear, obscenity, and wild ecstatic sexuality, which led to their persecution and demise. The phallic, playful, goat god of Old Europe—and of later traditions, such as the Knights Templar and Wicca—led to allegations of devil worship and then the total annihilation of those traditions. The androgynous half-goat, half-human deity Baphomet—an embodiment of the Dark God—is too provocative a figure to bring up even now. It is unfortunate that literal interpretation of the Bible has led to a dualism where belief in one god has created a devil. Such simplistic dualism engenders absolutes of "good" and "evil," instead of a complementary round. However, most Western readers have no difficultly examining the rich mytho-logical traditions of other native peoples. Here it is possible to glean an understanding of the ancient European mysteries without the fearfulness induced by our own biases.

Instead of digressing any further from the theme here, a discussion of how Western thought and consciousness developed a dualistic worldview is given in the Appendix, "Dualism and Deity."

Free of the division wrought in the Western worldview by excessive transcendentalism, it is now probable that only among remote tribal peoples can a sense of wholeness in spiritual practice be reached. The overwhelming characteristic of these cultures is an attitude of earth honouring. This emerges in reenactment of the myths of creation. The earth is directly perceived as the body of "our Mother." Spiritual practices include sacred sexuality or tantra and the aligning of the human consciousness with that of animals, with plants, and even with rocks in order to maintain the earth spirit. There is vision questing and progressive initiation that accesses deeper and "darker" levels of the unconsciousness. There is a complete ritual cycle that includes the dramatic appearance of Wrathful Deities, Otherworldly Guardians, and various Nature Spirits. Examples include the Dakinis of Tibetan Buddhism and the Kachinas of the Pueblo Indians. All these are held in a context that includes clowning, satire, parody, masquerade, sexuality, ferocity, profanity, lewdness, and other vulgar eccentricities which, although once recognized, are now entirely banished from the Christian Church.

The blood mysteries are central to the traditions of indigenous peoples, especially in the initiation of young men and women. The blood in the body is perceived as being directly analogous to the blood in the body of the Earth Mother. The magnetic lines of force upon the earth, locally affected by iron deposits—and by the waters of subterranean springs that collect this deposit—find a magical analogy in the blood of the human body. In this worldview, spirit and matter are homogenous. The earth is alive with vibrant, interconnected, and potentially renewable energies.

It is to ideas like these that we must look if our wish is to imagine the properties and powers originally associated with the iron-laden waters of the Blood Spring. The rituals enacted there maintained the flow of the earth spirit and ensured its continued presence among the people. Through sympathetic resonance between the human body and the body of the earth, life was maintained. This is not an idea of "primitive" people. The creative thinker and great artist Leonardo da Vinci held that rivers were the blood vessels of the living organism of the earth. Yet, sadly, the nature of the horn-bearing, spear-carrying, death-facing, and inseminating mysteries of the White Spring seem irretrievable to us in an age that has entirely lost its own rites of masculine spiritual-sexual initiation. Ironically, after such a long period of patriarchy, it will be easier to retrieve the face of the Goddess than it will be the face of the God. Whatever rites Gwynn ap Nudd, the Horned God, and the Wild Hunt performed are perhaps only retrievable now through personal archetypal experience.

> *A man, with a crown, stands upon the earth.*
> *Behind him is a sword entwined by two serpents.*
> *The right side of his body is painted red*
> *   and the other side white.*
> *Patterns of the two colours overlap.*
> *He holds a child in his left arm, the fruit of his*
> *   white semen-emitting red penis.*
> *In his right hand he holds a white spear*
> *   that drips red blood.*
>
> *His power can create and destroy.*
> *His power is like the spear and the two-edged sword.*
>
> *One edge of his power can bring order and purpose.*
> *It can organize, structure, clarify, create, and build.*
> *It can bring law, justice, and fairness.*
> *It creates ecstatic dance and trance states through which*
> *   all the levels of creation can be known.*
> *Through it he merges with the spirit of the animal he hunts.*
> *His power is playful, strong, sweet, energizing,*
> *   valiant, individualizing, and fulfilling through the order*
> *   it brings and the purpose it provides.*
>
> *The other edge of his power can destroy the life*
> *   of the matrix of the elements.*
> *It can force the elements to serve his ends.*
> *It can bend, monopolize, channel, and rigidify them.*
> *It can kill, dominate, push, and control.*
> *It can exploit, rape, hold, cut up, separate, and enforce*
> *   self-seeking tyrannies.*
> *His power over the world blinds him to his unity with it, and he knows*
> *   only the "waking" consciousness of the Sky Father.*

Male initiation taught men how to balance these powers. It taught a man how to direct the masculine energy into paths that connected him with every part of creation and enhanced the life of the whole community. The sword had to be contained within the scabbard of the twin serpents.

A woman, with a crown, stands upon the earth.
Behind her are the two serpents entwined around the sword.
The right side of her body is painted white and the left side red.
Patterns swirl between each side.
She holds the child in her right arm, the fruit of her womb.
In the other hand she cradles her red breast, out of
*   which streams drops of white milk.*

Her power can devour and give life.
It can reveal and conceal.
Her power is like that of a two-edged mouth—a "vagina dentata."

Her power is within the swirling matrix of the elements.
It can increase them and transform them, one into the other.
It can pour the water of life.
It can unify, make community, and bring all into the
*   one web of being.*
It creates the life of the matrix, through birth and
*   new combinations of elements.*
Through her power to embody every transformation
*   of the matrix, she knows within herself every facet of creation.*

The other side of her power can spin in never-ending chaos.
It can breed frenzy and monsters.
It can ceaselessly demand blood for blood.
It can suck dry every well.
It can lapse into chatter, lethargy, dark introspection,
*   or produce endless multiplications of matter*
*   without goal or purpose.*
Her unity with the world can blind her to the subtle realms
*   and she identifies only with the Earth Mother,*
*   who ultimately becomes the hag.*

Female initiation taught women how to balance this power. It taught women how to use and direct their feminine energy into paths that carried life on to fulfillment. The twin serpent scabbard had to contain the sword.

THE RED AND THE WHITE ROSE

The theme of polarity and conflict between two sides holding a red or a white symbol is taken up several times in British history. It is a dyad essential to British sovereignty. Before unification with Scotland and Wales, the British flag consisted of a red cross on a white background. During the War of the Roses, the Houses of Lancaster and York adopted the emblems of the red and the white rose. The victor in that war, Henry VII (1485-1509), understood the power present in symbols—the rose was an alchemical symbol for the Red Elixir—and he hastened to draw on ancient precedents to legitimate his reign. He claimed descent from King Arthur (through Offa and Cadwallader), named his first son Arthur, and inclined toward a balance of red and white elements on the royal coats of arms. Henry fought under the standard of the red dragon, and today, the red lion and the white unicorn prevail.

At the time of Uther Pendragon, the semi-mythical father of Arthur, it was said the standard of Britain was a red dragon and a white dragon. Pendragon means the "head of the dragon" and the Welsh Uthr Ben means "wonderful head." It may be related to the enchanted head of the cauldron keeper Bran. As long as Bran's head remained on the hill that is now the Tower of London, Britain was protected from invasion. The symbol of the dragon was used in battle as a sign of wisdom and courage. Because of the vision received by Arthur at the Chapel of St. Brigit at Beckery, Arthur put away the old standard (and the head of Bran) and created a new one based upon a cross, three crowns, and the Holy Mother and Child. Despite the success at Mount Badon, Arthur was defeated at Camlamn and retired to Avalon to die of his wounds. The old standard was divided, with the white dragon apparently going to the Saxons in the east and the red dragon going to the Welsh (the Celts) in the west. It was the unification of this ancient mythological division that Henry VII (Welsh Tudor) was aware of in his attempts to restore the Kingdom of the Britons after the Wars of the Roses. He was at least politically successful in this unification, and subsequent monarchs have always claimed sovereignty through the line of descent he established.

At the same time Henry VII was doing this, the hermetic tradition was enjoying a renaissance. Under the aegis of the Rose Cross, the Rosicrucians were able to reinstate some of the principles of the ancient mysteries. Both Alchemy and Freemasonry were inspired by the Rosicrucian initiative, which had at its heart the balance of male and female energies and the concepts of initiatic rebirth, immortality, or reincarnation. It is likely that the banner of Arthur—mother and child, three crowns, and the cross was a Rosicrucian emblem. The cross was another version of the cauldron. It symbolized the elements meeting in the crucible of life, death, and rebirth. The mother and child made manifest the invisible dynamic of the triple-crowned trinity. The rose—not on this banner, but on most others—represented the most sacred distillate of the transformational process, the "Heavenly Dew" of the Mother's breast, or the blood-red "Elixir of Life."

A remarkable synthesis of symbolic themes is expressed in the Avalonian Tradition. There is a mysterious alchemy which emerges wherever one turns. Whether one turns to the vesica design on the cover of Chalice Well; to the dynamic of the high Tor and the gentle Chalice Hill; to the Red and White Springs or to the red and white cruets of Joseph of Arimathea; to the two ancient oak trees Gog and Magog; to the contrast of the Isle of Avalon and its surrounding marshy plain; or to the alignment of the Tor to the world above and the world below; in all of these things there is a symbiosis of nature and spirit, each moulding and informing the other. The ancient Isle of Avalon seems to surpass all other places in Britain for the ability to sound the resonance between the inner and outer worlds.

Glastonbury means much to the British Church. It is the place where the faith was founded and the first church built. Glastonbury promoted the love of the feminine aspect of divinity, an element which hard-edged, patriarchal Christianity desperately needed. To the mystics, Glastonbury became the Grail Castle and the place of origin of Excalibur. It is the place of burial of King Arthur—who is not dead, but waits to return—and it is the entrance to the Christian heaven—or hell. Glastonbury also meant much to those of the ancient past who left no written record. But in the tradition they founded and in the markings they left behind in the landscape, it may be possible to read a message.

Waters have always represented the inner worlds and it is here, at the springs, that we must dive if we wish to gain access to the depths of our ancient inheritance.

THE ALCHEMY OF AVALON

By now it should be clear how closely the "Matter of Britain" is tied to Avalon and specifically to the Red and the White Springs. The fundamental cosmological polarity of red and white, represented by the two springs, sustains the synchronistic order of the inner and the outer worlds. This complementary polarity—the dragon currents of the earth spirit—maintains the nature, health, and harmony of the ancient land of Britain. It is central to the story of creation. It establishes the relationship of the people to the land. It establishes the source and character of their sovereignty. If we are to follow the Tibetan Tradition, the red and white streams establish the fundamental cosmological polarity of individual consciousness and life. The geomythical power of the springs originates from the time when the inseparability of the body, nature, and spirit was intrinsic to the worldview of the people and the landscape was seen as a sacred living thing.

This view allows an understanding of the alchemical mystery of Avalon that runs throughout its traditions. The Cauldron of Annwn, the Cauldron of the Great Goddess—the later Christian Grail, eventually represented by the cross—is the crucible of the transformational and creative alchemical process. The early dwellers upon the isle—and later followers of the hermetic tradition, like St. Dunstan—sought the transmutation of the base substance or the undeveloped soul within the Cauldron or the Grail. They sought the Elixir of Life. In terms of their worldview this was possible, as no division existed between the external world and its internal energizing potential. The realm of the ancestors and the unborn, the creative powers of the deities, were as immanent as the world of the living. The alchemical mystery was obtained through the emulation of nature—conceived of as the Divine Feminine—as the decay and regeneration of the forms, seeds, trees, plants, and creatures of the landscape provided the perfect symbol for all the transformative potentials of life.

To be close to this mystery, the first people on the Isle of Avalon lived in the simplest possible way. Their lives were a mirror of the seasons. They ate only what could be gathered. They performed a constant round of ritual in order to be in harmony with the energies of the inner world. Where these energies flowed to the surface of the land, at the caves, hills, trees, groves, and especially at the fountainous springs, they worshipped at the appropriate times and built nothing to interrupt the flow. The island was an "earthly paradise" because the balanced harmony of Nature, the generative power of the Great Mother, prevailed. The water they drank was of the essence of life. The food they ate, the apples of Avalon, gave immortality. The mystery kept upon the Isle was that of creation, of the cycle of birth, death, and reincarnation. It was they, the shamans—male and female—who took the initiates who came to the Isle through the rites of life passage.

During the late Neolithic or Megalithic Age, it was perceived that some adjustments to the landscape were necessary to maintain or increase the flow of energies. Perhaps the quality of the life energy was felt to be diminishing. It was thought necessary to enhance the Tor with a set of rising concentric rings. These allowed greater numbers of people to participate in the ceremonies. Perhaps by this time, a sense of slipping away from the pristine communion with nature and the world of mythologized ancestors was developing. The terraces represent an attempt to restore the original order of a "Golden Age." Perhaps the men were getting out of hand as a result of cultural changes where newly introduced agricultural and urban practices replaced their ancient role as hunters. Men's mystical communion with the spirits of the world achieved through the development of acute sensibilities and lifelong spiritual initiation was replaced by the repetitive demands of agriculture and of patriarchal civilization. A contradiction was created where masculine energy went into defending the fixed and women-defined towns and fields. Men became attackers of the towns and fields of others.

In later millennium, the Druids attempted to revive the ancient traditions. They abandoned the great ceremonial centres and returned to the original simplicity of the grottos and sacred groves. At the Red and the White Springs, nature presented the Druids with its most profound teaching. In the same way as the alchemists sought the transmutation of the soul through the practice of their art, so here on the Isle of Avalon nature transmuted life in the crucible of the earth. The process was exact. It required death or "putrefaction," represented by the black coagulate, or by the entry into the Underworld. Only

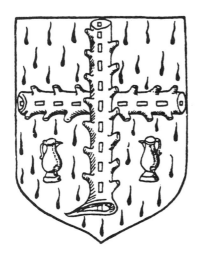

▲ *The coat of arms of Joseph of Arimathea.*

through the careful blending of the Red Elixir and the White Elixir could the purest water, the Mercury of the Philosophers, the Universal Solvent, or the "Heavenly Dew"—capable of creating new life—be formed. Then, from out of the earth, catalyzed by the red and the white streams, the soul returned—phoenix-like—purified from the ultimate initiation.

Echoes of this process are heard in the legends of journeys into the inner earth of Avalon. It is here that Excalibur, the sword of British sovereignty, was forged with its balanced, intertwined, fiery serpents. Excalibur lay in the keeping of the "Lady of the Lake," who must be none other than the spirit of sovereignty. It was into her lakes and rivers that the British gave innumerable treasures: swords, shields, cups, and coins as votive offerings. The process can be heard in the words of the sixteenth-century John Dee who reported finding the "red and white powders" of St. Dunstan in the Abbey grounds. It was Abbot Dunstan who mixed and channeled the waters of the two springs in the tenth century. Then there is the declaration of the sixth-century Glastonbury prophet, Melkin, which at least reveals the thinking of the monks of the Medieval monastery:

> For Joseph has with him in the tomb two white and silver vessels filled with blood and sweat of the prophet Jesus. When his tomb is found, it will be seen whole and undefiled in the future, and will be open to all the earth. From then on, neither water nor heavenly dew will be able to be lacking for those who inhabit the most holy island.[9]

Dewdrops are shown on St. Joseph's coat of arms, but the "heavenly dew" is not simply rain water. Avalon has plenty of that. It is the transformative distillate of the Red and White Elixirs, the water of life. The "blood and sweat of the prophet Jesus" is an allegory for the greatest alchemical transmutation of them all, initiatory death and rebirth, through the elements of the Underworld. All those who walked the path of knowledge employed Christian terms after the banishment of the hermetic or gnostic arts. But for those versed in the ancient mysteries, it was always the two springs that provided the tangible manifestation of the primary polarity of existence which continued its dynamic in the depths of the cauldron of the earth. This process could be emulated and enhanced through the ancient rites of blood, semen, initiation, song, dance, storytelling, ecstatic sexuality, and possibly, ritual death by drowning and resuscitation at the springs. What took place in the body also took place within the earth, and vice versa.

Although this may be reading too much into the issue, the reason for the covering up of the White Spring in Glastonbury lay in the arrival on the sanctuary of Avalon of the orthodox branch of a new transcendental cosmology. Its priests, seeking personal and corporate power, had no place for a sacred world and especially not for an entrance to—or worse, an exit from—an Underworld. In the new cosmology, the world—and the body—was full of sin and suffering. It was to be risen above. It was not to be acknowledged, let alone honoured and integrated. The sacred groves were burnt, springs were covered, the honouring of the many "spirits of place" was forbidden, male and female initiation ceased, worship was allowed only within a church—quite separate from nature—and the church itself was frequently placed upon the ancient, and apparently empty, sacred site.

If the people possessed a cosmology that allowed crossing between the worlds and thus could access their own deep and immanent psycho-physical inner powers, they would have spiritual revelations at odds with the prescribed doctrines of a monolithic and fiercely monotheistic ortho-doxy. They might, for example, access the mystery of the sovereignty of King Arthur which lies in a cave below the land. They might wish to cross the Wasteland and find the symbols of abundance and power: the sword, the cauldron, the cross, the spear, and the horn, which have their origin and final resting place—along with King Arthur—on the Isle of Avalon. They might find the way to dream into being the ancient spiritual way of life based upon harmony with the natural world. They might then oust a priest who reified spiritual power to a transcendent source and then claimed a monopoly upon it. The legend of St. Collen shows the Chris-tians wanted nothing to do with the doorway to the Underworld. They duly banished its champion and guardian, Gwynn ap Nudd. It follows that the actual physical entrance to his realm would meet with the same fate.

The Red and the White Springs represent the cycle around and the necessary balance between the light and the dark halves of existence. They represent the balance between the sexual powers, between masculine and feminine, between birth and death, between the inner world and the exter-nal world—the relationship between consciousness and unconscious-ness—the life of a whole cosmos. The two springs conjunctly rising from their deep and mysterious subterranean source, are physical representa-tions of a tremendous body of mythical and symbolic knowledge and power. They do not just symbolize this power, they are its vital currents in the greatest alchemical cauldron of them all—the body of Nature in its specific manifestation upon the cosmological centre of the Isle of Avalon.

The two springs are the twin currents of the Earth Spirit as it coils around the World Tree and the World Mountain. They are the creative spirit which sustains the health and well-being of the people and the sovereignty of the land of Britain. Viewed in this way, it becomes imperative that the water of the White Spring emerging from the calciferous caverns under the Tor be allowed to flow freely once again. Reunited as a living stream with the rubeate waters of its partner Chalice Well, there will be restored to the Avalonian landscape a physical expression of the ancient order, not just of Britain, but of the sacred world.

ENDNOTES

1. Geoffrey got his material from Nennius, a Welsh cleric who wrote about AD 800.

2. In *Owein, or the Countess of the Fountain*, two protagonists struggle with each other for the hand of the Countess, who is clearly a sovereign goddess. The meteorological phenomena which accompany this struggle, as well as the Otherworldly details, places the story in a cosmological context. But the two men, by the time this story was recorded, fight to the death.

3. See Nicholas R. Mann, *His Story: Evolving the New Male Archetype*, Llewellyn: St. Paul, 1994, ch. 5.

4. Robert Lawlor, *Voices of the First Day*, Inner Traditions, 1991, p. 107.

5. *The Tibetan Book of Living and Dying*, Rinpoche Sogyal, Harper Collins, 1993, p. 248.

6. Manly P. Hall, *The Secret Teaching of All Ages*, Los Angeles, 1977, p. CLIII-CLX.

7. C.G. Jung, *The Archetypes and the Collective Unconscious*, Bollingen Series XX, 1959, p. 184-5.

8. This is why in practically all traditions so many of the visible customs, songs, regalia, rites of passage, and so on are concerned with men.

9. James P. Carley, "Melkin the Bard and Esoteric Tradition at Glastonbury Abbey," *The Downside Review*, 99, 1981.

APPENDIX
DUALISM AND DEITY

Dualism as a dominant principle arose as a result of certain chance circumstances in the history of the Western world. It was not a predestined product of the development of human consciousness. The history of Western thought could have taken another course. A polarity always existed in the minds of those who lived in what we chauvinistically call the "prehistoric" world. It is the binary mode in which the mind thinks, e.g., hot or cold, dark or light, raw or cooked, right or left, edible or inedible, friend or foe. But the worldview or the context in which people held these ideas meant that pairs of critical opposites acted in a complementary rather than in an exclusive fashion. The concept of deity, for example—which is tremendously formative of the worldview—had aspects both positive and negative, dark and light. All aspects were a part of the whole. The practice of spirituality was geared for participation within the many categories of nature, not for personal apotheosis. Only later in "history" did Western religion develop the duality of good and evil, the "good" god and the "evil" devil and the chasm between spirit and nature. This came about because of a change in cosmology or worldview.

With the agricultural revolution—the domestication of animals, the cultivation of grains, and the development of permanent settlement sites— pressure on land and water resources brought previously nomadic tribes into conflict. In the Near East, where this process began especially early, the tendency was to portray the cultural traits, customs, and deities of another tribe in an unfavourable light. One's own gods and goddesses were expanded in power, privilege, and dimension while those of other people were diminished. Cultural heroes, myths, and religions provided a badge of distinction from others and a mark of belonging to one's own people.

The Jewish people, particularly hard pressed to find their own territory, developed a concept of deity which set them apart from all others. A monotheistic belief provided a strong set of boundaries and a unique badge of identity. At the same time, the deities of their enemies were branded in as negative a fashion as possible. The deities of the Canaanites and Babylonians became evil giants and wicked demons. The Jewish deity, beginning like most deities as a local spirit of place, became reified into a totalitarian, omnipotent, and transcendental god. All that was good—to the Jews—was attributed to their one god and all that was bad was attributed to the worship of other deities. They literally created—with all their furnishings—heaven and hell. The Jews, under the aegis of their one god, were highly successful at maintaining their identity in the face of adversity. Indeed, their enemies were necessary to reinforce their faith in the goodness of their own god. Christianity grew out of the Jewish worldview.

The one transcendent male god soon proved his worth to all the emerging urban and nationalist cultures. He provided a hierarchical model for effective and strong leadership in the home, in the towns, in the nation, and on the battlefield. He also provided a model for the divine right of the priest-king leaders. Under this model, the ruler could not be challenged. Patriarchal authority could not be usurped, laws and their upholders were divinely ordained. This worldview provided cohesion, decisiveness, efficiency, identity, and, at its best, justice—if you belonged to the "in group."

The fiercely combative Greek world found such a cosmos extremely attractive. The Greek pantheon of deities had become arbitrary and fickle. A new world order was required in which law and justice was brought by a god king. The centuries leading up to the time of Christ saw many attempts to establish such a ruler in the Egyptian and Hellenistic world. Egypt, at times, and Israel provided a model. Both countries were conquered by the Greeks. But the petty despotisms and dynasties of the Hellenistic rulers—including that of Alexander the Great—kept on collapsing, invoking the scepticism of the people. The Hellenistic philosophers knew an order based upon a transcendent reality and sustained by priest-kings was desirable and possible, but how could it be achieved?

With the military success of the Roman Republic in the Mediterranean, a solution became apparent. Around the time of Christ, the newly emerging Roman Empire placed a god in the form of an Emperor at its head. The monotheism of the Jews and the Christians merged with the need of the Roman Empire for a single ruler. In order for this ruler to keep dispensing patronage to his supporters, new lands had to be continually conquered. Christianity was literally carried across Europe on the arms of the Roman Empire. Through its conquests, Rome also planted the seeds for feudalism—the descending pyramidal model of power which was to characterize the subsequent monarchies and bureaucracies of Europe right up and through their colonial eras.

Jewish and then Christian monotheism, the Greek and then the Roman need for a worldview which legitimated invasion and hierarchical rule, and finally feudalism, with its concepts such as the divine right of kings, all conspired together to plant in the Western mind a dualistic concept of cosmos and deity. The ultimate good was to be found in the god king of the city state or nation. The ultimate evil lay in the other, the enemy.

To support the power of the priesthood, the king, and the hierarchical order, good and evil became reified to absolutes. What was good became a completely inaccessible transcendent god, up in heaven, utterly beyond the world. God became identified with the male, with light (and white skin), with authority, and with his earthly representatives—who built suitably inaccessible and splendid palaces for themselves. What was evil mirrored the structure of heaven, but in reverse. Hell became the all too ubiquitous earthly reality. Hell was identified with the body, with sexuality, with women, with the ethnic or cultural "other," and with the fearful images wrought by the human imagination—such as Satanism. Dualism created the one devil at the same time as it created the one god. "Anyone who is a Christian and believes in God, must also believe in the existence of Satan.[1] Dualism created the hierarchical class system of Europe. Dualism created the divide between the creator and the creation. Dualism created the divide between spirit and matter, between the mind and the body—with a clear valuation upon which was best.

By the Medieval age, the world was seen as a place of purgatory and suffering. Its creatures and resources were worth nothing, only existing to be used by man. The work ethic which accompanied the Industrial Revolution saw gruelling labour as "taming the flesh" for the "glory of god."

Slavery was justified for the same reason. Women were merely servants and "carriers of the seed" of men. War was necessary for the purging of heretical and other undesirable traits. These concepts formed the present era and are still prevalent in our institutions. It is the denial of the body and the attempt to eradicate those things identified with the "devil" which constitute the only truly evil acts of history. To know that God really exists for those in this worldview there must be an enemy, a scapegoat. The Inquisition and the burning of women, slavery, the Holocaust, the purging of out groups, and the ethnic-cleansing of modern regimes are the products of this worldview.

A similar situation exists in parts of the world dominated by any of the monotheistic desert religions. In places where other traditions, such as Buddhism, predominate, deities retain an aspectual character. These aspects are viewed as creations of the mind. The division in the worldview between spirit and nature tends to disappear. Conversion is not sought. There is no external enemy. From the evidence which remains of the pre-Classical and Christian world—and from the evidence of those cultures which were not subjected to them—the mind-body split, "Us and the Other" consciousness, and the reification of "good and evil" are non-issues. These cultures may retain the cruelty, superstitions, and immobility of the negative aspects of matriarchy, but on the whole they do suggest a valid and alternative course of human development. What this may have been, or may be as the Western world and its colonies reassess themselves after centuries of religious proselytizing and expanding feudal hegemony, remains to be seen. The long-standing mystery teaching of the Avalonian Tradition suggests a worldview which allows integration of the whole cycle of existence rather than the false elevation—and mirroring denigration—of any of its parts.

ENDNOTES

1. Quoted from *Satanic Panic: The Creation of a Contemporary Legend,* by Jeffrey S. Victor, Open Court, Chicago, 1993, p. 99.

BIBLIOGRAPHY

Alcock, Leslie. "Excavations at South Cadbury Castle, 1967,"
  Antiquities Journal, vol. 48, 1968.

Ashe, Geoffrey, editor. *The Quest for Arthur's Britain.* Paladin,
  1968.

——*The Glastonbury Tor Maze.* Glastonbury: Gothic Image
  Publications, 1979.

——*Avalonian Quest.* London, 1982.

——*The Rediscovery of King Arthur.* Anchor Press, 1985.

Benham, Patrick. *The Avalonians.* Glastonbury: Gothic Image
  Publications, 1993.

Bligh Bond, Frederick. *The Architectural Handbook of Glastonbury Abbey.* Glastonbury, 1909.

——*The Gate of Remembrance.* Oxford, 1918.

Bord, Janet and Colin. *Mysterious Britain.* Paladin, 1974.

Bryant, N., trans. *Perlesvaus (High Book of the Grail).* Cambridge, 1978.

Bullied, Arthur. *The Lake Villages of Somerset* (5th edition).
  Glastonbury, 1958.

Caradoc of Llancarfan. "Vita Gildae" in *Gildas: The Ruin of*

Britain, ed. Williams, Hugh, *Cymmrodorion Record Series,* No. 3, Pt. 2, London, 1901. Also contains 'De Excidio et Conquestu Britanniae" by Gildas.

Carley, James P. "Melkin the Bard and Esoteric Tradition at Glastonbury Abbey," in *The Downside Review,* 99. 1981.

——*Glastonbury Abbey,* 1988.

Cohn, Norman. *Europe's Inner Demons.* Basic Books, New York, 1975.

Coles, J. & Orme, B. *Prehistory of the Somerset Levels.* Somerset Levels Project, 1982.

——*Sweet Track to Glastonbury: The Somerset Levels in Prehistory.* London, 1986.

Eliade, Mircea. *Shamanism: Archaic Techniques of Ecstasy.* Translated by Willard R. Trask. Bollingen Series 76, Princeton University Press, 1964.

Fortune, Dion. *Avalon of the Heart.* Aquarian Press, 1971.

Gantz, J., trans. *The Mabinogion.* Penguin, 1976.

Gennaro, Gino. *The Phenomena of Avalon: The First Heliocentric Book for Two Thousand Years.* Cronos Publications, 1979.

Geoffrey of Monmouth. *The History of the Kings of Britain.* Translated by L. Thorpe. Penguin, 1966.

Gildas, see "Life of Gildas" and "Life of St. Collen" in *Baring-Gould, S. & Fisher, J., Lives of the British Saints.* 1911. Also Caradoc of Llancarfan, (above).

Giraldus Cambrensis. *The Historical Works.* Translated by T. Wright and G. Bohn. 1863.

Graves, Robert. *The White Goddess.* Faber, 1961.

Hearne, Thomas. *The History and Antiquities of Glastonbury, 1722.*

Howard-Gordon, Frances. *Glastonbury: Maker of Myths.* Glastonbury: Gothic Image Publications, 1982.

Jones, Kathy. *The Goddess in Glastonbury.* Glastonbury, 1990.

John of Glastonbury. *Chronicle.* Translated by B. Carley. Boydell, 1985.

Jung, Carl C. *The Archetypes and the Collective Unconscious.* Bollingen Series 20. Princeton University Press, 1959.

Knight, Gareth. *The Secret Tradition in Arthurian Romance.* Wellingborough: Aquarian Press, 1983.

Lawlor, Robert. *Voices of the First Day.* Inner Traditions, 1991.

Loomis, R. S. *Arthurian Tradition and Chrétien de Troyes.* New York, 1949.

——*The Grail: From Celtic Myth to Christian Symbol.* New York, 1963.

Maltwood, Katherine. *A Guide to Glastonbury's Temple of the Stars.* London, 1929.

McCrickard, Janet. *Eclipse of the Sun: An Investigation into Sun and Moon Myths.* Glastonbury: Gothic Image, 1989.

Mann, Nicholas. *The Cauldron and the Grail.* Glastonbury, 1985.

——*Glastonbury Tor.* Glastonbury, 1986 and 1993.

——*The Red & White Springs.* Glastonbury, 1992.

——*His Story: Maculinity in the Post-Patriarchal World.* St Paul, 1994.

Matthews, Caitlín. *Arthur and the Sovereignty of Britain.* Arkana, 1989.

Matthews, John. *Taliesin: Shamanism and the Bardic Mysteries in Britain and Ireland.* London: Aquarian, 1991.

Michell, John. *The New View Over Atlantis.* Thames & Hudson, 1983.

——*The Dimensions of Paradise.* Thames & Hudson, 1988.

——*New Light on the Ancient Mysteries of Glastonbury.* Glastonbury: Gothic Image Publications, 1990.

Nichols, Ross, *The Book of Druidry.* Wellingbourough: Aquarian Press, 1990.

Pike, Albert. *Morals and Dogma (of the Ancient and Accepted Scottish Rite of Freemasonry).* Southern Jurisdiction of the United States, 1985.

Pixley, Olive. "Psychometry." Gun Pelham, 1937.

Rahtz, Philip, *Excavations on Glastonbury Tor, Somerset, 1964-6.* R.A.I, 1971.

——*Glastonbury.* London, 1993.

Rahtz, P. & Hirst, S. *Beckery Chapel, Glastonbury, 1967-68.* Glastonbury, 1974.

Roberts, Anthon., *Glastonbury: Ancient Avalon, New Jerusalem.* Rider, 1978.

Saward, Jeff. *Caerdroia 14.* 1984.

Sogyal, Rinpoche. *The Tibetan Book of Living and Dying.* Harper Collins, 1993.

Spence, Lewis. *The Mysteries of Britain.* Rider, Aquarian, 1979.

Squire, Charles. *Celtic Myth and Legend.* London, 1905.

Thom, Alexander. In *Glastonbury, a Study in Patterns,* edited by M. Williams. R.I.L.K.O., 1969.

——*Megalithic Sites in Britain.* Oxford, 1967.

Bromwich, Rachel, ed. *Trioedd Ynys Prydein (The Welsh Triads).* Cardiff, 1961.

Victor, Jeffrey S. *Satanic Panic: The Creation of a Contemporary Legend.* Chicago: Open Court, 1993.

Walsh, Terry. *Global Sacred Alignments.* Glastonbury: University of Avalon Press, 1993.

Warner, Rev. Richard. *An History of the Abbey of Glaston.* Bath, 1826.

Westwood, Jennifer. *Albion: A Guide to Legendary Britain.* London, 1985.

William of Malmesbury. "De Antiquitate Glastoniensis Ecclesiae." In *Scott, J., The Early History of Glastonbury.* Woodbridge: Boydell, 1981.

Wright, George W. "The History of Glastonbury During the Last Forty Years." In *Bulleids of Glastonbury.* Armynell Goodall: Taunton, 1984.

INDEX

Aborigines, Australian, 84, 120, 149, 182

Alchemy, 25, 185, 187, 191-192

Amaethon, god, 126

Anne, St., 59, 87, 91

Annwn, 20, 23, 26, 118, 123-125, 127, 130-131, 140-142, 144, 146, 171, 178, 180, 193

Arawn, king, 20, 125-126

Arianrhod, goddess, 102, 126, 139, 142, 145-146

Arthur, king, 3, 12, 14, 20, 23, 38-40, 45, 47-48, 53-56, 87, 89, 91-92, 100, 110, 113, 117, 124, 126-128, 130-136, 138, 143-146, 151, 161, 175-176, 178-179, 191-192, 196

Ashe, Geoffrey, 48, 55-56, 77, 101-102, 120, 138, 172

Avallach, king, 20, 54, 130

Avalon

Isle, 1-4, 7-10, 12, 14, 16, 18-20, 22-26, 29-30, 32, 34-36, 38-40, 42, 44, 46, 48, 50, 52-56, 58-60, 62, 64, 66, 68, 70, 72, 74, 76, 78, 82, 84-86, 88, 90, 92, 94, 96, 98, 100, 102, 104, 106-110, 112-116, 118, 120, 124, 126, 128, 130-136, 138-146, 148, 150-152, 155-158, 160, 162, 164, 166, 168-170, 172, 175-176, 178,

180, 182-184, 186, 188, 190, 192-194, 196, 200, 202, 204, 206, 204, 206

mysteries, 2-3, 20, 26-27, 50-51, 56, 61, 81, 83, 85, 87, 89, 91, 93, 95, 97, 99, 101, 103, 105, 107, 109, 111, 113, 115, 117, 119, 121, 127, 131, 180, 182, 185, 187-189, 191, 195

name, 7, 10, 18, 23, 26-27, 33, 42, 48, 81, 102, 109, 123, 125-127, 130-131, 136, 142, 145, 155-156, 170, 180, 185

Avebury, henge, 31, 34-35, 81, 104, 179

Baboquivari, 101-102, 148

Baptism, 25

Beckery, Isle of, 36, 41, 65, 91, 132, 135-138, 140, 146, 152, 191

Bedivere, knight, 131, 145, 176

Bel, god, 64, 104, 179

Beltane, 64, 82, 87, 98, 104, 134, 179, 185

Bligh Bond, Frederick, 61, 110-111, 114, 116, 119, 121, 161

Blood, 1-3, 17, 23-27, 130-132, 136, 139-141, 155-156, 159-160, 163, 171, 175-176, 180-182, 184-185, 187-190, 195

Bran, Bron, king/god, 20, 23, 92, 123, 125-126, 132, 149, 179, 191

Brigit, St., 41, 50, 54, 64-65, 91, 104, 132, 135-137, 139, 171, 191

Buckton, Alice, 161-162

Burrowbridge Mump, 81-83, 86-87, 91, 104, 179

Cadbury Castle, 33, 46, 68-69, 87, 89, 91, 113, 143, 176

Caer Arianrhod, 145-146

Caer Sidi, 22, 142, 144-146

Calvary Mount, 14, 65-66, 76

Cambrensis, Giraldus, 20, 39, 130

Campbell, Iris, 73

Cauldron of Plenty, Rebirth, 2-4, 20, 22-24, 123, 132, 140, 142, 144-145, 179, 193, 195-196

Caradoc of Llancarfan, 7, 39, 48

Carnac, 34, 85, 89

Cernunnos, god, 125, 128

Cerridwen, goddess, 20, 22-23, 26, 104, 139, 142, 145

Chalice Hill, 10, 13, 17, 19-20, 23, 71-72, 93, 95-97, 99, 114, 132, 138, 140, 142, 155-156, 160, 173, 176, 192

Chalice Well, 16-17, 26, 36, 74, 95, 100, 107, 136, 140, 142, 155-157, 159-164, 168-169, 171-173, 176, 184, 187, 192, 197

Christ, Jesus, 3, 12, 23-25, 51, 55, 57, 59, 61, 110, 113, 132, 137-141, 176, 186, 195, 200-201

Collen, St., 3, 100, 124-125, 129, 150-151, 170-171, 196

Corbenic, 66, 92

Creiddylad, 77, 125-127, 129, 151, 178

Crewkerne, 85, 120

Cross, 3, 16, 42, 49, 53, 61-62, 65-66, 72, 91, 112-114, 119, 132, 135-136, 138-139, 146, 191-193, 196

Cuthbert, St., 85

Cwm Annwn, 20

David, St., 50, 55, 117

Dee, John, 25-26, 105, 109, 195

Dod Lane, 60, 86, 99

Don, goddess, 22, 125-126, 179

Dragon, 26, 64, 81, 84, 125, 130, 132, 150, 164, 179, 191, 193

Dualism, 25, 87, 187-188, 199, 201, 205

Dundon Hill Fort, 18

Dunstan, St., 12, 25-26, 55, 64, 150, 163, 193, 195

Durrington Walls, henge, 34-35, 153

Druids, 3, 37, 46, 50, 54, 78, 141, 150, 160, 185, 187, 194

Eliade, Mircea, 146, 149, 153

Excalibur, 12, 100, 130-131, 134-135, 176, 178, 192, 195

Fisher King, 23, 132-133, 135, 140, 176, 180

Fortune, Dion, 74, 78, 173

Freemasonry, 111-113, 121, 191

Gawain, 126, 149

Gennaro, Gino, 74, 78

Geoffrey of Monmouth, 20, 39, 130, 176

Gildas, 27, 39-40, 46, 127

Glastonbury
Abbey, 3, 12, 16, 18, 20, 24-26, 29, 39-41, 48-51, 53-57, 60-62, 64, 66, 68, 71-73, 86-87, 91, 93, 95-97, 99-100, 110-111, 114-115, 121, 132, 138, 140-141, 148, 160-161, 176, 181, 195

foundation, 23-26, 41, 50, 54, 57, 81, 89, 93, 111, 119-120, 132, 140-141

town, 7, 12, 19, 68, 73, 85, 136, 142, 156, 163, 165-166, 168, 171

Zodiac, 2, 23, 25-26, 51, 61, 85, 105-107, 109-110, 113, 115, 119, 127, 145

Gog and Magog, 93, 95, 97-98, 141, 150, 192

Golden Age, 130, 194

Golden Section, Mean, 95, 162

Goodchild, John, 137

Govannon, god, 126

Guinevere, queen, 40, 53, 55, 127-128, 133, 135, 151, 176, 178

Gundestrup Cauldron, 128

Grail, Holy, 3, 22-25, 27, 41, 66, 91-92, 95, 130-135, 137, 139-140, 145, 152, 176, 180, 192-193

Graves, Robert, 125-126, 145, 172

Gwyddbwyll, 112

Gwydion, god, 22-23, 125-126, 128, 142, 145, 149, 179

Gwynn ap Nudd, 20, 27, 123-125, 127-128, 133, 141-143, 150-151, 170, 178, 180, 189, 196

Gwythyr ap Greidyawl, 64, 125-128, 178, 180

Henry VII, king, 191

Henry VIII, king, 24, 60, 65

Herne the Hunter, 123, 143

Horn, 66, 91-92, 107, 196

Horned God, 123, 127, 131, 186, 189

Imbolc, 64, 82, 87, 89, 104, 179

Ine, king, 48, 50, 54

Isis, 178

John of Glastonbury, 27, 132, 140, 152-153

Jones, Kathy, 138, 153

Joseph of Arimathea, 3, 12, 22-23, 40-41, 50, 54, 57, 59, 85, 93, 110-111, 116, 139, 141, 192, 194

Jung, Carl G., 143-144, 153, 184, 197

Lady of the Lake, 130-131, 134-136, 195

Lake Village, 10, 129

Leodogranz, king, 127

Ley Lines, 74, 83-85, 120

Living Rock, 74, 82, 99, 102-103

Llud, Lludd, 77, 125-127, 151

Llyr, god, 123, 126-127, 151, 179

Lugh, Llew, 104, 126, 179

Lughnasad, 82, 87, 98, 104, 152, 179

Lydney, 123

Mabinogion, 20, 76, 113, 125, 127-128, 134, 151, 175-176

Magdalene, 26, 65, 132, 135

Maiden Castle, 37, 69

Maltwood, Kathryn, 105-107

Manannan, god, 126

Mary Chapel, 24, 51, 53-55, 57, 83, 87, 91, 93, 95, 97, 111, 113-116, 118-121, 141, 161

Mary, St., 24, 40, 57, 59, 64, 87, 93, 95-96, 116, 118-119, 131, 138

Melkin, bard, 110, 113, 119, 140, 195

Melwas, 40, 45, 48, 127-128, 133, 145, 178-179

Mendip Hills, 7, 29, 33, 157, 170

Merlin, 105, 130, 176

Michael, St., 3, 14, 41, 60, 62-66, 71, 81-84, 86-87, 89, 91, 93, 95, 97-100, 103, 110, 128, 130, 170-171, 179

Michell, John, 50-51, 53, 56, 81, 111, 115, 119-121, 153

Modron, goddess, 20, 130-131

Montacute, 91

Mordred, 126, 133-134

Morgan, queen, 20, 22, 130-131, 133-136, 139

Morrighu, goddess, 131

Newgrange, passage mound, 34, 82, 143

Nichols, Ross, 98, 173

Nudd, Nodens, Nuada, god, 20, 27, 123-128, 133, 141-143, 150-151, 170, 178, 180, 189, 196

Odin, god, 124

Old Church, 24, 39-41, 50-51, 55, 57, 93, 95, 110-111, 114-117, 138, 140

Osiris, 128, 178

Owein, 113, 130, 197

Patrick, St., 40-41, 45, 50-51, 53-54, 72, 93, 153

Pelagius, 54

Peredur, 149, 176

Perilous or Pomparles Bridge, 102, 131, 135, 176

Perpetual Choir, 141

Persephone, goddess, 126, 178, 184

Philosopher's Stone, 26, 55, 183

Phoenix, 26, 107-108

Pixley, Olive, 73, 78

Ponter's Ball, 2, 9, 18-19, 33, 36, 38, 40, 76-77, 107, 127

Priddy, 33-34, 59

Pryderi, 125, 142, 144

Pwyll, king, 20, 22, 125-126, 142, 144

Red
  colour, 26, 115, 125, 155, 169, 180, 205
  elixir, 183, 191-194
  essence, 182-183, 186, 193

Red Spring, see Chalice Well

Rahtz, Philip, 27, 29, 44, 49, 56, 95, 101, 120, 152, 173

Rhiannon, goddess, 26, 125

Romans, 3, 9, 12, 18, 46, 50, 136-137

Rosicrucian, 191-192

Samhain, 73, 82, 87, 89, 104, 124, 130, 179

Saward, Jeff, 105, 120-121

Seven, number, 2, 17, 35, 65-66, 87, 89, 92, 102, 113-115, 144, 148

Sidhe, 123, 131, 142-143

Silbury Hill, 35, 148

Stanton Drew, stone circle, 33

St. Joseph's Well, 95, 156

St. Michael Line, 81-82, 84, 86-87, 98-99, 110

St. Michael's Mount, 81, 179

Somerton, 91

Stone Down, 71, 97-100

Stonehenge, 34-35, 37, 51, 60, 78, 82, 85-86, 89, 99, 102, 141, 153

Stoney Littleton, longbarrow, 33, 82

Sulis Minerva, goddess, 136

Summer Land, country, 1, 127, 151

Sutton Montis, 89

Taliesin, bard, 23, 130, 144

Taranis, god, 128

Templars, Knights, 51, 85, 187, 204

Thom, Alexander, 98, 100, 120

Tibetan tradition, 186, 193

Tohono O'odham, 101, 148

Tor
  labyrinth, 14, 68, 73, 99, 101-105, 109, 142, 148

monastery, 14, 18, 41-42, 44, 59-60, 62, 65-66, 71-72, 76-77, 93, 95, 136-137, 170-171, 195

mythology, 22, 55, 107, 128, 130-131, 152, 178

settlements, 10, 32-33, 35

terraces, 2, 9, 14, 29, 33, 35, 38, 65-66, 68-69, 71-73, 76-77, 100-102, 110, 145, 150, 157, 164, 169, 194

Trackways, 9-10, 30, 32-33, 35-36

Tuatha de Danaan, 123, 131, 140, 142

Tudor Pole, Wellesley, 136-137, 156

Twelve, number, 2-3, 41-42, 50-51, 54, 85, 91, 106, 110-111, 119, 141

Uther Pendragon, king, 46, 191

Vesica Piscis, 95, 113-114, 161-163

Vortigern, king, 46, 176, 178

Wearyall Hill, 10, 20, 23, 37, 76, 85, 93, 95, 131-132, 135, 138, 140, 176

West Kennet, long barrow, 34

Weston, William, 66, 77

White

colour, 26, 115, 125, 155, 169, 180, 205

elixir, 183, 191-194

essence, 182-183, 186, 193

White Spring, 2, 17, 20, 26-27, 74, 107, 140, 142, 150-151, 155-156, 163-166, 168-173, 189, 195-196

William of Malmesbury, 40, 51, 54, 110, 119

Wild Hunt, 4, 20, 123-124, 130-131, 143, 152, 180, 186, 189

Woden, god, 123-124, 149

Wookey Hole, 29, 168, 170

Wright, George, 165-166, 168, 173

Yder, 128, 133, 151

Yggdrasil, 149

Ynis Witrin, 7, 126, 145

Zodiacs, 2, 23-26, 51, 61, 74, 81, 85, 105-107, 109-110, 113, 115, 119, 127, 145

On the following pages you will find listed, with their current prices, some of the books now available on related subjects. Your book dealer stocks most of these and will stock new titles in the Llewellyn series as they become available. We urge your patronage.

TO GET A FREE CATALOG

You are invited to write for our bimonthly news magazine/catalog, *Llewellyn's New Worlds of Mind and Spirit*. A sample copy is free, and it will continue coming to you at no cost as long as you are an active mail customer. Or you may subscribe for just $10 in the United States and Canada ($20 overseas, first class mail). Many bookstores also have *New Worlds* available to their customers. Ask for it.

In *New Worlds* you will find news and features about new books, tapes and services; announcements of meetings and seminars; helpful articles; author interviews and much more. Write to:

Llewellyn's New Worlds of Mind and Spirit
P.O. Box 64383-459, St. Paul, MN 55164-0383, U.S.A.

TO ORDER BOOKS AND TAPES

If your book store does not carry the titles described on the following pages, you may order them directly from Llewellyn by sending the full price in U.S. funds, plus postage and handling (see below).

Credit card orders: VISA, MasterCard, American Express are accepted. Call us toll-free within the United States and Canada at 1-800-THE-MOON.

Special Group Discount: Because there is a great deal of interest in group discussion and study of the subject matter of this book, we offer a 20% quantity discount to group leaders or agents. Our Special Quantity Price for a minimum order of five copies of *The Isle of Avalon* is $59.80 cash-with-order. Include postage and handling charges noted below.

Postage and Handling: Include $4 postage and handling for orders $15 and under; $5 for orders *over* $15. There are no postage and handling charges for orders over $100. Postage and handling rates are subject to change. We ship UPS whenever possible within the continental United States; delivery is guaranteed. Please provide your street address as UPS does not deliver to P.O. boxes. Orders shipped to Alaska, Hawaii, Canada, Mexico and Puerto Rico will be sent via first class mail. Allow 4-6 weeks for delivery. **International orders:** Airmail – add retail price of each book and $5 for each non-book item (audiotapes, etc.); Surface mail – add $1 per item.

Minnesota residents add 7% sales tax.

Mail orders to:
Llewellyn Worldwide, P.O. Box 64383-459, St. Paul, MN 55164-0383, U.S.A.
For customer service, call (612) 291-1970.

HIS STORY
Masculinity in the Post-Patriarchal World
Nicholas R. Mann

His Story was written for men of European descent who are seeking a new definition of being. The patriarchal worldview dominating Western thought has cut men off from the traditions which once directly connected them to the nature of their masculinity. This book offers them a means to locate and connect with their birthright—the "native tradition" that lives in the deepest core of their being—by drawing on the pre-Christian era's conception of a man's true masculine nature.

His Story contrasts patriarchal and pre-patriarchal ideas about masculine identity, self-definition, sexuality, symbology and spirituality—then provides a wealth of information on traditions and mythology that encompass many masculine archetypes, from those of the Grail legends to the Green Man, the Wild Man and the Horned God. Finally, the book reveals how men can connect again with these traditions and their own inherent source of personal power, thus transforming their relationships to those around them and to the world.

ISBN: 1-56718-458-8, 6 x 9, 336 pp., softbound   **$16.95**

ANCIENT MAGICKS FOR A NEW AGE
Rituals from the Merlin Temple, the Magick of the Dragon Kings
Alan Richardson and Geoff Hughes

With two sets of personal magickal diaries, this book details the work of magicians from two different eras. In it, you can learn what a particular magician is experiencing in this day and age, how to follow a similar path of your own, and discover correlations to the workings of traditional adepti from almost half a century ago.

The first set of diaries are from Christine Hartley and show the magick performed within the Merlin Temple of the Stella Matutina, an offshoot of the Hermetic Order of the Golden Dawn, in the years 1940-42. The second set are from Geoff Hughes and detail his magickal work during 1984-86. Although he was not at that time a member of any formal group, the magick he practiced was under the same aegis as Hartley's. The third section of this book, written by Hughes, shows how you can become your own Priest or Priestess and make contact with Merlin.

The magick of Christine Hartley and Geoff Hughes are like the poles of some hidden battery that lies beneath the Earth and beneath the years. There is a current flowing between them, and the energy is there for you to tap.
0-87542-671-9, 320 pgs., 6 x 9, illus., softcover **$12.95**

THE ARTHURIAN QUEST
Living Legends of Camelot
Amber Wolfe

Wherever you are in your own quest for meaning, *The Arthurian Quest* reveals how you can
use the legends of Arthur, Merlin, and
Camelot as a catalyst for personal evolution
and empowerment. Drawing from a wide variety of sources—historical, mythological, psychological, and magickal—*The Arthurian
Quest* takes you through guided journeys,
experiential exercises and spiritual ceremonies
to activate the transformative power of these ancient legends. Learn to uti-
lize practical mysticism to awaken your unconscious wisdom, and develop
your own personal myths for self-transformation. Release the deep
insights and magickal gifts which lie at the heart of the Arthurian saga and
connect with this mighty current of mystical power.
ISBN: 1-56718-806-0, 7 x 10, 432 pp., softcover   **$24.95**

THE CELTIC HEART
Kathryn Marie Cocquyt

The *Celtic Heart* tells the adventurous, epic tale of spirit, love, loss, and the difficult choices made by three generations of the Celtic Brigantes tribe, who once lived off the coast of North Wales on an island they named *Mona mam Cymru* ("Mother of Wales," or Anglesey).

Follow the passionate lives of the Brigantes clan and the tumultuous events during the years leading up to the Roman Invasion in A.D. 61, when Anglesey was a refuge for Celts struggling to preserve their inner truths and goddess-based culture against the encroachment of the Roman Empire and Christianity. As their tribal way of life is threatened, the courageous natures of the Chieftain Solomon, the Druidess Saturnalia, and the young warriors Kordelina and Aonghus are tested by the same questions of good and evil that face us today.

Filled with ritual, dream images, romance, and intrigue, *The Celtic Heart* will take you on an authentic and absorbing journey into the history, lives, and hearts of the legendary Celts.

ISBN: 1-56718-156-2, 6 x 9, 624 pp., softbound   **$14.95**

CELTIC MAGIC
D. J. Conway

Many people, not all of Irish descent, have a great interest in the ancient Celts and the Celtic pantheon, and *Celtic Magic* is the map they need for exploring this ancient and fascinating magical culture.

Celtic Magic is for the reader who is either a beginner or intermediate in the field of magic. It provides an extensive "how-to" of practical spell-working. There are many books on the market dealing with the Celts and their beliefs, but none guide the reader to a practical application of magical knowledge for use in everyday life. There is also an in-depth discussion of Celtic deities and the Celtic way of life and worship, so that an intermediate practitioner can expand upon the spellwork to build a series of magical rituals. Presented in an easy-to-understand format, *Celtic Magic* is for anyone searching for new spells that can be worked immediately, without elaborate or rare materials, and with minimal time and preparation.

0 87512-136-9, 240 pgs., mass market, illus. **$4.99**

THE HANDBOOK OF CELTIC ASTROLOGY
The 13-Sign Lunar Zodiac of the Ancient Druids
Helena Paterson

Discover your lunar self with *The Handbook of Celtic Astrology*. Solar-oriented astrology has dominated Western astrological thought for centuries, but lunar-based Celtic astrology provides the "Yin" principle that has been neglected in the West—and author Helena Paterson presents new concepts based on ancient Druidic observations, lore and traditions that will redefine Western astrology.

This reference work will take you through the Celtic lunar zodiac, where each lunar month is associated with one of the 13 trees sacred to the Druids: birch, rowan, ash, alder, willow, hawthorn, oak, holly, hazel, vine, ivy, reed and elder. Chapters on each "tree sign" provide comprehensive text on Celtic mythology and gods/desses associated with the sign's ruling tree and planet; general characteristics of natives of the sign; and interpretive notes on the locations of the planets, the Moon, the ascendant and Midheaven as they are placed in any of the three decans of each tree sign. A thorough introduction on chart construction, sign division and the importance of solstices, equinoxes, eclipses and aspects to the Moon guarantees this book will become *the* definitive work on Celtic astrology.

1–56718–509–6, 7 x 10, 288 pp., illus. $15.00

CELTIC MYTH & MAGIC
Harness the Power of the Gods & Goddesses
by Edain McCoy

Tap into the mythic power of the Celtic goddesses, gods, heroes and heroines to aid your spiritual quests and magickal goals. *Celtic Myth & Magic* explains how to use creative ritual and pathworking to align yourself with the energy of these archetypes, whose potent images live deep within your psyche.

Celtic Myth & Magic begins with an overview of 49 different types of Celtic Paganism followed today, then gives specific instructions for evoking and invoking the energy of the Celtic pantheon to channel it toward magickal and spiritual goals and into esbat, sabbat and life transition rituals. Three detailed pathworking texts will take you on an inner journey where you'll join forces with the archetypal images of Cuchulain, Queen Maeve and Merlin the Magician to bring their energies directly into your life. The last half of the book clearly details the energies of over 300 Celtic deities and mythic figures so you can evoke or invoke the appropriate deity to attain a specific goal.

This inspiring, well-researched book will help solitary Pagans who seek to expand the boundaries of their practice to form working partnerships with the divine.

1–56718–661–0, 7 x 10, 464 pp., softbound $19.95

THE GRAIL CASTLE
Male Myths & Mysteries in the Celtic
Tradition
Kenneth Johnson & Marguerite Elsbeth

Explore the mysteries which lie at the core of being male when you take a quest into the most powerful myth of Western civilization: the Celtic-Teutonic-Christian myth of the Grail Castle.

The Pagan Celtic culture's world view—which stressed an intense involvement with the magical world of nature—strongly resonates for men today because it offers a direct experience with the spirit often lacking in their lives. This book describes the four primary male archetypes—the King or Father, the Hero or Warrior, the Magician or Wise Man and the Lover—which the authors exemplify with stories from the Welsh Mabinogion, the Ulster Cycle and other old Pagan sources. Exercises and meditations designed to activate these inner myths will awaken men to how myths—as they live on today in the collective unconscious and popular culture— shape their lives. Finally, men will learn how to heal the Fisher King—who lies at the heart of the Grail Castle myth—to achieve integration of the four archetypal paths.

1–56718–369–7, 6 x 9, 224 pp., illus., index **$14.95**

THE NINE DOORS OF MIDGARD:
A Complete Curriculum of Rune Magic
Edred Thorsson

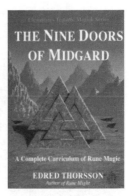

The Nine Doors of Midgard are the gateways to self-transformation through the runes. This is the complete course of study and practice which has successfully been in use inside the Rune-Gild for ten years. Now it is being made available to the public for the first time.

The runic tradition represents a whole school of magic with the potential of becoming the equal of the Hermetic or Cabalistic tradition. The runic tradition is the northern or Teutonic equivalent of the Hermetic tradition of the south. *The Nine Doors of Midgard* is the only manual to take a systematic approach to initiation into runic practices.

Through nine lessons or stages in a graded curriculum, the books takes the rune student from a stage in which no previous knowledge of runes or esoteric work is assumed to a fairly advanced stage of initiation. The book also contains a complete reading course in outside material.
0-87542-781-2, 320 pgs., 5 1/4 x 8, illus.   **$12.95**

THE CRAFTED CUP
Ritual Mysteries of the Goddess and the Grail
by Shadwynn
The Holy Grail—fabled depository of wonder, enchantment and ultimate spiritual fulfillment—is the key by which the wellsprings of a Deeper Life can be tapped for the enhancement of our inner growth. *The Crafted Cup* is a compendium of the teachings and rituals of a distinctly Pagan religious Order—the *Ordo Arcanorum Gradalis*—which incorporates into its spiritual way of worship ritual imagery based upon the Arthurian Grail legends, a reverence towards the mythic Christ, and an appreciation of the core truths and techniques found scattered throughout the New Age movement.

The Crafted Cup is divided into two parts. The first deals specifically with the teachings and general concepts which hold a central place within the philosophy of the *Ordo Arcanorum Gradalis*. The second and larger of the two parts is a complete compilation of the sacramental rites and seasonal rituals which make up the liturgical calendar of the Order. It contains one of the largest collections of Pagan, Grail-oriented rituals yet published.

0–87542–739–1, 420 pgs., 7 x 10, illus., softcover   **$19.95**

BY OAK, ASH & THORN
Modern Celtic Shamanism
by D. J. Conway

Many spiritual seekers are interested in shamanism because it is a spiritual path that can be followed in conjunction with any religion or other spiritual belief without conflict. Shamanism has not only been practiced by Native American and African cultures—for centuries, it was practiced by the Europeans, including the Celts.

By Oak, Ash and Thorn presents a workable, modern form of Celtic shamanism that will help anyone raise his or her spiritual awareness. Here, in simple, practical terms, you will learn to follow specific exercises and apply techniques that will develop your spiritual awareness and ties with the natural world: shape-shifting, divination by the Celtic Ogham alphabet, Celtic shamanic tools, traveling to and using magick in the three realms of the Celtic otherworlds, empowering the self, journeying through meditation and more.

Shamanism begins as a personal revelation and inner healing, then evolves into a striving to bring balance and healing into the Earth itself. This book will ensure that Celtic shamanism will take its place among the spiritual practices that help us lead fuller lives.

1–56718–166-X, 6 x 9, est. 288 pp., illus., softcover   **$12.95**